THE WILLIAM PINKNEY RATLIFF FAMILY SAGA
1847-1988

THE WILLIAM PINKNEY RATLIFF
FAMILY SAGA
1847-1988

THE LIVES OF WILLIAM PINKNEY
AND CORNELIA MITCHELL RATLIFF
AND THEIR ELEVEN CHILDREN

BY JOHN BARTON RATLIFF III

Copyright © 2014 John Barton Ratliff III

All rights reserved.

ISBN: 1492283622
ISBN-13: 9781492283621
Library of Congress Control Number: 2013915996
CreateSpace Independent Publishing Platform
North Charleston, South Carolina

Visit *www.ratliffsaga.com*

To Diane,

my sweet wife of fifty-five years,
whose love and support
I will treasure all of my life

ACKNOWLEDGMENTS

I could not have written this book without the generous assistance, interest, and support of many members of the extended Ratliff family, and also of those who were not direct relatives but went out of their way to share information to which they had access.

First of all, I owe a debt of gratitude to all those who came before me in researching the Ratliff family genealogy. They include the following:

My father, **John Barton Ratliff Jr.**, whose stories about my Ratliff great-grandparents, grandparents, and great aunts and uncles whetted my interest in the family history and gave me an added appreciation for those who were only names until my research began in earnest.

My uncle **Pinkney Brooks Ratliff**, who along with my uncle **Paul Adams Ratliff** invited me to live with them in their Washington, DC, apartment my first year at Georgetown University. Uncle Brooks shared many family stories with me (including those about my father that I otherwise would never have known) and especially the story of "when Grandpa Pink shot Old Man Jackson."

My cousin **Ed Ratliff**, who researched the family from Maryland to Mississippi and beyond; published and distributed the *Ratliff's Ferry* newsletter (named for a ferry across the Pearl River in Mississippi operated by his great-great-grandfather John Ratliff); compiled an extended family tree and made it available to interested family members; organized and coordinated Ratliff reunions in Texas, South Carolina, and Mississippi; supported my research efforts from the time we first met in El Paso at a Ratliff cousins reunion in 1992; and continued to offer encouragement and support in the writing of this book. In addition, Ed volunteered to proofread the entire manuscript before submission for publication. His astute suggestions were invaluable.

My cousin **Charles Ratliff**—brother of Ed Ratliff—who traced the movements of the Ratliff family from Alabama to Mississippi by examining the land records. His knowledge and background in oil land leasing were invaluable in locating and examining many of these land records. His work was published in the *Ratliff's Ferry* newsletter of January 18, 1985 (Vol. 2, No. 1).

Howard S. Hazlewood and my cousin **Betty J. Ratliff Carson** for their research on our early Ratliff ancestors as reported in their unpublished booklet entitled *The William Ratcliff/Ratliff Family of Maryland and Anson County, North Carolina* (about 1989). This booklet may be found in the genealogical sections of many of the major libraries in Maryland, North Carolina, and Mississippi.

Marion Ratliff—early Ratliff historian for Anson County, North Carolina Ratliffs—for his effort in collecting and maintaining Ratliff Family information in Anson County, North Carolina.

May MacCallum for preserving the early Ratliff family records of Marion Ratliff and for her own extensive research into the Ratliff family of Anson County, North Carolina. She also found and catalogued many of the small Ratliff family cemeteries in and around Anson County. She was a major planner for the large Ratliff Family Reunion held in Cheraw, South Carolina, in February of 1995.

ACKNOWLEDGMENTS

Clarence Earl Ratcliff *for* providing early encouragement to Ed and Charles Ratliff in their family research, as well as for his publishing the definitive work on the Quaker Ratcliff Family from Talbot County, Maryland.

My cousin ***Bessie Corean Ratliff Herrin***, daughter of Tom Watson Ratliff, who extensively researched the Ratliff family history.

I am also deeply grateful to the many family members who generously shared family photos, official records, newspaper clippings, and memories, without which this book would not have been possible:

My aunt ***Martha Ratliff Whetzel***, daughter of John Barton (John B.) Ratliff, who made invaluable contributions to the book by sharing her family experiences and knowledge and identifying family members in various photos. And her daughter, ***Marlyn Wilkinson***, who generously shared hundreds of family photos belonging to her mother and our mutual Ratliff grandparents after the death of her mother.

My cousin ***Barton Wade Ratliff***, son of Albert Wade Ratliff, who sent me the first copies of photos of the 1939 Ratliff family reunion and shared information and memories about his direct family as well as other branches.

My cousin ***Tommie Jane Ratliff Allen***, daughter of Tom Watson Ratliff, who generously shared the suitcase full of family photos and letters to her father going back as far as 1910, as well as her personal memories and knowledge of the family. These letters opened a window into the lives and travels of not only Tom but also those of many of his ten siblings, particularly in the period from 1910 through the end of World War I.

My cousin by marriage ***Patricia Everly Ratliff***, who shared many photos of her husband Philip Grady Amidon Ratliff's family, as well as information about her father-in-law Paul Grady Ratliff and her mother-in-law Beulah Amidon Ratliff. And I am also grateful to her daughter and my cousin, **Alison Ratliff**, who shared more photos, including those of medals her grandfather Paul Grady Ratliff earned in World War I and those her father Philip Grady Amidon Ratliff was awarded in World War II.

My cousin **Ellen Oakes Pettit** and cousin-by-marriage **Sally Sloss Wasson** for sharing much information about our family in Kosciusko and Attala County, Mississippi, including photos, newspaper clippings, diaries, etc. In addition, for generously taking much of their personal time to take my wife Diane and me all around the Kosciusko and Attala County sites important to our family history, including the courthouse, the genealogy room of the library, and many old cemeteries, not to mention entertaining us at their homes and camps.

My cousins—the great-grandchildren of Sarah Anna Lee Ratliff Donoho—especially **Connie Hazelwood Brown**, who shared family photos and letters from her uncle Edward Lee Hazlewood, and **Pamela Hazelwood Cooke**, who copied and shared family photos from a number of her siblings, as well as **Robert Hazelwood** and **Kathy Hazelwood Roy**.

My cousin by marriage **Beverly Smith Herrin**, wife of Bessie Corean Ratliff Herrin's son Tom, for a number of high-resolution photos of Tom Watson Ratliff and his family.

Patricia Jenkins Hartman (related to the Ratliff family indirectly through her husband, Alan Hartman, who was the step-grandson of Mary Belle Ratliff Wilson's daughter Sudie), who took time from her busy schedule as a teacher and pastor's wife and used her impressive genealogical research skills to track down newspaper articles, death certificates, legal documents, and grave sites connected to the Mary Belle Ratliff Wilson family. Without her generous assistance, much of what we know about Belle's family would never have been discovered, particularly since there are no living direct descendants.

ACKNOWLEDGMENTS

Barbara Ann McNeil Mingee and her daughter ***Susan Mingee*** of Natchez, Mississippi, the niece and great-niece respectively of William Henry Kimberlin Jr., who was married to Sarah Elizabeth Donoho, one of Sarah Anna Lee Ratliff Donoho's twin daughters. Barbara cared for her uncle Henry Kimberlin in his declining years, and, upon his death, she put away in a closet for safekeeping all photos, documents, and letters pertaining and belonging to Sarah Elizabeth Donoho Kimberlin and her family in hopes of eventually finding someone in Elizabeth's family to whom she could pass them on. By chance, our paths crossed twenty-five years after Henry's death. Thanks to the foresight of Barbara and the generosity of both Barbara and her daughter Susan in sending these treasures to me for the purposes of my research and returning them to Aunt Elizabeth's family, I have been able to include much of the information about and many of the photos of Elizabeth, Henry, and other members of Anna's family in the book.

My cousin ***Robert Edmond Ratliff***, son of Zack Mitchell Ratliff, who shared photos and stories about his family.

My cousin ***Judith Ratliff Evans***, granddaughter of Zack Mitchell Ratliff, who shared stories and photos of her father, Joseph Pinckney Ratliff, and his family and, with the assistance of her husband, the late ***Larry Trcka***, researched various documents, newspaper articles, and legal documents about her grandfather and his family.

My cousins ***Kathryn Naylor Prenevost*** and ***Michael Naylor***, who shared information about and photos of their grandmother Katherine Elaine Ratliff and her family.

My cousin ***Curtis Alden Deyrup***, son of Paul Grady Ratliff's daughter Beulah Curtis Ratliff Deyrup, for stories about his family, as well as priceless letters and telegrams providing information about the POW status of his grandfather Paul Grady Ratliff in the RAF in World War I.

My cousin **Beulah Tacey Deyrup,** daughter of Paul Grady Ratliff's daughter Beulah Curtis Ratliff Deyrup, for photos of her family.

Trenton Cecil Cole Jr.—who shared his recollections of Mitchell Carruth Ratliff (Mitchell married Trenton's mother after his father was killed in a plane crash).

Ann Breedlove, genealogy clerk at the Attala County Library, for her assistance in locating information in the library about my great-grandfather and his family.

Our son **Andrew Michael Ratliff** for his generous and masterful restoration of many old family photos used in the book, including of the 1887 photo of William Pinkney Ratliff, his parents, and his nine siblings.

My wife, **Diane Moffat Ratliff**, for her support and active participation throughout the years of research and writing this book and for proofreading the manuscript many times as well.

And finally, my first cousins—the grandchildren of John B. and Emma Jenkins Ratliff—who shared family photos and information about their families. They include **Frances Roxana Ratliff Green**, daughter of my uncle Pinkney Brooks Ratliff; **Dr. Harry Milton Thomas Jr.**, son of my aunt Anabel Ratliff Thomas; **James Grady Ratliff Jr.,** son of my uncle James Grady Ratliff; **Mava Ratliff Fowler**, daughter of my uncle William "Billie" Rodgers Ratliff; **Susan Ratliff Thompson**, daughter of my uncle Albert Wade "Bevo" Ratliff; and **Marlyn Wilkinson**, daughter of my aunt Martha Ratliff Wilkinson Whetzel.

TABLE OF CONTENTS

ACKNOWLEDGMENTS		vii
PART ONE		
WILLIAM PINKNEY RATLIFF		1
Chapter 1	A TRIBUTE	3
Chapter 2	MARCH 3, 1894	5
Chapter 3	WHO WAS WILLIAM PINKNEY RATLIFF?	7
Chapter 4	WHO WAS SAMUEL ANDERSON JACKSON?	13
Chapter 5	SHOWDOWN AT THE COURTHOUSE	17
Chapter 6	ON TRIAL FOR MURDER	29
Chapter 7	LIFE AS A FARMER	43
PART TWO		
CORNELIA MITCHELL		57
Chapter 1	THE EARLY LIFE OF CORNELIA MITCHELL	59
Chapter 2	MOVING ON	65
Chapter 3	BACK HOME IN KOSCIUSKO	69
PHOTOS OF THE 1939 REUNION		73
PART THREE		
THE CHILDREN OF WILLIAM PINKNEY AND CORNELIA		
MITCHELL RATLIFF		81
Chapter 1	SARAH ANNA LEE RATLIFF	85
Chapter 2	MARY BELLE RATLIFF	117
Chapter 3	JOHN BARTON RATLIFF	135

THE WILLIAM PINKNEY RATLIFF FAMILY SAGA 1847-1988

Chapter 4	SUDIE RATLIFF	201
Chapter 5	ZACK MITCHELL RATLIFF	209
Chapter 6	KATHERINE ELAINE RATLIFF	239
Chapter 7	FLORENCE CORNELIA RATLIFF	255
Chapter 8	ALBERT WADE RATLIFF	261
Chapter 9	PAUL GRADY RATLIFF	277
Chapter 10	BESSIE GRACE RATLIFF	321
Chapter 11	TOM WATSON RATLIFF	329

PART FOUR
THE SIBLINGS OF WILLIAM PINKNEY AND
CORNELIA MITCHELL RATLIFF 351

| Chapter 1 | THE SIBLINGS OF WILLIAM PINKNEY RATLIFF | 353 |
| Chapter 2 | THE SIBLINGS OF CORNELIA MITCHELL | 361 |

EPILOGUE 365

APPENDICES 367

APPENDIX ONE: WILLIAM PINKNEY RATLIFF, WRITING
IN THE ALLIANCE VINDICATOR JULY 14, 1891
"RATLIFF'S ATTEMPT TO REPLY TO THE NINE QUESTIONS" 369

APPENDIX TWO: WILLIAM PINKNEY RATLIFF, WRITING
IN THE ALLIANCE VINDICATOR SOMETIME AFTER
JULY 14, 1891
"RATLIFF PUT ON ANOTHER BLISTER" 373

APPENDIX THREE: AN EDITORIAL IN SUPPORT OF
WILLIAM PINKNEY RATLIFF AND THE SUB-TREASURY PLAN
PROBABLY W.P. RATLIFF IN THE ALLIANCE VINDICATOR,
SOMETIME AFTER JULY 14, 1891
"WHO COMMENCED IT?" 377

TABLE OF CONTENTS

APPENDIX FOUR: EDITORIAL IN THE MERIDIAN
MISSISSIPPI NEWS ADVOCATING A POLICY OF REFUSAL
TO PUBLISH INFLAMMATORY ATTACKS
REPRINT IN THE MEMPHIS APPEAL-AVALANCHE
(SOMETIME AFTER MARCH 3, 1894)
"EDITORIAL RESPONSIBLITY"   381

APPENDIX FIVE: DUELING NEWSPAPER ARTICLES
BETWEEN W.P. RATLIFF AND JACKSON, LATE FEBRUARY 1894   385

APPENDIX SIX: LETTER OF RESPONSE TO W.P. RATLIFF
FROM COL. WILLIAM LEWIS NUGENT
FEBRUARY 26, 1894   389

APPENDIX SEVEN: THE ANCESTORS OF
WILLIAM PINKNEY RATLIFF   393

APPENDIX EIGHT: THE ANCESTORS OF
CORNELIA MITCHELL   395

BIBLIOGRAPHY   **397**

ABOUT THE AUTHOR   **403**

INDEX OF NAMES   **405**

THE LIVES OF WILLIAM PINKNEY
AND CORNELIA MITCHELL RATLIFF
AND THEIR ELEVEN CHILDREN

PART ONE

WILLIAM PINKNEY RATLIFF

1

A TRIBUTE

If there were ever a true American renaissance man of the nineteenth and early twentieth century, William Pinkney Ratliff was such a man. As a farmer, soldier of the Confederacy, businessman, journalist, preacher, and politician, his influence on his family and community, as well as the circumstances in which he found himself, are still being felt and discussed today. What follows is the story of his life and that of his wife, Cornelia Mitchell Ratliff, and their eleven children.

William Pinkney Ratliff was born in Leake County, Mississippi, on February 9, 1847, and died in Hope, Arkansas, on May 10, 1927. After his funeral, which was held in Attala County, Mississippi, the following tribute appeared in the Kosciusko newspaper:

A Tribute to the Memory of W.P. Ratliff

> Another good man has left us, has crossed the Great Divide, and passed into the valley of silence, and we are left to mourn his loss.
>
> He was born in Attala County on February 9, 1847, and died at Julia Chester Hospital in Hope, Arkansas, on May 10, 1927, and left surviving him the following children, to wit: Mrs.

R. E. Donoho, Mrs. O. W. Wilson, Jr., J. B. Ratliff, Mrs. Claude Spain, Z. M. Ratliff, Mrs. Kate Naylor, Miss Florence Ratliff, A.W. Ratliff, Mrs. K. H. Causey and T. W. Ratliff.

Mr. Ratliff lived in Attala County all his life until about twenty-five years ago he moved to Arkansas and perhaps other Western States, and died in Hope, Arkansas. He was brought here and buried at Springdale on the 12th day of May, 1927, and with Revs. W. W. Milligan and R. P. Neblett holding the funeral services, and a large crowd of our people in attendance to the last sad rites.

Mr. Ratliff was one of the best known men in Attala County, honored and respected by all, was at one time a member of the Legislature of the State of Mississippi from Attala County, and filled other places of trust and confidence in our people. He was a brave and courageous man, and acted well his part in the battle of life, for a braver, a more serene, a more chivalrous spirit never passed from life to enrich the realms of death. It was proper that his remains should be brought to his old home, and be laid to rest with his neighbors, his father and other dear ones, to sleep his last sleep. And we never knew a braver spirit than the one that once inhabited this silent form of dreamless clay.

Farewell, Mr. Ratliff, we think the world is better for your life and braver for your death, generous to your fellowman, and whose hands were stretched to save and help those who could not help themselves. Many are well and happy now, because you lived the life you did. This is enough. It puts a star above the gloom of death.

S.L.Dodd[1]

---

1   Presumably the *Kosciusko Star-Herald,* May 1927. With permission.

2

MARCH 3, 1894

When William Pinkney Ratliff awoke on the morning of March 3, 1894, he presumably had no thought of shooting anyone. Although he'd put his Colt .38 revolver in his coat pocket when he left the house, he later said that he had been carrying a pistol for some time because his friends warned him that a certain enemy threatened to "do him up."[1]

It was true that W. P. Ratliff and Sam Jackson had been on opposite sides of the political fence as members of the Mississippi legislature. Moreover, with the dispute publicly aired through articles in rival newspapers over the past few weeks, their differences had escalated into name calling and accusations. The Farmers Alliance, which had been formed because farmers felt that they were not being paid fairly for their cotton crops, had hopes of getting laws passed that would ease the distress of farmers. These proposals included a federal government takeover of the railroads in order to bring down the costs of agricultural shipments and the "Sub-Treasury Plan," which entailed the creation of government warehouses where farmers could store their cotton until prices rose, thereby freeing farmers from the vagaries of the marketplace.

The Farmers Alliance had tried to work with Democrats in the state legislature, the majority of whom were lawyers, not farmers. When it

---

[1] W.P. Ratliff's own testimony at his trial, as reported by the *Kosciusko Star,* March 23, 1894.

became clear that their legislators did not support the farmers' economic interests, the Farmers Alliance formed a new party called the "People's Party" or "Populist Party."

When the Mississippi legislature met in special session in January of 1894, twenty-two state legislators left the Democratic Party and joined the Populist Party. The Populist Party caucus, aligned with agrarian Democrats, was able to have some success with their proposals in the legislature, leading to tensions between members of the two parties.[2]

So it was in this tense atmosphere that Jackson had called Ratliff a traitor to the Democratic Party because of Ratliff's decision to leave the Democratic Party to join the new Populist Party.

In response, Ratliff accused Jackson of voting for a member of Ratliff's Populist Party in the Mississippi legislature to fill a vacancy in the US Senate, in spite of Jackson's being a Democrat. While not backing down from his original accusation, in an editorial in late February in his own newspaper, the *Alliance Vindicator*, Ratliff admitted that his accusations had been intended to make sport of Jackson and to get his goat.[3]

In response, Jackson paid for an advertisement in the *Kosciusko Star*, in which he called Ratliff "an infernal liar," which Ratliff could have considered "fighting words." Jackson told the editor of the *Jackson Clarion-Ledger* privately that "in Attala, where party lines are so tightly drawn, I do not think I can afford…to let him go unnoticed."[4] Ratliff responded in print to Jackson's taunt, and conceded that he had made an error but did not apologize. Jackson may have thought the matter settled.

But when Ratliff left his home that fateful morning to visit a sheriff's bankruptcy auction at the Attala County Courthouse, he had no idea that the lives of his family and others would be so dramatically and tragically affected by the events at the courthouse that day.

---

[2] Stephen Cresswell, *Multi-Party Politics in Mississippi 1877-1902* (University Press of Mississippi, 1995), 110-114, 127-130.

[3] *Alliance Vindicator*, late February 1894.

[4] Cresswell, *Multi-Party Politics in Mississippi 1877-1902*, 130.

3

WHO WAS WILLIAM PINKNEY RATLIFF?

William Pinkney Ratliff[1] was the eldest son of Zachariah Lfonzo Ratliff[2] and Sarah Lucretia Adams's[3] eleven children. His ancestors can be traced back to William Ratliff[4] and Susannah Thomas,[5] who married in Queen Anne County, Maryland, on June 3, 1759.[6] Sarah Lucretia Adams's ancestors are known as far back as William Adams, born in Ilton, Somerset, England, in 1670. The assumption is that William Ratliff's forebearers emigrated from England, but no documentation for ancestors in England has been found as of this writing. Susannah Thomas's ancestors

---

1 Information regarding the early Ratliff Family in Maryland comes from Betty J. Ratliff Carson and Howard S. Hazlewood, *The William Ratcliff/Ratliff Family of Maryland and Anson County, North Carolina* (Sun Valley, Arizona, 1989). Names and dates for ancestors in England previously reported by various genealogists are repeated here but are without documentation and therefore cannot be substantiated.

2 Born in Stewart County, Tennessee, on March 10, 1818, married Sarah Lucretia Adams in Attala County, Mississippi, on December 19, 1842, died in Ethel, Attala County, Mississippi, on June 26, 1906. Sometimes listed as Zachariah Llonzo Ratliff.

3 Born in Amite County, Mississippi, on November 9, 1825.

4 Born in Talbot County, Maryland, on February 19, 1727; died in Anson County, North Carolina, on February 10, 1777.

5 Born in Queen Anne County, Maryland, about 1722; died in Anson County, North Carolina, on January 6, 1778.

6 US and international marriage records 1560-1900.

can be traced to England as far back as 1522, starting with Tristram "Rev" Thomas.[7]

William Pinkney (W.P.) Ratliff was born in Leake County, Mississippi, on February 9, 1847. The family moved to Attala County a year later.

Although he was only fourteen years old at the outbreak of the Civil War in 1861, he joined the Confederate forces, first as a substitute for his father but later on his own account.[8] The July 6, 1864, Company Muster Roll of the 20th Calvary, Col. L. Lay's Regiment of the Army of the Confederate States of America lists W.P. Ratliff as having enlisted on June 4, 1864.[9] He served in Louisiana until the end of the war.[10]

Biographical and Historical Memoirs of Mississippi reports that Ratliff "received his primary education in the common schools" and that he was mostly self-educated once reaching maturity, had an extensive library, and kept well posted on the topics of the day.[11]

MARRIAGE AND CHILDREN

On October 22, 1868, William Pinkney Ratliff married Cornelia Mitchell (full name: Nancy Ophelia Mary Jane Bethany Cornelia Mitchell), a member of one of the old families of Attala County.[12] At the time of their marriage, the couple lived in Ethel. The first child was stillborn; a second, William Franklin Ratliff, lived only a year and a half, passing away on September 16, 1872. Cornelia bore eleven children who lived to adulthood, six girls and five boys.[13]

---

7   Born in Surrey, England, in 1522, died in Chevening Parish, Kent, England, on March 28, 1624.
8   *Biographical and Historical Memoirs of Mississippi* (Chicago: Goodspeed, 1891), 642.
9   CSA Muster Roll for W.P. Ratliff, July 6, 1864.
10 *Biographical and Historical Memoirs of Mississippi*, 642.
11 Ibid.
12 Ibid.
13 John Barton (John B.) Ratliff, the third child and oldest living son, born in Ethel on May 14, 1878, was the grandfather of the author.

In 1870, W.P. and Cornelia were living in Ethel with no children.[14] In 1880, they were living in the same place, now with four children.[15]

WILLIAM PINKNEY RATLIFF - MAN OF MANY OCCUPATIONS

Farmer

As described in *Biographical and Historical Memoirs of Mississippi*, upon returning home from the Civil War, William Pinkney Ratliff purchased a small amount of land in Attala County on credit and began farming. He soon paid off the debt and purchased more land. By 1890, he had three plantations consisting of 1,100 acres, including eleven acres in strawberries at the plantation in Ethel.[16] He was a farmer until his death in 1927.[17]

Businessman

W.P. Ratliff, as he referred to himself in his business affairs (he was called "Pinkney" or "Pink" by his friends),[18] had a store near Springdale and "in February 1897, erected a telephone line from Kosciusko to his residence and store."[19] The Hughes Post Office was moved to his store in 1906, where it remained until 1908.[20] And, of course, he was engaged in the growing and sale of cotton, strawberries, and other produce from his farms.

---

14   1870 US Census, Township 15, Range 6, Attala Co., Mississippi, sheet 15A, National Archives Microfilm, M593, roll 722.
15   1880 US Census, Township 14, Range 6, Attala Co., Mississippi, ED 18, sheet 17, National Archives Microfilm, T9, roll 641.
16   *Biographical and Historical Memoirs of Mississippi*, 642.
17   Much of the information about the occupations of William Pinkney Ratliff is quoted directly from Kosciusko-Attala Historical Society, *Kosciusko-Attala History* (Walsworth Publishing Company, 1976), an open source.
18   Unpublished manuscript: Bernard L. Trippett, *The Jackson-Ratliff Duel: A Memoir of Family History* (1991). Trippett was married to a descendant of Sam Jackson.
19   Kosciusko-Attala Historical Society, *Kosciusko-Attala History,* 72.
20   Ibid., 148.

Preacher

In 1866, W.P. Ratliff joined the Methodist Church and was ordained as a preacher in 1878.[21] Ratliff was listed as one of the speakers at the Attala County Sunday School Convention at McCool, Mississippi, on July 7–8, 1886.[22] In a July 14, 1891, *Alliance Vindicator* article, apparently in response to a charge in a rival newspaper accusing him of having given up his calling as a preacher, Ratliff wrote, "And as to the desertion of my calling, you are reckoning without your host. I preached to an appreciative audience last Sunday and expect to fill an appointment at Forest on next Sunday."[23]

Newspaperman

With T.J. Fowler, W.P. Ratliff founded the *Alliance Vindicator* newspaper around 1891 as an organ of the People's (Populist) Party.[24] His career as a journalist appears to have been motivated by his interest in politics and the Populist Party. The newspaper lasted until 1896, by which time he had moved from Kosciusko to a farm in Zilpha.

Politician

W.P. Ratliff began his political career at a relatively young age. In 1875, when he was only twenty-eight years old, he was elected Attala County assessor and conducted two assessments during his term.[25] In 1891, he ran for the Mississippi House of Representatives as a Democrat and won.[26] Later, Ratliff changed parties after being elected as a Democrat. Also elected from the same district was Major L.S. Terry, a Democrat. Terry died in 1893 and was replaced by Samuel Anderson Jackson for the rest of his term.

---

21   *Biographical and Historical Memoirs of Mississippi*, 642.
22   Kosciusko-Attala Historical Society, *Kosciusko-Attala History*, 154.
23   W.P. Ratliff, "Ratliff's Attempt to Reply to the Nine Questions," *Alliance Vindicator*, July 14, 1891. See Appendix One.
24   Kosciusko-Attala Historical Society, *Kosciusko-Attala History*, 65.
25   *Biographical and Historical Memoirs of Mississippi*, 642.
26   Kosciusko-Attala Historical Society, *Kosciusko-Attala History*, 63.

WHO WAS WILLIAM PINKNEY RATLIFF?

In 1893, Ratliff ran for US Congress to represent the Fifth Congressional District of Mississippi, consisting of the counties of Attala, Clarke, Holmes, Jasper, Lauderdale, Leake, Neshoba, Newton, Scott, Smith, Wayne, and Yazoo.

Ratliff represented the Populist Party, while his opponent, John Sharp Williams, was the Democratic Party's candidate. While presumably Ratliff's *Alliance Vindicator* newspaper supported Ratliff for Congress, Williams was supported by the *Kosciusko Star*. Ratliff lost—3,028 votes to Williams's 7541. John Sharp Williams went on to serve eight terms in the US House of Representatives and two terms in the US Senate.[27]

---

27 *Biloxi Herald,* August 22, 1896; also Trippett.

William Pinkney Ratliff

4

WHO WAS SAMUEL ANDERSON JACKSON?

The following description of Samuel Anderson Jackson, his ancestors, his background, and place in the community is from an unpublished paper by Bernard Trippett, the husband of a Jackson descendant, and is reproduced here with his permission.

> Sam Jackson was born on November 7, 1854, the son of John Anderson Jackson and Susan Anna Zollicoffer Jackson. His father was a farmer and merchant in Kosciusko, who died in 1861.
>
> The Jackson family had been prominent in Attala County from the earliest years of the Nineteenth Century. They were substantial, aggressive, energetic, and successful. Three Jackson men were colonels in the Mexican War, including John Anderson Jackson. A Jackson man was active in an anti-secessionist movement, but in 1861, all Jacksons joined the Confederate Army when it was necessary, in the words of one Jackson, "to battle a common enemy."
>
> Sam Jackson's mother was from the distinguished Zollicoffer family, which included General Felix Kirk Zollicoffer, the

first Confederate general officer killed in the Civil War. His mother—called Sue or Annie by friends—was a woman of means who was a skillful investor of funds. In 1884, she gave her son Sam and his bride Lillie Clower Jackson a house as a wedding present.

Sam Jackson was educated at Ole Miss (University of Mississippi) in pharmacy. He entered business in Kosciusko as Samuel A. Jackson & Company, Wholesale and Retail Drugs. The store later expanded to include general merchandise.

Sam Jackson married Susan Clower at the Methodist Church in Lexington, Mississippi on February 28, 1878.

Susan Clower Jackson died February 3, 1881 for causes not known. She was 21.

Samuel A. Jackson married Lillie P. Clower, who was his first wife's sister, on March 28, 1882. They had four children:

Eva Lillian, born in March, 1883, married Lester Ethel Barr of Lexington, Mississippi.

Frederick Zollicoffer, born in October, 1886, married Elizabeth Durfy in 1906.

Lavinia Ethel, born in August 1888, married Dalton McBee of Lexington, Mississippi in December 1913.

John Felix, born February 6, 1892, married Julia Riley in 1930.

In a few years, Sam Jackson became interested in the law and local politics. He returned to Ole Miss to study law and also studied law at the University of Virginia.[1]

According to the *Daily Blade*:

...Jackson was one of the most popular businessmen of Kosciusko. A short time ago, he attended one of the best law schools in the land; came away in every way fitted to the profession, and was a few months ago elected to represent his county in the state legislature, defeating a populist by a good majority.[2]

---

1   Bernard L. Trippett, *The Jackson-Ratliff Duel: A Memoir of Family History,* 1991. The author met with Mr. Trippett on three occasions at Mr. Trippett's home in Northern Virginia. Mr. Trippett stated that all of the information in his manuscript was gleaned from open source materials.

2   *Chicago Daily Blade*, March 10, 1894.

5

SHOWDOWN AT THE COURTHOUSE

So it was on March 3, 1894, that Ratliff and Jackson met by chance or fate in Kosciusko at the Attala County Courthouse. Below is a photo of the courthouse around 1894.[1]

---

1   Framed photo on the wall of the current Attala County Courthouse. Photo taken by author in 2009.

Below are photos of how the courthouse square would have appeared in 1894.

Cotton going to compress on northwest corner of Courthouse Square

Cotton going to compress on west side of Courthouse Square[2]

---

2   Thanks to both Bill Mitchell, who has the original photos, and Sally Wasson, who gave the author access to her copies.

The account below is taken from the testimony of many who witnessed some part of the incident, as well as from Ratliff himself. As often happens, not every witness saw the same thing or agreed on exactly what happened. However, the following basic story emerged.

Thirty to forty persons, including Jackson and Ratliff, had congregated in the courthouse for a bankruptcy auction of goods by the sheriff.[3] It was near the front door of the courthouse, about ten feet from the south door and not far from the law offices of Allen and McCool.[4] The *Daily Blade* reported that "Saturday about noon Messrs. Jackson and Ratliff met on the lower floor of the courthouse and just in front of the sheriff's office, where Deputy Sheriff Wallace was auctioning some goods."[5]

Ratliff and Jackson did not acknowledge one another, as far as witnesses saw. Jackson had his head bent, looking over some inkstands. Frank Arrington said he was standing next to Jackson when Ratliff approached. Ratliff shook Arrington's hand.[6] Then without warning, Ratliff walked around behind Jackson and struck Jackson on the side of the head with his fist.[7] A scuffle ensued, with the two ending up on the floor—Ratliff on top. A doctor would testify later that Jackson had an abrasion on his right cheek and a bruise on the ear, consistent with injuries caused by a blow.[8]

---

3   *New York Times*, March 4, 1894.
4   Testimony of J.C. Clark at the trial of W.P. Ratliff, as reported by the *Kosciusko Star*, March 23, 1894. Clark was an attorney, mayor of Kosciusko (1886-91), and a state senator. According to the *Kosciusko-Attala County History*, pg. 70, citing the *Kosciusko Star-Ledger* of August 12, 1898, he died tragically as a result of a fall from an upstairs window at the courthouse while leaning out to shoot at sparrows.
5   *Chicago Daily Blade*, March 10, 1894.
6   Testimony of Frank Arrington at the trial of W.P. Ratliff, as reported by the *Kosciusko Star*, March 23, 1894.
7   Ratliff's grandson Barton Wade Ratliff wrote, in a note to the author in 2008, that being called a liar and a traitor and a scoundrel in print would have been fighting words to his grandfather, who would have felt that his honor was impugned.
8   Testimonies of J.C. Clark and Dr. J. R. Roby at the trial of W.P. Ratliff, as reported by the *Kosciusko Star*, March 23, 1894.

Jackson was not expecting an attack from Ratliff that day. A newspaper dated March 5, two days after the incident, reported as follows:

IT WAS A FOUL CRIME

Ugly Testimony Against Parson Ratliff

The Difficulty Entirely Unexpected
By Representative Jackson

His First Intimation was the Blow that Knocked Him Down.

The Victim Thought the Matter was Dropped and Expressed His Intention of Withdrawing the Offensive Language on Account of (Ratliff's) Family

Kosciusko, Miss. March 5 --- There is no doubt that the difficulty which culminated so fatally on Saturday last between Ratliff and Jackson was entirely unexpected by Jackson, he being led to believe from Ratliff's publication in the last issue of his paper that the matter would be dropped.

Jackson expressed to his friends only a short time before ... that he was sorry he had used the offensive language on account of Ratliff's family. As it had not been resented, he would withdraw the same in the next issue of the *Kosciusko Star*.[9]

This was not the first instance of fisticuffs involving Ratliff. Writing after the incident with Jackson at the courthouse, a Memphis newspaper reported:

---

9 Unidentified newspaper, March 5, 1894, probably the *Kosciusko Star*.

>...It would appear that Ratliff... has on previous occasions been involved in difficulties growing out of a somewhat free-handed exercise of his privileges and opportunities as the editor and publisher of a Populist newspaper. Only last August he came in contact with F. P. Johnson, the publisher of a rival paper at Kosciusko, and came off with a sanguinated face. Kosciusko enjoys two papers, the *Alliance Vindicator*, of which Ratliff is the publisher, and the *Kosciusko Star*, a sturdy Democratic paper, edited by F.P. Johnson. Ratliff is known in his community and outside of it for that matter, as "the fighting parson." During last August he published an article reflecting on Mr. Johnson's veracity, and on the occasion of their next meeting, Mr. Johnson showed a spirited resentment by landing an uppercut on the parson's forehead. The municipal authorities interfered before any serious damage was done. It was thought then that this experience would serve to attenuate the bitterness of the parson's writings, but the sequel shows otherwise.[10]

In the courthouse altercation, as bystanders separated the two men, Jackson got up, pulled his gun, and raised it above his head. He appeared to be trying to turn it toward Ratliff when bystanders intervened by grabbing at the gun.[11] Ratliff put his hand on his gun. Two shots were fired, both hitting the door. Witnesses agreed that Jackson had fired. Ratliff drew his pistol but was immediately forced out the door. Witness accounts varied as to whether Ratliff fired or not.[12]

---

10 Unidentified Memphis newspaper, March 4, 1894.
11 Testimony of Will Jamison at the trial of W.P. Ratliff, as reported by the *Kosciusko Star*, March 23, 1894.
12 Testimony of W.P. Ratliff at his trial, as reported by the *Kosciusko Star*, March 23, 1894.

The *Kosciusko Star* of March 15, 1894[13] reported this part of the struggle as follows:

> Shortly after twelve o'clock Saturday, Mr. Jackson was at the south end of the court house inspecting some stationery and other articles that were being sold at auction by the sheriff. While he was looking at the goods, Ratliff walked up unperceived by him and hit him in the back of the head and a little to the right with his fist without warning. Jackson made an effort to face his assailant, when Ratliff tripped him and threw him violently to the brick floor. Ratliff then made an effort to get down on Jackson's body, but was prevented. Both men then drew their pistols, but who did so first is unsettled, as the testimony of each witness depended upon whom he was looking at. The men were then separated by the officers and bystanders. Jackson was forced into the space between the steps and the wall on the east side, while Ratliff was carried to a similar place on the west side. At this moment the men came near getting together again and it was decided to take Ratliff out the south door and to hold Jackson inside.[14]

Reverend J. B. George tried (unsuccessfully) to take Jackson's gun from him. Sheriff Dave F. Love and Deputy Sheriff Newt Love escorted Ratliff out of the courthouse through the south door. They tried to take his gun, but Ratliff refused. Meanwhile, men inside were trying to restrain Jackson, who was trying to get out of the courthouse to pursue Ratliff. Jackson was heard by one witness to say, "I'm going to kill the scoundrel."[15] No doubt, Ratliff felt he had reason to be ready to protect himself should Jackson try to make good on his threat. As the officers took Ratliff outside,

---

13   The author is indebted to Sally Wasson for sharing clippings about the shooting and trial from many newspapers around the country.

14   *Kosciusko Star,* March 23, 1894.

15   Testimony of Charles Listner at the trial of W.P. Ratliff, as reported by the *Kosciusko Star,* March 23, 1894.

moving westward, Bob Gunter closed the south door to keep Jackson inside, whereupon Jackson placed his pistol to Gunter's head and told him to let him out.[16] Gunter refused. Jackson then rushed to the west door of the courthouse and ran outside.

As he exited the courthouse, Ratliff was being led away by the officers and had his back to Jackson. Witnesses heard someone shout, "Look out!" One witness testified that he heard Jackson say, "Turn the rascal loose!"[17] Another witness who was sitting in front of the Hines Hotel on the south side of the courthouse square heard shots and saw Ratliff holding "a very black pistol."[18] Officers carried Ratliff off in an oblique direction across the square, with Ratliff still in possession of the pistol. The witness said that he saw officers release Ratliff with pistol in hand.[19] Yet another witness testified that he saw Ratliff led off by officers and that he "appeared to be resisting."[20]

Note: Ratliff family legend, as related by W.P.'s grandson Pinkney Brooks Ratliff to the author in 1957, was that the sheriff had taken Ratliff's pistol, and when Jackson began shooting, Ratliff said, "Sheriff, You aren't going to let him shoot a good man, are you?" whereupon the sheriff returned Ratliff's gun to him and Ratliff returned fire. That this account is likely only a family legend (Pinkney Brooks Ratliff was born more than ten years after the shooting) is supported by the preponderance of witnesses to the shooting who stated that Ratliff still had his pistol when Jackson approached.

Note: According to Ellen Oakes Pettit (great-granddaughter of John Whitfield Ratliff, W.P.'s brother), her grandfather Charles "Charlie"

---

16   Testimony of Earnest Allen at the trial of W.P. Ratliff, as reported by the *Kosciusko Star*, March 23, 1894.

17   Testimony of J.M. Hughes at the trial of W.P. Ratliff, as reported by the *Kosciusko Star*, March 23, 1894.

18   Reported to be a Colt .38 revolver.

19   Testimony of H.P. Casey at the trial of W.P. Ratliff, as reported by the *Kosciusko Star*, March 23, 1894.

20   Testimony of M. M. Hull at the trial of W.P. Ratliff, as reported by the *Kosciusko Star*, March 23, 1894.

Franklin Oakes (married to W.P.'s niece Mary Ella Ratliff) said that he was told by Ratliff kin and others that the sheriff said, "Pink, defend yourself."

According to the testimony of Sheriff D. F. Love, Ratliff broke away from Deputy Newt Love and himself and returned fire.[21] One witness saw Jackson running toward Ratliff. Jackson fired at Ratliff, running about five or six steps after firing. Ratliff turned and returned fire. Jackson fired two shots; Ratliff fired three.[22] Other witnesses thought Ratliff fired two shots, though three shots were more likely. At least one of the shots may have been deflected by someone trying to seize Ratliff's gun.[23] Jackson went down. When the smoke had cleared, two were dead: Jackson, shot in the head,[24] and one innocent bystander—Sam Russell. The *New Orleans Times Democrat* described the scene as follows:

> Six pistol shots rang out with sickening clearness at the courthouse, and before the excited crowd that rushed there realized its deadly import, Hon. S.A. Jackson, Democratic Representative from this county in the Legislature, lay dead with a gaping wound in his forehead, while his life's blood poured out on the sod beneath him, and just behind lay Sam Russell gasping for breath, and Will Sanders, another innocent bystander, moaning from a mortal wound. There also, stood Hon. W.P. Ratliff, the Populist member of the Legislature, with a smoking revolver in his hand, seemingly unmoved by the dreadful havoc he had wrought. The terrible tragedy is made sadder by the killing of Russell and the probable fatal wounding of Sanders, because neither were parties to the difficulty, and their death was purely accidental.[25]

---

21 Testimony of Sheriff D.F. Love at the trial of W.P. Ratliff, as reported by the *Kosciusko Star*, March 23, 1894.
22 Testimony of H.P. Casey at the trial of W.P. Ratliff, as reported by the *Kosciusko Star*, March 23, 1894.
23 Testimony of W.P. Ratliff at his trial, as reported by the *Kosciusko Star*, March 23, 1894.
24 Testimony of Dr. J. R. Roby at the trial of W.P. Ratliff, as reported by the *Kosciusko Star*, March 23, 1894.
25 Special to the *New Orleans Times-Democrat*, March 4, 1894.

The innocent bystander Will Sanders was wounded in the hip—a wound thought to be fatal. However, he recovered. Brought into the courthouse on a litter to appear as a witness in the trial, Sanders described the circumstances of his shooting as follows: He heard two shots behind him. He ran toward the west corner, but saw Jackson coming and ran back east and was shot in the right hip by Ratliff as he (Sanders) crossed the brick walk on the south side of the courthouse.[26]

The tragic story of the death of the innocent bystander Sam Russell was recounted in *The Russell and May Family History*. With the permission of authors Barbara Gail Russell Brien and Bill Gary Russell, their description of the circumstances of Sam Russell's death is included below:

> One day in 1894, Allen left their Sallis farm to go to Kosciusko to pick up his brother, Sam, who had been released from prison and was arriving by train. (Sam and his brother, Seborn, and two Teague brothers had robbed a train. Sam was sent to the penitentiary. I am not sure if anyone else was caught and sentenced.) In any event, Sam arrived in Kosciusko, and while waiting for Allen, noticed two men arguing over politics on the courthouse lawn. The argument was heated and resulted in a duel, with one man killing the other. Two other bullets, however, strayed and hit two bystanders, seriously wounding one and killing Sam. Allen arrived a few minutes after the duel to find his brother dead. He loaded his brother's body in the wagon and took him the ten long miles back to the Sallis farm. Since they didn't have telephones, the rest of the family didn't know about what had happened until Allen got home.[27]

---

26 Testimony of Will Sanders at the trial of W.P. Ratliff, as reported by the *Kosciusko Star*, March 23, 1894.
27 Barbara Gail Russell Brien and Bill Gary Russell, *The Russell and May Family History* (Greenville, Mississippi: BGR Brien, 1997). Out of print. Thanks to Barbara Gail Russell Brien and Bill Gary Russell for permission to quote this passage from their book.

The *Kosciusko Star* of March 9, 1894, described the chaotic scene after Ratliff had been taken out of the courthouse and Jackson pursued him:

> Ratliff was then forced away from the door in an oblique direction towards the Southwest corner of the yard. In the meantime Jackson had broken away from those who were holding him and rushed out the West door just as Ratliff had passed the North and South line of the Courthouse on the West side. Jackson called out to those who were holding Ratliff to look out, he was going to shoot. Deputy Newt Love, who was assisting the sheriff to hold Ratliff, then rushed towards Jackson to prevent his shooting. He reached the latter just as he got to the corner of the Courthouse; when Jackson fired once over Love's shoulder, though the bullet evidently went wide of the mark. Ratliff returned fire and this was the shot that is supposed to have killed Russell, who was standing about the West window on the South side.
>
> Now occurred a strange feature of the tragedy. Instead of rushing directly towards Ratliff, whom he was evidently anxious to reach, Jackson bore away to the East and went in towards Ratliff in a sort of semi-circle. When almost in line between the South door of the Courthouse and Ratliff the latter again fired, and the best evidence is that that shot struck Sanders. When almost directly East of Ratliff Jackson started directly towards him with his pistol tightly gripped in both hands.
>
> All this time he had had his head hung forward on one side with his body drawn up in a most singular fashion. A plausible explanation of this is that he was dazed by the blow from Ratliff on the back of his head. The contortion of his body

might be explained by his pulling down with all his might on the trigger on his self-acting revolver, when the fact is that if such weapons have been fired, the trigger must be momentarily released in order to fire again. In the excitement, Mr. Jackson no doubt forgot this.

When in about eight feet of Mr. Ratliff, with his head still down, the latter shot him directly in the top of his head, and his life went out instantly.[28]

According to the *Kosciusko Star* of March 23:

After the shooting, Ratliff was taken back into the court house, still in possession of the Colt .38 revolver he used in the shooting. Mr. McCool had come into the sheriff's office and told them that the people were very much excited and they should best be prepared. Other parties began to load their pistols.[29]

The *Jackson Clarion-Ledger* reported the following:

Before further violence could occur, Ratliff was arrested, taken to the jail, and charged with murder. Ratliff said from his jail cell that he would not have killed Sam Jackson for anything in the world, save in defense of his own life.[30] Later, in a statement in his own *Alliance Vindicator* newspaper, Ratliff wrote that "if he possessed the wealth of a Vanderbilt, he would gladly give every dollar if he could call back to earth the spirits of the dead, and restore the ties of broken friendship."[31]

---

28 *Kosciusko Star*, March 9, 1894.
29 Testimony of W.P. Ratliff at his trial, as reported by the *Kosciusko Star*, March 23, 1894.
30 *New Orleans Times-Democrat*, March 4, 1894.
31 *Jackson (MS) Clarion-Ledger*, March 19, 1894.

Thus a battle between two opposing politicians that started with a war of words and festered over a period of weeks or months finally ended in a brawl and a gun fight with tragic consequences.

Friends of Sam Jackson removed a door from the courthouse and used it as a makeshift stretcher to carry him to his home three blocks away. Funeral services were conducted at the Jackson residence on the evening of March 4 by Rev. J.H. Alexander. Sam Jackson's body was interred at the Kosciusko Cemetery. The *Clarion-Ledger* reported that "never before in the history of Kosciusko was there such an outpouring of people at a funeral. The Masons, Knights of Pythias, and Knights of Honor turned out in force."[32] At the time of his death, Jackson was only thirty-nine years old.

According to the March 10, 1894, account in the *Chicago Daily Blade*:

> The obsequies of S. A. Jackson occurred here Monday. The burial was conducted by the Masons, the deceased having been a member of that order. The Knights of Pythias and the Knights of Honor also took part. Parson Ratliff watched the funeral procession from the window of his cell as it passed the jail. He showed no emotion until after it had passed, when he burst into tears and between sobs expressed the deepest regret for killing Jackson.[33]

W.P.'s nephew Zachariah Alexander "Zack" Wasson was in town when W.P. shot Sam Jackson. Zack stopped by the home of his Aunt "Duck," who was W.P.'s sister Louisa Matilda "Duck" Ratliff Hines. He reported that when she heard about the shooting, she cried and cried.[34]

---

32 Bernard L. Trippett, *The Jackson-Ratliff Duel: A Memoir of Family History*, 1991.
33 *Chicago Daily Blade,* March 10, 1894.
34 Letter to author from Sally Wasson, widow of Zachariah Alexander Wasson's son William Eugene "Billie" Wasson, dated June 11, 2009.

6

ON TRIAL FOR MURDER

Grand Jury Called

A grand jury was convened the week of March 5, 1894, and "W. P. Ratliff, editor, legislator, and leader of the third party in this district," was indicted on two counts: assault with intent to kill and murder of "S.A. Jackson, druggist and legislator."[1]

The trial was to begin March 10, and the prosecution's team, consisting of District Attorney W.S. Hill and the law firm of Anderson, Hayden and Davis, announced itself ready for trial. However, the defense team, comprised of the law firms of Allen and McCool and Dodd and Armistead, requested a continuance on the grounds that many of the witnesses who had been called had not yet reported. Additional arguments for continuance were to be heard on Monday, March 12.[2]

Unprecedented Publicity and Attention

Needless to say, the violence and tragedy at the courthouse was the talk of Kosciusko and Attala County and attracted notable attention in other parts of the country. Newspaper coverage was extensive. The *New York*

---

1   *Atlanta Constitution*, March 11, 1894.
2   Ibid.

Times reported that feelings were so high in Kosciusko that the jail was "strongly guarded to prevent Ratliff being lynched by Jackson's friends."[3]

The story of the shooting drew particular attention because the two principals were not only both politicians, but also members of the Mississippi legislature, both from the same district. The story, as dramatic it was on the face of it, also lent itself to hyperbole.

The *New York Times* headline on March 4, 1894, about the incident read as follows:

HE KILLS HIS ENEMY AND FATALLY WOUNDS TWO BYSTANDERS

> The Rev. Mr. Ratliff, Populist, ends a Political Quarrel
> by Shooting a Leading Democratic Politician
> – Both were Members of the Mississippi Legislature –

Two Witnesses of the Encounter Victims of the Clergyman's Revolver[4]

The *Atlanta Constitution* opined that the case "promises to be one of the most prominent "cases célèbres" in the annals of Mississippi on account of the political prominence of the parties."[5]

From the *New Orleans Times-Democrat*:

> It is a trial that commands the public interest for more than one reason. First, it grew out of the intense political excitement, occasionally reaching fever heat that has agitated the county for the past two years. The defendant is one of the best known members of the Populist Party in this state, while the deceased was a prominent leader.[6]

---

3   *New York Times*, March 4, 1894.
4   Ibid.
5   *Atlanta Constitution*, March 11, 1894.
6   *New Orleans Times-Democrat*, March 16, 1894.

The *Times-Democrat* further said this of the trial:

> It will pass into local history as a most important event and for years will be discussed over the firesides of the people.[7]

The *Chicago Daily Blade* of March 10, 1894, published the following sketches of Ratliff and Jackson:[8]

W. P. Ratliff, the Slayer.

S. A. Jackson, the Slain.

---

7   Ibid.
8   *Chicago Daily Blade*, March 10, 1894. Thanks to Ellen Pettit for providing clippings from the newspaper with these sketches.

The same article in the *Daily Blade* of March 10, 1894, printed the sketch below of the shooting.⁹

it Was a Duel to Death.

The sketch of the courthouse that follows, showing the particulars of the shooting outside the courthouse and where each of the principals was located also comes from the *Daily Blade* article of March 10, 1894.

---

9   Ibid.

THE COURTHOUSE AT KOSCIUSKO.

Notes on photo:

1. South entrance, just inside of which occurred the first meeting, where Ratliff struck Jackson and wrestled him to the floor, and from which Ratliff was ushered out of the building…
2. West door, where Jackson came out after he and Ratliff were separated
3. Where Jackson fell mortally wounded
4. Where Ratliff stood when the fatal shots were fired that killed Russell and Jackson
5. Where Sam Russell fell, pierced through the head by a stray shot from Ratliff's pistol
6. Where W.P. Saunders was shot, on the brick walkway[10]

---

10   Ibid.

Assembly of Witnesses and Selection of Jurors

On Thursday, March 15, 1894, the trial began.[11] W.P. Ratliff, neatly dressed in a long black coat, appeared in court at 9:00 am, appearing composed and calm. Having been jailed for almost two weeks, he looked pale and thin.[12] His daughter Florence Cornelia Ratliff would later recall that, as an eight-year-old child, she took food from home to her father at the jail.[13]

The names of more than eighty-five witnesses were called. Forty-nine persons were called for the jury pool. The state and the defense each were allowed twelve challenges without cause. The process of jury selection consumed most of the afternoon, and by around 5:00 pm, all parties declared themselves satisfied with the twelve jurors selected. Court was adjourned, with the trial set to begin on March 16.

The Trial Begins

Trial began on the morning of Friday, March 16, with the testimony of prosecution witnesses. The following witnesses, in order of appearance, testified throughout the day:

J. C. Clark, Dr. J. R. Roby, Charles Listner, Edgar Sanders, Will Jamison, Frank Arrington, W.T. Riley, H.P. Casey, J. J. Furr, W.J. Sanders, Will Stingley, J. H. Redding, W. C. Whitehead, W. N. Dorrill, George McMillan, L. Glazier, N. O. Thompson, Rev. J. B. George, Ed Stingley, Will Sanders (wounded bystander), T. V. Jones, C. G. Kuykendall, L. S. Blackstock, W. L. Allgood, Earnest Allen, Sheriff David F. Love, Bob Gunter, Will Hull, V. H. Wallace, J. F. McCool, W. M. Yandell, Sr., J. W. D. White, Ephraim Dodd, and Zack Dailey.

After a supper break, the court held a night session, with defense witness testimony commencing. The following witnesses testified during the evening session: L.W. Hoffman, W.L. Ray, J. A. Emerson, C.M. Bruce,

---

11 The primary source for this account of the trial was *the Kosciusko Star*, March 23, 1894. The account appears to include a summation of the *Star's* daily coverage of the trial, with the March 23 article including the full account of the trial from the first day through the final verdict.
12 *New Orleans Times-Democrat*, March 16, 1894.
13 As told to Florence's nephew Barton Wade Ratliff in Phoenix, Arizona, November 1963.

George Bullock, W.A. Ward, John Hughes, Isaac Lansdale, C.F. Rowell, Will Curry, G.W. Curry, Dick Cottrell, J.M. Hughes, and W.M. Cooper.

The defense attorneys stated that the presentation of their witnesses would take about one more hour. At this point, the judge adjourned court, to resume at 8:00 am on Saturday, March 17.

As the trial reconvened on Saturday, the defense called its witnesses in the following order: M.M. Hull, Sam Williams, Asa Robinson, R.B. Meek, and William Pinkney Ratliff (the defendant).

It was clear from the testimony of the witnesses that, although Ratliff initiated the physical attack, Jackson was first to draw his weapon and fire at Ratliff in the courthouse. After the two protagonists were separated and Ratliff was hustled outside and was being led away by the sheriff and his deputy, Jackson wrested free of those who were holding him and pursued Ratliff, firing shots at him yet a second time.

After the testimony of the defendant, the defense rested its case. The prosecution called witnesses to rebut defense testimony. Called were Sheriff David F. Love, George Bullock, J.H. Sullivant, and Dr. F.D. Smythe. The state rested its case about 11:00 am. The court allowed the defense until the afternoon to prepare their final statement. Speeches were limited to two for each side.

Court reconvened at 2:00 pm.

The following instructions to the jury are quoted directly from the *Kosciusko Star* of March 23, 1894:

> The District Attorney read the following instructions:
>
> The court instructs the jury that one who prepares a deadly weapon intending to use it if necessary in overcoming resistance, approaches his antagonist, brings on the attack, and then uses the said weapon, cannot plead self-defense when his antagonist makes it necessary to use said weapon and if, from all the evidence in this cause, the jury conscientiously believe that W. P. Ratliff armed himself with a pistol, and that it was a deadly weapon, and that he intended to use it

if necessary in overcoming resistance; approached S.A. Jackson, brought on the attack and while then and there overcoming Jackson's resistance of the attack so brought on, fired with said pistol at and towards Jackson, he is guilty of the second count in the indictment[14] and the jury will so find.

Mr. Haden, of the prosecution, also read the following instructions:

No language, however violent or defamatory, either spoken, written or published by one man about another, will justify even an assault unless it is uttered in the presence of the party and resented at the time of utterance. And although the jury may believe from the evidence that Jackson, in reply to a newspaper article by Ratliff, published the article in *The Kosciusko Star*, in which he said "The villain still pursues me" and in substance that Ratliff was an infernal damned lie or liar—this did not justify or authorize the defendant in assaulting Jackson, or in shooting at or killing him. But if the jury believe from the evidence that the defendant started the difficulty at the time it occurred by striking Jackson, the defendant being at the time armed with a pistol which was a deadly weapon, which he intended to use if necessary, then he is guilty of an assault with intent to kill and the jury will so find.

The court instructs the jury that the newspaper articles in evidence before them cannot be considered by them only as showing the State of feeling between the defendant and deceased, and in arriving at a verdict the jury are not to consider said articles or any of them as justifying defendant in any attack or assault upon or shooting at or killing deceased.

---

14   Assault with intent to kill.

If the jury believe from the evidence that the defendant provoked the difficulty at the time it occurred in the Court House by striking Jackson, being armed with a pistol which was a deadly weapon which the defendant intended to use if necessary to overcome any resistance or attack Jackson might make in the difficulty thus provoked, and that the defendant fired or shot at Jackson with said pistol, then he is guilty of an assault with intent to kill, although the jury may further believe from the evidence that Jackson, after being assaulted, first drew his pistol and fired at the defendant.

The instructions of the court to the jury for the defendant were as follows:

The court instructs the jury that from all the evidence in the case, both from the State and the defendant, that they will find the defendant not guilty as to the first count in the indictment:

If, from the whole evidence and all the circumstances in the case the jury can only say there is a probability of the defendant's guilt; the jury will acquit.

If there is any reasonable hypothesis or supposition arising out of the evidence, or want of evidence, which is inconsistent with the guilt of the accused, the jury should acquit.

Neither a preponderance of evidence nor any amount of weight of preponderance of evidence warrants the jury in convicting the defendant unless it generates full belief of the prisoner's guilt to a moral certainty.

The court instructs the jury for the defendant W. P. Ratliff, that although they may believe from the evidence that

Ratliff brought on the difficulty with Jackson by striking Jackson with his fist, and was armed with a deadly weapon at the time he did it; yet if they further believe that Ratliff did not intend to use said weapon to overcome Jackson or to kill him, or in any other way to do Jackson any great bodily harm, then Jackson was not authorized to shoot Ratliff; and if they further believe from the evidence that when Jackson and Ratliff were first separated, that Ratliff abandoned the fight in good faith and that Jackson then drew his pistol and struggling to run upon him shot at Ratliff and, that Ratliff returned the fire only to protect himself, then Ratliff is not guilty as charged and they must so find.

The jury are instructed that although they may believe from the evidence that the defendant commenced the fight in question, and made the first attack upon the deceased with his fist, still if the jury further believe from the evidence that the defendant afterwards and before Jackson drew his pistol and attempted to shoot him, ceased to fight and in good faith withdrew from the conflict by retreating in the custody of the officers, then the right of Jackson to shoot at defendant ceased, and if the defendant [sic][15] did not then desist from attempting to use violence toward defendant, then the defendant's right to defend himself (survived?) and if he then found himself (in real?) or apparent danger of losing his life or of sustaining great bodily injury at the hands of the deceased, he had the same right to defend himself that he would have had if he had not originally commenced the conflict.

The court further instructs the jury for the defendant Ratliff that a mere blow with the fist upon Jackson which would not

---

15 Author's note: Could this be a mistake? Perhaps the writer intended to write "deceased" (Jackson) rather than "defendant" (Ratliff).

endanger his life, or do him any great bodily harm, would not authorize Jackson to shoot Ratliff, and if they believe from the evidence that Jackson drew his pistol after being so struck, and attempted to shoot Ratliff after he (Ratliff) had wholly abandoned the difficulty, and that Ratliff did not intend to use the deadly weapon at the time the difficulty occurred, nor attempt to do so; and that Ratliff shot as he was retreating only to protect himself from being killed by Jackson, then they must find the defendant not guilty of the crime charged.

The court instructs the jury that to justify the killing of deceased or of shooting at him at the door of the court house, it is not necessary that the danger to defendant need be actual nor the killing unavoidable at the time, and if the jury believe that he honestly shot at Jackson to save his own life, and that he did not provoke the difficulty armed with a deadly weapon, nor to use his pistol to overcome deceased if necessary, then the law is for the defendant and the jury will so find.

The law presumes the defendant to be innocent of any and all crime, and it is the duty of the jury to reconcile this presumption with all the facts and circumstances in the case if they can reasonably do so. And by his pleas of not guilty he puts upon the State the burden of proving each and every material allegation in the indictment to a moral certainty; and while there may be many facts and circumstances in the case that point to the defendant's guilt, yet if from a single fact or circumstance in the whole case as shown from the evidence, the jury have a reasonable doubt as to defendant's guilt, they will acquit.

The court further instructs the jury that the evidence for the State must be so satisfactory and convincing that the conclusions of the defendant's guilt must be reasonably unresistable; and if from all the evidence in the case there is a single fact or circumstance that raises a reasonable doubt as to the defendant's guilt as charged, or fails to make it morally certain to their minds that the defendant is guilty as charged in second count of indictment, then they must find him not guilty.

At this point, on a motion of the defense, the first count of the indictment—for murder—was dismissed, and the case went to the jury on the second count, charging Ratliff with shooting with intent to kill. The *Star* reported the following:

> Mr. Haden, for the State, opened the argument at 3:15 p.m., and spoke about fifty minutes. He was followed by Messrs. McCool and Armistead for the defense. Mr. Anderson then spoke for the prosecution and court adjourned for supper.
>
> Upon the reassembling of court for the night session Major Allen addressed the jury for the defense; followed by Mr. Dodd on the same side. District Attorney Hill then closed the argument.
>
> The case was given to the jury about 11:30 o'clock Saturday night. Court adjourned until Monday a few minutes before 12 o'clock.
>
> It is said that the jury reached a verdict a few minutes after 12.[16]

---

16   *Kosciusko Star,* March 23, 1894.

The *Kosciusko Star* ended its extensive account of the trial proceedings with the following statement:

> Court met Monday morning early and the jury was brought in. They rendered the following verdict: "We, the jury, find the defendant not guilty," and Mr. Ratliff was a free man.[17]

Could this tragedy have been avoided? Yes, without question. Below are actions that were taken and accusations hurled that, had any one of them not occurred, the chances of escalation and loss of life would have been reduced significantly:

- As emphasized in an editorial in the *Meridian News*, the fact that the dispute was carried out in writing in rival newspapers for all the public to read raised issues of honor and possible impact on future political careers, not to mention intensifying the quarrel the longer it went on. Had the quarrel played out in a face-to-face confrontation, or even through third parties, the two might have encountered one another and fought it out. The injuries would have been minor and the dispute would likely have blown over. The fault lies not only with the antagonists but also with the newspaper companies for permitting such accusations to be printed without regard for their confrontational nature.[18]

- Both antagonists employed inflammatory language in their newspaper articles, impugning one another's character and ultimately laying down clear challenges to one another to "do your worst." Even as presented in the newspapers, had the arguments been well-thought-out airings of differences

---

17 Ibid.
18 Editorial. *Meridian (MS) News*, reprinted by the *Memphis Appeal-Avalanche*, sometime after March 3, 1894. See appendix 4.

between the two parties rather than personal attacks, the chance of violence would likely have been ameliorated.[19]

- The original animosity was thought to stem from the fact that Jackson called out Ratliff in a newspaper article as a traitor for leaving the Democratic Party. Ratliff retaliated by accusing Jackson of voting for a Populist for the US Senate during a session of the Mississippi legislature. Within days, it became clear that Ratliff was mistaken—that Col. Nugent, for whom Jackson cast a meaningless "complimentary vote," was a loyal Democrat, not a Populist, although Nugent's brother had been the Populist Party candidate for governor of Texas in 1892.[20] Yet Ratliff refused to completely withdraw the charge, even when he received a letter from Nugent himself attesting that he was not a Populist.[21] Had Ratliff acknowledged unequivocally in his newspaper that he was wrong, that too could have been the end of it.

- And, finally, each of the two men armed themselves with pistols before leaving home that morning. If neither had been armed, it would not have escalated beyond fisticuffs and scuffling.

---

19 Dueling articles between Ratliff in the *Alliance Vindicator* and Jackson in the *Kosciusko Star*. See appendix 5.
20 Letter from Col. W.L. Nugent to W.P. Ratliff, February 26, 1894. See appendix 6.
21 Ibid.

7

LIFE AS A FARMER

Although the charge of murder was dismissed and W. P. acquitted of the charge of assault with intent to kill by reason of self-defense, life could not have easily returned to normal for the Jackson and Ratliff families.

The Jackson family enjoyed great respect in Kosciusko and Attala County. The pharmacy and general goods store operated by Sam Jackson presumably provided a good livelihood. Jackson's widow was reportedly left financially comfortable, thanks to her husband's industrious and entrepreneurial ways.

Nevertheless, life without a husband and father must have been difficult for Sam Jackson's family.

Both Ratliff and Jackson were respected pillars of the community. Their children went to school and played together. It must have been hard for them to be in the same school, attending classes together after the shooting and trial.

About two years after the shooting, Ratliff, who in 1890 had moved into Kosciusko with his family to give his children access to the town schools, moved his family back to the country, this time to his farm in Zilpha, north of Kosciusko.[1]

---

1   Zilpha is north of Kosciusko on Zilpha Creek, which flows into the Big Black River. Zilpha had a post office in 1895, but it no longer exists as an incorporated or unincorporated community.

In an October 12, 1946, letter to the editor of the *Kosciusko Star-Herald*, W.P.'s son Zack Mitchell Ratliff wrote to set the record straight about his father's departure from Attala County after the shooting. Zack wrote about the loss of the prior close relationship of the two families and expressed his regret at the tragedy:

> This is an incident I very much dislike to mention or even think of, and very much regretted by Dad and all his family. I trust what I say will not be misunderstood and that I say not a word to offend anyone. I'm sure that all the Ratliffs' hearts hold nothing but kindness and friendship for all the Jackson people. We kids were playmates and schoolmates of Mr. Sam and Mr. F.Z. Jackson. Claude and Doty were nearer my age, in (the) same room and classes at school under Prof. Boyd and Sisson.
>
> I will never forget the happy days I spent with these boys as well as the nights I spent with Claude and Doty. I am so sorry it becomes necessary for me to speak of the tragedy of 1894, which was brought about only by politics. No man is to blame, but politics alone.[2]

Return to a Normal Life

W.P. resumed his life as a farmer in Zilpha, maintaining his three farms and 1,100 acres of farmland.

Below are two photographs of the family, presumably taken on the same day in 1897, one in the garden and the other in front of the house on the farm in Zilpha.

---

2   Zack Mitchell Ratliff, letter to the editor, *Kosciusko Star-Herald*, October 12, 1946. With permission.

LIFE AS A FARMER

Photograph in garden of house in Zilpha 1897

Top row, standing from left, Florence Cornelia, Zack Mitchell, Katherine Elaine, Albert Wade; *middle row, seated, from left,* William Pinkney Ratliff, Cornelia Mitchell Ratliff, Sudie, Mary Belle; *front row, from left,* Tom Watson, Bessie Grace, Paul Grady.

Missing are daughter Sarah Anna Lee, born in 1873, and son John Barton, born in 1878.

Photograph in front of house in Zilpha 1897

From left, standing, Cornelia Mitchell Ratliff (*behind fence to right of left window, wearing black*), daughter Kate Elaine, William Pinkney Ratliff (*behind fence*), daughter Sudie; *from left, on bench,* son Tom Watson, son Albert Wade, daughter Bessie Grace, *to the right of the bench, standing, from left,* daughter Florence Cornelia, daughter Mary Belle; *in foreground from left,* son Zack Mitchell on mule called Sam, son Paul Grady on pony named Dixie.

Missing are daughter Sarah Anna Lee and son John Barton.

In 1900, W.P. and Cornelia and the nine children depicted in the 1897 photos above were still living in Zilpha.[3] In 1905, their Zilpha farmhouse was destroyed in a fire. W.P. then sold his farm in Zilpha and bought another farm near Winona, in Montgomery County, about forty miles

---

3 1900 US Census, Zilpha, Attala Co., Mississippi, ED 7, sheet 6B, National Archives Microfilm, T623, roll 800.

north of Kosciusko. They remained there until 1909, when W.P. traded his farm in Winona for one in western Illinois.[4]

The 1910 census reported W.P. and Cornelia's residence as Munson Township in Henry County, Illinois, though the post office may have been in Cambridge. By that time, there were only daughters Florence (age twenty-four) and Bessie (eighteen) and youngest son Tom (fifteen) still at home. W.P.'s occupation was listed as farmer.[5]

In 1910, Tom received two letters from his brother Grady, sent to their home in Illinois. Grady was writing from Chicago where he was working and attending Northwestern University.[6]

In a June 10 letter, Grady asked Tom if they had all of their land in cultivation and wondered if they had planted corn. A July 17 letter asked if they had gotten the hay in yet and would Tom tell his sisters Florence and Bessie to write.

The following year, 1911, W.P., Cornelia, daughters Florence and Bessie, and son Tom moved to Hempstead County, Arkansas. Why they made another move after only a couple of years in Illinois is unknown. Perhaps for a family from the Deep South, the cold winters and shorter growing season in Illinois were not attractive.

The actual month of the move to Arkansas is unknown, but on April 12, 1911, Tom received a letter in Arkansas from a school chum named Adolph Gustafson in Cambridge, Illinois. According to Adolph, "This year, we have a lot of fun in school. There are eight kids in school now."[7]

According to a warranty deed and lien dated May 11, 1911, William Pinkney Ratliff purchased 200 acres of farmland in Hempstead County, Arkansas, from George W. Bell and Joanna Bell, residents of Kentucky, for the sum of $6,000 in cash and time payments of $4,000 as follows: $800 before one year from date of purchase, $800 before two years from date

---

4   Zack Mitchell Ratliff, letter to the editor, *Kosciusko Star-Herald*, October 12, 1946.
5   1910 US Census, Munson, Henry County, Illinois, ED 114, sheet 7A, National Archives Microfilm, T624, roll 291.
6   Letters from Paul Grady Ratliff to his brother Tom on June 26 and July 16, 1910, copies of which were provided by Tommie Jane Ratliff Allen, Tom Watson Ratliff's youngest daughter.
7   Letter from Adolph Gustafson to Tom Watson Ratliff, April 12, 1911.

of purchase, $700 before three years from date of purchase, $800 before four years from date of purchase, and $900 before five years from date of purchase.[8]

The land W.P. purchased was described as

> E ½ of NE ¼ of Section 22
> E ½ of E ½ of SW ¼ of Section 15
> W ½ of SE ¼ of Section 15
> Township 11, South Range 26W comprising approximately 200 acres in Hempstead Co., Arkansas.[9]

Also in 1911, son Tom received a letter from his oldest sister, Anna Ratliff Donoho, about her plan to visit the family in Arkansas with her twin baby girls, Mary Lee and Sarah Elizabeth, born June 28, 1910. The letter states that her trip with the twins had to be postponed because Tom had chicken pox. Anna also requested Tom to ask "Mama" when he will be well and if Florence and Bessie have had chicken pox.[10]

In October of 1915, Tom left from New Orleans on a freighter filled with horses for England, having enlisted in the British army.[11] He was twenty-one years old. About the same time, Tom's mother, Cornelia Mitchell Ratliff, left her husband and Arkansas for good.

After Cornelia left W.P., the two had different stories about their marital status. In the 1920 census, when Cornelia was living near Jacksonville, Cherokee County, Texas, with her son Albert Wade Ratliff, either Cornelia or Albert Wade reported her status as a "widow." In the same 1920 census, William Pinkney Ratliff, living in Ozan Township, Hempstead County,

---

8   Warranty deed and lien, May 11, 1911, filed in the Hempstead County Clerk's Office May 22, 1911.
9   Ibid.
10   Letter from Sarah Anna Lee Ratliff Donoho to her youngest brother, Tom, undated, but probably sometime in 1911.
11   Article from the *Washington (AR) Telegraph* sometime in October or November of 1919, shortly after Tom's return from service in WWI.

Arkansas, reported that he was "divorced," though no divorce documentation has been found.

It was rumored within the family that W.P. brought a "mistree"[12] (mistress) over to Arkansas from Mississippi. This was presumably someone he had known when they still lived in Mississippi. Alternatively, the family may have used its contacts in Mississippi to bring a cook from there to help out in Arkansas. In 1957, Pinkney Brooks Ratliff, uncle of the author and son of W.P. and Cornelia's son John B., told the author that "Grandpa Pink had another family across the [Mississippi] River." Since Brooks was twenty years old by the time his grandfather Pinkney died, presumably the story of a mistress went beyond rumor.

As reported above, in the 1920 census, W.P. was listed as a divorced farmer on a farm in Ozan Township, Hempstead County, Arkansas.[13] Listed directly below William Pinkney Ratliff, and presumably on the same property and in the same household, was a woman named Callie Thompson, age twenty-nine, who was listed as widowed, black, and working as a cook. She had three young daughters, Vivian, age five, Pollyanna, age four, and Mildred, age two. The race of all three was listed as "mulatto," which would indicate a white father.

There was also an older daughter, Bessie Clark, age eleven, whose race was indicated as "black," obviously a reference to a different father from the three youngest daughters. The birth state of Callie, the mother, was "Mississippi" and the birth state of the father of Bessie Clark was also "Mississippi." However, the birth state of the father of the three younger children was listed as "United States," which could have been used to obscure the identity of the father. Curiously enough, in the 1900 census, when W.P. and family were living in Zilpha, they had a black male boarder and farm worker named Sam Thompson.[14] Could he have been a relative

---

12 Undated letter from Bessie Corean Ratliff Herrin (daughter of W.P.'s son Tom Watson Ratliff) to her cousin Zack Abernathy Ratliff (son of W.P.'s son Zack Mitchell Ratliff).

13 1920 US Census, Ozan, Hempstead Co., Arkansas, ED 104, sheet 4A, National Archives Microfilm, T625, roll 64.

14 1900 US Census, Beat 3, Attala Co., Mississippi, ED 17, sheet 6B, National Archives Microfilm, T623, roll 800.

of the Callie Thompson who was living with W.P. in Arkansas in the 1920 census?

Could the three youngest children have been daughters of William Pinkney Ratliff and Callie Thompson? The 1930 census ten years later provides something close to conclusive proof. In this census, Callie Montgomery (no longer Thompson), a widow, was living in Natchez, Mississippi, with her two daughters, Pollyanna and Mildred. It is suggestive that these two are the same daughters who were listed in the 1920 census in Arkansas. The whereabouts of the older daughter, Vivian, who would have been fifteen or sixteen in 1930, is not known.

For Pollyanna and Mildred, their race was now listed as "black" rather than "mulatto." The birth state of their father was now listed as "Mississippi." But, most importantly, the last name of both Pollyanna and Mildred in the 1930 census was "Ratliff."[15] The appearance in the 1930 census of a mother named Callie with two daughters named Pollyanna Ratliff and Mildred Ratliff, all in the same household, cannot simply be a coincidence. Moreover, in the 1940 census, a Polly Ann Ratclift, born in Arkansas, is listed in the same neighborhood where Callie, Pollyanna, and Mildred had been living in 1930. That census record indicated that Polly Ann had also lived there in 1935.[16] One is compelled to conclude that W.P. was the father of these three children, and that this liaison with their mother, Callie, probably prompted Cornelia to leave W.P. by 1915, when Vivian, the oldest of the three daughters, was born.[17]

After Cornelia's departure from Arkansas, W.P. continued his life as a farmer. There are indications that he wrote many letters to his son Tom while Tom was a soldier in World War I. Tom saved a couple of those letters.

---

15 1930 US Census, Natchez, Adams Co., Mississippi, ED 1, sheet 22B, National Archives Microfilm T626, roll 1137.

16 1940 US Census, Natchez, Adams Co., Mississippi, ED 1-1, sheet 5B, National Archives Microfilm, T627, roll 2005.

17 Attempts by the author to trace Vivian, Pollyanna, Mildred, and/or their descendants after 1940 proved fruitless.

LIFE AS A FARMER

In a letter to Tom, who was serving in the British army in Bangalore, India, W.P. wrote the following (on a typewriter):

Washington, Ark. 9/29/18
Mr. T. W. Ratliff
Bangalore, India

My Dear Boy:
I received your letter written July 17, yesterday. I was glad to hear from you again, for it had been quite a while since I had a letter from you. I wrote you over where you were when running the Motor Armored Battery and the letter was returned saying you could not be found.

Yes, Tom, I am in Washington now. I have sold my blackland farm and have bought a farm just 1 mile from town. I am in sight of the depot, between Tom Bearden & Mr. Frazier. It's a small farm of (illegible - 91?) acres. I like to live here much better than out on the blackland. I got $45.00 per acre for my farm.[18] I got your picture all right.

I guess hunting pheasants is fine sport, but I never found anything in the hunting line that I liked as well as duck hunting over in the Delta. This is my 7th year in Ark. and I have not been hunting since I have been in the state, except when the snow was on the ground, hunting rabbits.

Yes, Tom, the Americans are the best shots in the world. They carry the Transports over in groups of 3 or 4 in a group, and have 3 or 4 of those Torpedo destroyers with them. The destroyers are very swift vessels and they go in a circle around the Transports all the way, so you can see they can scan the seas in every direction.

---

18 Presumably the 200 acres in Hempstead County that W.P. bought on May 11, 1911.

There never has been but one of our transports sunk, and then we did not lose a man. It had ten thousand men on it and all of them were saved.

(page 2)

Yes, the Americans have surprised the world, and have surprised the Germans most of all. We now have one million six hundred thousand men over there now and by the time you get this, we will have over two million men in France. We expect to put three and a half million men in France by the 30th of next June.

We have just had a new registration from 15 to 45. There were 13 million registered. The 4th Liberty loan started yesterday. They are going to raise 8 billion dollars this time. We will soon have the elements full of Air ships too. Then if Berlin is so well fortified that we can't get in by land, we will send enough bombs in our airships to blow up Berlin & all the country nearby.

Yes, you wrote me that you were torpedoed in the Mediterranean but did not give me as much of the particulars as you did this time. I hope you won't have that kind of experience anymore.

Well, Tom, I will close for this time. Write when you can for I am always glad to hear from you. Then the folks are always asking about you. Old man Ab Smith asks me about you nearly every time I see him.

With love from your father,
(signed) W.P. Ratliff

In a letter to Tom, who was still in the British army, but by then in Tiflis (also known as Tbilisi), Russia (present-day Georgia), W.P. wrote the following (also on a typewriter):

LIFE AS A FARMER

Washington, Ark 5/25/19
Mr. T.W. Ratliff
Tiflis, Russia

My Dear Son,

How are you getting on by this time? I hope you are enjoying good health. I have been looking for you back in the U.S. but it seems they will hold on to you. But I guess you will be here sometime this year. The people of Washington will be glad to see you. You won't hardly know the old town, there have been so much improvement since you left.

There are now two big brick buildings on the old Weiderman lots, one two story brick with one dry goods store and one Drug store on the ground floor and quite a lot of office rooms above; then there is another big brick building with general merchandise called the Farmers Mercantile Co. Then on the other side of the street is a brick Hardware and Furniture co. 100X50 ft. And now W.J. Johnson & Co. have their store moved out in the street, right in the Hope road and are building a new brick store 100 X 50 ft.

The old P.O. building has been pushed back off its place and Mr. Stroud is going to put up a brick store on the old spot and put in a stock of goods. Quite a lot of our people have died since you were here. Sterling Gold, Mrs. Parsons, Henry Trimble, Trav Holt, old man Phillips and others.

Now we are going to have rock roads; the bonds have been sold. One from here to Columbus and from here to Hope and from here to Blevins, and from Blevins to Hope, then from Fulton to Hope and on to Emmet. All these are assured and others will be built. Yes, from Hope to Columbus.

Well, Tom, our crop prospect is good, we have had good seasons up to this time, It's been a little cool and the crops are a little late but otherwise, they are all right. I got a letter from Sudie[19] today and she said they had been too wet and the crops were grassy. We have had good seasons up this far but I can't tell what is in store for us in the future. I have 10 acres in cantaloupes this year and I think I will make some money on them.

Everybody is planting cantaloupes this year, they made good money on them last year, and the prospects are for a good price this year. Tom, I may have told you some things that I have told you before but I have had so many of my letters returned that I hardly know what you have heard from here.

Well I will close for this time for you may not get this one. Write me when you can and come home when you get out of the army.

With best wishes from your father
I am yours truly
W.P. Ratliff[20]

The last communication from W.P. Ratliff that has been found is a postcard from Hope, Arkansas, to his son Tom in Corsicana, Texas, on April 22, 1927. W.P. seems to have been in the hospital in Hope when he wrote it and to have recently had a visit from Tom. He wrote as follows:

Hope, Arkansas April 22, 1927

My Dear Tom,
How are you and fam. by today? Hoping you found them all well when you got here. I am still ____ and may

---

19 Sudie Ratliff Spain, W.P.'s daughter, who lived in Kosciusko, Mississippi.
20 Letter from W.P. to Tom, May 25, 1919.

have only about 5 days to stay in bed. I will be so glad when they let me out.

Love to all,
Your father,
W.P. Ratliff[21]

William Pinkney Ratliff died of chronic nephritis less than three weeks later, on May 10, 1927. He was eighty years old.[22] His body was transported back to Attala County, where he was buried on May 12, 1927, in the Springdale Cemetery, near the graves of his parents.

W.P.'s obituary listed the names of all the family who attended the funeral. The name of his estranged wife, Cornelia, was not among them.[23] After his funeral, the family mailed out a printed thank you card that read as follows:

> Mrs. W.P. Ratliff and Family
> wish to express
> their sincere appreciation
> of your
> sympathy and kindness

Also, W.P.'s daughter Sudie in Kosciusko wrote to her sister Anna in Marshall, Texas, as follows:

> ...Claude[24] and I went down to Springdale Sunday, we picked up Uncle Ed's[25] family as we went by, carried some fresh flowers. There is room for several graves in the row with papa. I am going to stake off a space for Claude and

---

21 Letter from W.P. to Tom, April 22, 1927.
22 Death certificate, May 11, 1927.
23 *Kosciusko Star-Herald*, May 1927.
24 Claude Spain, Sudie's husband.
25 W.P.'s younger brother Zachariah Edmond Ratliff.

me, and if any of the others want a place, I will be glad to reserve a place for them too. Do you know if mama wants to be laid to rest by papa or not? Anyway, I am going to save three places…[26]

---

26   Letter, May 24, 1927. Letter is courtesy of Barbara and Susan Mingee, who found the letter among things that Anna's twin daughter Sarah Elizabeth Donoho Kimberlin saved from her mother's house after Anna's death.

PART TWO

CORNELIA MITCHELL

1

THE EARLY LIFE OF CORNELIA MITCHELL

CORNELIA MITCHELL - A SURVIVOR

Cornelia Mitchell Ratliff lived to be ninety years old. Within that long life span, she experienced

- the joys of marriage and motherhood,

- the love of her children and grandchildren,

- a somewhat nomadic existence with her husband for almost twenty years after the shooting,

- the trauma and sense of loss caused by an unavoidable permanent separation from her husband,

- life with four of her children and their families, in turn, for the next twenty-five years after the separation,

- the death of two of her children, and

- the institutionalization of a child.

By all accounts and from her appearance in every known photo, Cornelia was a rather dour woman who rarely smiled. Her granddaughter Martha Ratliff Whetzel said that she was domineering, and Martha had memories of being told harshly when she was in her grandmother's presence, "Go brush your hair!"[1]

Cornelia (full name Nancy Ophelia Mary Jane Bethany Cornelia) Mitchell was born October 11, 1851, in Attala County, Mississippi. Her Mitchell ancestors can be traced as far back as 1534 in England. Abraham Mitchell, born in Halifax, Yorkshire, England, in 1626, immigrated to York, Virginia, where he married Jane Taylor in 1650. Cornelia's great-grandfather, Nimrod Mitchell, was a lieutenant in the South Carolina Militia during the Revolutionary War.[2] Cornelia's father, Albert Washington Mitchell, born in South Carolina, married Susan Anne Cone, also of South Carolina. They settled in Georgia around 1833, moving to Attala County, Mississippi, around 1850. Cornelia was the youngest of eight children and the only one born in Mississippi.

According to *The Civil War Record and Diary of Captain William V. Davis, 30th Mississippi Infantry, C.S.A - "Oh for Dixie"* by Joe and Lavon Ashley, Albert Washington Mitchell served in the Confederate army in the Civil War. Four of Cornelia's brothers also fought for the Confederacy, serving in the 30th Mississippi Infantry, Company D. The oldest, Whitman William Mitchell, was killed at the Battle of Murfreesboro, Tennessee, while coming to the aid of his wounded brother, Albert Pierce Mitchell. After Albert Pierce recovered from his wounds, he returned to service but was captured at the Battle of Lookout Mountain in 1863. Benjamin Franklin Mitchell was killed near Atlanta in 1864. A fourth brother, George Fellows Mitchell, also served in the same unit.[3]

---

1 Conversations between the author and his Aunt Martha, in Nokesville, Virginia, around 2008.
2 Bobby G. Moss, *Roster of South Carolina Patriots in the American Revolution* (Baltimore: Genealogical Publishing Company, 1983), 687. With permission.
3 Joe and Lavon Ashley, *The Civil War Record and Diary of Captain William V. Davis, 30th Mississippi Infantry, C.S.A - "Oh for Dixie"* (Colorado Springs: Standing Pine Press, 2001), 180-181. Thanks to Joe and Lavon Ashley for permission to use this information about the Mitchells from their book.

In 1860, nine-year-old Cornelia, along with her parents and older brothers, Pierce, Franklin, and Robert, were living in Attala County. Her father, Albert, was a farmer.[4]

Marriage and Children

Cornelia married William Pinkney (W.P.) Ratliff on October 22, 1868, in Attala County, only a few days after her seventeenth birthday. On August 28, 1869, her first child was stillborn and buried in the Liberty Chapel Cemetery in Ethel.

In 1870, Cornelia and W.P. were living in Ethel, and W.P. was a farmer.[5]

William Franklin Ratliff was born on February 19, 1871, but passed away on September 16, 1872. He also is buried in Liberty Chapel Cemetery next to the unnamed sibling who was born and died August 28, 1869.

Over the next twenty-one years, Cornelia would give birth to eleven children, all of whom were born in Attala County, Mississippi, and lived into adulthood:

- **Sarah Anna Lee Ratliff:** Born in Ethel on January 31, 1873

- **Mary Belle Ratliff:** Born in Ethel on June 22, 1875

- **John Barton (John B.) Ratliff:** Born in Ethel on May 14, 1878[6]

- **Sudie Ratliff:** Born in Ethel on January 31, 1880

- **Zack Mitchell Ratliff:** Born in Ethel on December 7, 1881

- **Katherine Elaine Ratliff:** Born in Ethel on January 20, 1884

---

4   1860 US Census, Township 16, Range 7, (Wells Post Office), Attala Co., Mississippi, sheet 385, National Archives Microfilm, M653, roll 577.

5   1870 US Census, Township 15, Range 6, Attala Co., Mississippi, sheet 15A, National Archives Microfilm, M593, roll 722.

6   The author's grandfather.

- **Florence Cornelia Ratliff:** Born in Ethel on January 30, 1886

- **Albert Wade Ratliff:** Born in Ethel on November 29, 1887

- **Paul Grady Ratliff:** Born in Ethel on December 31, 1890

- **Bessie Grace Ratliff:** Born in Kosciusko on February 26, 1892

- **Tom Watson Ratliff:** Born in Kosciusko on July 29, 1894

Life after the Shooting

Cornelia was four months pregnant with her youngest son, Tom, when her husband shot Sam Jackson on March 3, 1894. The events obviously would have been traumatic for her, not only as W.P.'s wife and the mother of his children but also as a Mitchell, a well-established and long-respected family in Attala County. Within a year or two after Tom was born, the family returned to their farm in Zilpha, Mississippi, just north of Kosciusko. For Cornelia, it would be one of many moves to take place over the rest of her life.

According to the 1900 census, Cornelia and W.P. were living in Zilpha, Attala County, with nine of their eleven children.[7] The oldest daughter, Anna, had married in 1898.[8] The oldest son, John Barton (John B.), had left home and was working in another part of the county and boarding with another family.[9]

---

7 1900 US Census, Beat 3, Attala Co., Mississippi, ED 17, sheet 6B, National Archives Microfilm, T623, roll 800.

8 1900 US Census, Kosciusko, Attala Co., Mississippi, ED 1, sheet 6A, National Archives Microfilm, T623, roll 800.

9 1900 US Census, Liberty Chapel, Attala Co., Mississippi, ED 5, sheet 10A, National Archives Microfilm, T623, roll 800.

"Mammy"
Becoming a Grandmother

In 1901, daughter Belle married Overton Welch Wilson and between 1902 and 1910 gave Cornelia and W.P. three grandchildren—two boys and a girl.

Also in 1901, oldest son John Barton (John B.) married Emma Jenkins, and between 1905 and 1909, they became the parents of two boys and a girl.

In 1910, Cornelia and W.P.'s oldest daughter Anna and husband Robert E. Lee Donoho had twin girls.

Cornelia's children referred to her as "Mama." However, the grandchildren all called Cornelia "Mammy" as long as she lived. Perhaps that is what Cornelia wanted to be called.[10]

Cornelia (Mammy)

---

10   The author first heard his father, J. Barton Ratliff Jr., refer to his grandmother Cornelia Mitchell Ratliff as "Mammy."

2

MOVING ON

As described earlier, the family's home in Zilpha was destroyed by fire in 1905. This set in motion a series of moves, first from Zilpha to Winona in Montgomery County, and then to Henry County, Illinois. As also mentioned earlier, perhaps the crops did not do well or the family found the climate too severe in Illinois. In any case, by April 1911, they were settled in Arkansas.[1] Florence, Bessie, and Tom made the move to Arkansas, though Florence and Bessie would not stay long.

In 1915, as mentioned previously, Cornelia left W.P. and Arkansas for good. When Cornelia left W.P., she first went to live with daughter Belle in Sealy, Texas, where Belle's husband, O.W. Wilson, owned a furniture store.[2] In addition to their three children, Belle's younger sister Florence, who worked as a bookkeeper in the furniture store, also lived with them.

Cornelia's son Zack Mitchell was employed by the railroad in Texas in those days. Since Zack's son Mitchell Carruth was born in Sealy, Texas, on April 4, 1916, they must have spent some time there,

---

1   Letters to Tom from a friend in Cambridge, Illinois, and his brother Grady in Chicago.
2   Postcard from son Tom in London, England, to his mother in Sealy, Texas, January 1, 1916.

or perhaps Zack's wife, Frances, went to Sealy to have the child.[3] When Cornelia's son Albert Wade registered for the draft on June 5, 1917, he gave a Sealy, Texas, address, although he was on the road with a carnival most of the time.[4]

So it appears that Cornelia had abundant family around her in Sealy. From Sealy, it appears that she moved to Galveston. On April 14, 1919, she wrote her son Tom from Galveston, using an envelope from O.W. Wilson Furniture Co., Galveston, Texas.[5] About June of 1919, she moved to San Antonio with Belle and her family.[6]

In July 1915, Tom enlisted in the British army in London, before the United States entered WWI. Cornelia saved the letters written to him by his family beginning when he was a child in Illinois. Tom himself saved some of the letters from his overseas service in WWI, providing a priceless record of his whereabouts during the war as well as the activities of his family members at home.[7]

Within six months of arriving in San Antonio, Cornelia moved once again, this time to Jacksonville, Texas, where her son Albert Wade had moved in December of that year.[8] Albert Wade was engaged in farming there, and Cornelia lived with him on the farm.[9]

But before the end of 1921, Cornelia and her son Albert Wade were on the move again. They moved to Sunflower County in the Mississippi Delta, where Cornelia's oldest son, John Barton (John B.), and his family had lived since 1909. Before long, Cornelia moved to a house in Drew behind the house of her son John B. and his family. This was on First

---

3   Zack's son Robert said his parents lived in a railroad car, moving by train to wherever the work was.
4   WWI draft registration for Albert Wade Ratliff, June 5, 1917.
5   Letter from Cornelia in Galveston to her son Tom, April 14, 1919.
6   Letter from Cornelia's daughter Sudie to her brother Tom, May 28, 1919, stating that "Mr. Wilson and family and Mama will move to San Antonio soon. Mama and Florence will live to themselves."
7   Copies of these letters, a few dating back more than one hundred years, were generously provided to the author by Tom's daughter Tommie Jane Ratliff Allen.
8   Letter from Cornelia to her son Tom, December 3, 1919.
9   1920 US Census, Justice Precinct 3, Cherokee Co., Texas, ED 23, sheet 4A, National Archives Microfilm, T625, roll 1786.

Street, near the corner of Shaw Street, and catty-cornered across the street from the house on Shaw Street that would later become the home of her son Albert Wade and his family.

And by 1926, Cornelia's son Zack Mitchell and his family had also moved to Sunflower County where, on April 19, 1926,[10] Zack's third son, Zack Abernathy Ratliff, was born. So three of Cornelia's sons and their families lived near her in Drew.

---

10 Their fourth son, Robert Edmond Ratliff, was also born in Sunflower County in 1927.

3

BACK HOME IN KOSCIUSKO

Around 1926, when Cornelia was living behind the house of her son John B. and his family, John B.'s house burned down. With no place to live, the family moved into Cornelia's house, sending her to live with her daughter Sudie and her husband, Claude Spain, in Kosciusko, in Attala County where Cornelia had been born. According to her granddaughter Martha Ratliff Whetzel, Cornelia was unhappy about leaving Drew.[1] Perhaps it was hard to leave a place where three of her children and their families lived, and which had provided her a sense of stability after those years of moving about. Or was Cornelia reluctant to return to Kosciusko because of a feeling of shame about her estranged husband's notorious past, including the shooting at the courthouse and his other family in Arkansas?

However, by 1928, Zack and his family had moved from Sunflower County to a farm in Sallis, Mississippi, south of Kosciusko, so Cornelia would have seen Zack, his wife, Frances, and their sons regularly. Cornelia's two sons, John B. and Albert Wade, and their families, who

---

1 Conversations between the author and his Aunt Martha Ratliff Whetzel, daughter of John B. and granddaughter of W.P. and Cornelia.

were still living in Sunflower County in the Mississippi Delta, also came visiting in Kosciusko with their families.

On at least one occasion, Cornelia's daughter Kate Ratliff Naylor came to visit from Chicago, bringing Kate's grandson, Peter Frederick Naylor Jr., to see his great-grandmother and other relatives.[2]

---

2   As told to the author by Zack's son Robert.

In May 1939, Cornelia's children orchestrated a Ratliff reunion, held at Zack's farm in Sallis, Attala County. Cornelia was eighty-seven years old and walked with a cane. Nine of Cornelia's eleven children were present, along with their spouses, children, and grandchildren, as well as W.P.'s sister Sarah Elizabeth (Aunt Bettie), totaling more than forty members of the Ratliff family. Families prepared food for a family lunch, and photos were taken to memorialize the occasion.

Cornelia at the 1939 reunion

PHOTOS OF THE 1939 REUNION

THE WILLIAM PINKNEY RATLIFF FAMILY SAGA 1847-1988

1939 Ratliff Reunion - Group Photo[3]

Top row, standing, from left, Zack Mitchell Ratliff, Frances Abernathy Ratliff, Tom Watson Ratliff, Rissie Corean Page Ratliff, Kirby Hall Causey, Florence Cornelia Ratliff, Bessie Grace Ratliff Causey, Albert Wade Ratliff, Ruth Bullock Ratliff, Sarah Anna Lee Ratliff Donoho, Sarah Elizabeth Ratliff (Aunt Bettie, sister of William Pinkney Ratliff), John B. Ratliff, Emma Roxana Jenkins Ratliff, Ernest Claude Spain, Sudie Ratliff Spain, Robert Henry Bopp, Kate Elaine Ratliff Naylor Bopp, Arthur Lee Hazlewood; *middle row, squatting/seated, from left*, Hattie Maye Sanders Ratliff, Pinkney Brooks Ratliff, Bessie Corean Ratliff, Margaret Grace Ratliff, Barton Wade Ratliff, Martha Cornelia Ratliff Wilkinson, Tom Jerome Ratliff, Cornelia (Mammy) Mitchell Ratliff, J. Barton Ratliff Jr., Vera Mixon Ratliff, James Grady Ratliff, Ana Belle (Anabel) Ratliff, Albert Wade "Bevo" Ratliff, Cornelia Ruth Ratliff, Mary Lee Donoho Hazlewood; *bottom row, center to right, mostly seated, from left, in front of Mammy*, Frances Roxana Ratliff, Neil Mixon Ratliff, John B. Ratliff III, Arthur Robert Hazlewood,[4] Edward Lee Hazlewood, Tommie Jane Ratliff, Robert Edmond Ratliff, Zack Abernathy Ratliff

---

3   See photo on opposite page.
4   Misspelled on birth certificate.

THE WILLIAM PINKNEY RATLIFF FAMILY SAGA 1847-1988

The children of W.P. and Cornelia

Standing, from left, Sudie Ratliff Spain, Zack Mitchell Ratliff, Florence Cornelia Ratliff, Sarah Anna Lee Ratliff Donoho, Kate Elaine Ratliff Naylor Bopp, Albert Wade Ratliff, Bessie Grace Ratliff Causey; *seated, from left,* John Barton (John B.) Ratliff, Cornelia (Mammy) Mitchell Ratliff, Tom Watson Ratliff

Missing from picture: Paul Grady Ratliff and Mary Belle Ratliff Wilson

The grandchildren of W.P. and Cornelia and their spouses

Standing, from left, J. Barton Ratliff Jr. (son of John B. Ratliff), Bessie Corean Ratliff (daughter of Tom Watson Ratliff), Vera Mixon Ratliff (wife of J. Barton Ratliff Jr.), James Grady Ratliff (son of John B. Ratliff), Cornelia Ruth Ratliff (daughter of Albert Wade Ratliff), Maye Sanders Ratliff (wife of Pinkney Brooks Ratliff), Barton Wade Ratliff (son of Albert Wade Ratliff), Pinkney Brooks Ratliff (son of John B. Ratliff), Albert Wade "Bevo" Ratliff (son of John B. Ratliff), Mary Lee Donoho Hazlewood (daughter of Sarah Anna Ratliff Donoho), Martha Cornelia Ratliff Wilkinson (daughter of John B. Ratliff), Arthur Lee Hazlewood (husband of Mary Lee Donoho Hazlewood); *seated, from left,* Tommie Jane Ratliff (daughter of Tom Watson Ratliff), Margaret Grace Ratliff (daughter of Tom Watson Ratliff), Tom Jerome Ratliff (son of Albert Wade Ratliff), Robert Edmond Ratliff (son of Zack Mitchell Ratliff), Zack Abernathy Ratliff (son of Zack Mitchell Ratliff), and Anabel Ratliff (daughter of John B. Ratliff)

Youngest grandsons and great-grandchildren
of W.P. and Cornelia Ratliff

Three children in front, John B. Ratliff III (grandson of John B. Ratliff), Frances Roxana Ratliff (granddaughter of John B. Ratliff), Neil Mixon Ratliff (grandson of John B. Ratliff*); older children, from left,* Arthur Robert Hazelwood (grandson of Anna Ratliff Donoho), Zack Abernathy Ratliff (son of Zack Mitchell Ratliff), Tom Jerome Ratliff (son of Albert Wade Ratliff), Edward Lee Hazlewood (grandson of Anna Ratliff Donoho), Robert Edmond Ratliff (son of Zack Mitchell Ratliff)

Cornelia with her grandson Barton's wife
Vera, and great-grandsons John[5] and Neil

June 18, 1942

Cornelia passed away on June 18, 1942, at ninety years of age. She was buried next to her husband, W.P. Ratliff, in Springdale Cemetery. Although her life had its troubles, she loved her children and they loved her to the end. The 1939 reunion gave them a special opportunity to honor and show their love for their mother. In some ways, it served as the capstone to her life and the large family that she left behind.

---

5   The author.

PART THREE

THE CHILDREN OF WILLIAM PINKNEY AND CORNELIA MITCHELL RATLIFF

The eleven children of William Pinkney and Cornelia Mitchell Ratliff, born between 1873 and 1894, were in many ways typical and ordinary citizens of their day. They established loving relationships and experienced success and failure, triumphs and tragedy. Among the eleven, some never married, some had no children, and some saw their children die in childhood.

Three of the sons tried farming at one time or another. Two served in the British armed forces during WWI, and one was a POW. One son died of a gunshot wound, thought by some family members to have been self-inflicted. Another son was involved in three shooting incidents, two in which he accidentally shot himself and one in which he killed someone and was tried in a court of law.

One daughter stole her sister's husband, and another daughter was committed to a mental institution.

Through the course of their lives, the children found themselves scattered among many states: Mississippi, Florida, Texas, Illinois, Arkansas, California, Oregon, Virginia, and Arizona. They lived and they died, and they are part of the history of the Ratliff family. Here now are their stories.

1

SARAH ANNA LEE RATLIFF

January 7, 1929 – A Feeling of Dread

Life had not been easy on the farm with a mortgage to meet every month. Anna's husband, Robert, took a job with the railroad as a boilermaker's helper, presumably to bring in a steady income to supplement the proceeds from the fields and dairy. But with the onset of the Depression, he lost that job. He was lucky to find a job in Santa Rita, New Mexico. It's easy to imagine that he didn't like to be separated from Anna and their twin daughters, but they needed the income.

On the last day of December of 1928, Anna received a telegram informing her that Robert was in the hospital—seriously ill with pneumonia. Her son-in-law Arthur Lee Hazlewood took the train to Santa Rita to do whatever he could for Robert, while keeping Anna posted on his condition.

A week later on January 7, when Anna was told that a telegram had arrived from her son-in-law in Santa Rita, her heart must have sunk as she no doubt feared the worst.

THE LIFE OF SARAH ANNA LEE RATLIFF

Sarah Anna Lee Ratliff was born January 31, 1873, on the family farm in Ethel. She was the eldest daughter, presumably named after her maternal grandmother, Sarah Lucretia Adams Ratliff. Her family called her "Anna."[1]

In the 1880 census, "Sarah L. Ratliff" was listed along with her family on the farm in Ethel.[2] On December 27, 1898—a month shy of her twenty-sixth birthday—Anna married Robert E. Lee Donoho in Attala County. The following account of the wedding appeared in the *Kosciusko Star-Ledger*:

Donoho-Ratliff

Mr. R. E. Donoho and Miss Anna Ratliff were happily married at the residence of the bride's father, Mr. W.P. Ratliff, on the 27th, Rev. J. S. Oakley officiating. Mr. Donoho is one of our most successful young business men with a bright future before him. High-toned, moral, honest, in fact possessing all the qualifications that go to make up an exalted manhood, while his lovely winsome bride is richly endowed with all the womanly graces that have made her sex the joy and solace of men since the creation.

The Star Ledger feels assured this union will be a happy one."[3]

---

1   The author is indebted to Connie "Cissy" Elaine Hazelwood Brown, who shared much information, many family photos, and also letters about family history from her uncle Edward Lee Hazlewood. The author is also indebted to Pamela Joyce Hazelwood Cooke, who shared many family photos copied from her siblings. The author is also grateful to Barbara Ann McNeil Mingee and her daughter Susan, who preserved family photos/letters/documents belonging to Anna's daughter Elizabeth and her husband, William Henry Kimberlin, for decades after Henry's death in hopes that they would someday be able to give them to members of Elizabeth's family.

2   1880 US Census, Attala Co., Mississippi, ED 18, sheet 144B, National Archives Microfilm, T9, roll 641.

3   *Kosciusko Star Ledger,* sometime after December 27, 1898.

Robert E. Lee Donoho was born on January 7, 1871, in Attala County. His father, W. B. Donoho, a farmer, was born in Virginia, of parents also born in Virginia. His mother, Martha Eakin, was born in Mississippi, with a father born in Ireland and a mother born in Alabama.[4] Robert had a brother who died at age six and a sister who died at age two.

Robert E. Lee Donoho

In 1900, Robert and Anna were living in Kosciusko, with Robert's occupation listed as "grocer."[5]

Around 1909, Robert and Anna migrated west—to Harrison County, Texas. By May 1910, Robert was a truck farmer.[6] On June 28, 1910, Anna gave birth to identical twin girls: Mary Lee and Sarah Elizabeth Donoho. They were called Mary and Elizabeth.

---

4   1880 US Census, Attala County, Mississippi, ED 12, sheet 8C, National Archives Microfilm, T9, roll 641.

5   1900 US Census, Kosciusko, Attala Co., Mississippi, ED 1, sheet 6A, National Archives Microfilm, T623, roll 800.

6   1910 US Census, Justice Precinct, Harrison Co., Texas, ED 40, sheet 15A, National Archives Microfilm, T624, roll 1562.

Mary and Elizabeth Donoho

In 1920, Robert and Anna had a twenty-five-acre mortgaged farm on Port Caddo Road, Precinct 3, Harrison County, near Marshall, Texas. The twins were almost ten years old. Employed by the Texas & Pacific Railroad, Robert's occupation was "Helper – railroad boiler shop." A neighbor, John Quick, was a boilermaker in the same shop and his son, George, was also an apprentice in the railroad tin shop. So perhaps Robert got his job through John Quick.[7]

---

7   1920 US Census, Gulfport, Harrison Co., Texas, ED 50, sheet 15A, National Archives Microfilm, T625, roll 1815.

Robert Donoho with Elizabeth and Mary

In the late twenties, Robert lost his job with the railroad. Jobs were "scarce as hens' teeth,"[8] but he finally managed to find work as a boilermaker for the Chino Copper Company in Santa Rita, New Mexico, a mining town.[9] In August 1928, he went there alone, leaving Anna and the twins back in Harrison County.

On December 31, 1928, only four months after Robert left home, Anna received a collect telegram from Santa Rita, New Mexico, which read as follows: "Mr. Donoho sick in hospital with pneumonia. Will keep you posted if any change. Dr. S. J. Hanks."

Anna's son-in-law Arthur Lee Hazlewood (husband of daughter Mary) went to Santa Rita to be with Robert. Sadly, a week later on

---

8   Letter from Anna's grandson Edward Lee Hazlewood to his niece Cissy Hazlewood, May 4, 1997.

9   Robert Donoho obituary, *Marshall (TX) News-Messenger*, about January 12, 1929.

January 7, 1929, Anna received the following telegram: "Dad passed away at 9:35 this morning. Arthur Hazlewood."

Robert's death certificate indicated that the primary cause of his death was influenza, with pneumonia as a contributing factor, and that he had been under treatment since December 22, 1928.[10]

Money was short and there was a question of how transportation and burial expenses would be covered. Coworkers of Robert's in Santa Rita took up a collection and, in what had to be both a surprising and comforting letter dated January 31, 1929, they wrote the following:

> To Mrs. R.E. Donoho and family,
>
> We are sending you a Post Office money order for $51.50, the balance we have on hand after all bills were paid in Santa Rita.
>
> We collected a fund of $301.50 among the many friends of your husband and father. His shop mates here extend our deepest sympathy for your loss.
>
> Santa Rita Store Co. $180.00
> Two railroad fares paid to Mr. Hazlewood $70.00
> Balance to Mrs. R. E. Donoho $51.50[11]

A second letter, from W. R. Hawksworth, a member of the Boilermakers Union, postmarked May 4, 1929, brought welcome news:

> Dear Madame,
>
> The boilermakers have been able to secure the thousand dollars ($1000.00) insurance of Mr. Donoho. The same will have to go through some reliable bank in Marshall with a Notary Public to stand for your identification.

---

10   New Mexico death certificate, January 8, 1929.
11   This letter is courtesy of Susan and Barbara Mingee.

Please notify me at once which bank you wish to handle this matter.

Sincerely yours,
W.R. Hacksworth[12]

Robert's body, accompanied by Arthur, arrived in Marshall on January 10, 1929. On January 11, funeral services were conducted at home, and he was buried in Greenwood Cemetery in Marshall.[13] Since Robert was a member of the Masons, the Masonic Lodge assisted with the funeral.[14] A bill from Hains and Herndon Funeral Home dated May 27, 1929, itemized the funeral expenses as follows: "Hearse, $30; Plot, $50; and Brick vault, $57.50 – Total: $137.50."[15]

Among Robert's personal papers was found a pocket-sized case containing his membership card for the International Brotherhood of Boiler Makers, Iron Ship Builders and Helpers of America. Behind some copies of receipts for union dues was found a folded note from his daughter Elizabeth. On the outside of the note were written these words: "Just a little gift to Daddy. Watch out, you will lose it. It is inside of this paper." When the paper was unfolded, there was a note with a tiny photo of Elizabeth:

> Daddy, does it look like the little girl Elizabeth you left four months ago? Now look good and see if it is me, Elizabeth. I am not kidding you. I mean it and you would say it is just like me if you could see me. I have changed, haven't I?

---

12   This letter also from Susan and Barbara Mingee.
13   Robert Donoho obituary, *Marshall (TX) News-Messenger*, about January 13, 1929.
14   Letter from Anna's grandson Edward Lee Hazlewood to his niece Cissy Hazlewood, May 4, 1997.
15   Courtesy of Susan and Barbara Mingee.

The photo showed Elizabeth with her hair cut very short. When Elizabeth wrote this note, it would have been no more than two months before her father passed away. She was eighteen years old.

Elizabeth

As previously mentioned, there was a mortgage that had to be met each month on the Donoho farm in Harrison County. After Robert's death, the twenty-five-acre farm was split three ways between Anna, Mary, and Elizabeth. In that manner, Anna had to pay only a third of what was owed, while Mary and Elizabeth would have been responsible for the remaining two thirds.[16]

In 1930, Anna and her daughter Elizabeth were living on the farm near Marshall. Anna was listed as the owner of a dairy farm and Elizabeth was a telephone operator.[17]

Also in 1930, Anna's daughter Mary and her husband Arthur (who married in 1928) and their one-year-old son Arthur Robert Hazelwood[18] were living in Pine Bluff, Arkansas. Arthur worked in a candy factory, and

---

16 Letter from Edward Lee Hazlewood to his niece Connie "Cissy" Hazlewood, May 4, 1997.
17 1930 US Census, Precinct 3, District 13, Harrison County, Texas, ED 13, sheet 3B, National Archives Microfilm, T626, roll 2354.
18 Letter from Uncle Edward Hazlewood to his niece Cissy Hazlewood dated May 18, 1997. The doctor misspelled the Hazlewood name on Arthur Robert's birth certificate, and he kept the spelling throughout his life, as did his children.

the family lived next door to the owner of the factory.[19] So Arthur became a professional candy maker and Mary worked in the shop as well. In 1931, the couple welcomed another boy, Edward Lee Hazlewood, born on December 1, 1931.

Mary and Arthur moved to Baton Rouge, Louisiana, in the mid-1930s. Both took jobs with the Capitol Candy and Cookie Company. Sons Robert and Edward stayed with their grandmother Anna on the farm near Marshall, Texas. In a 1997 letter to his niece Cissy, Edward wrote that if he had to make a declaration about who had made the greatest impact on his life, his grandmother Anna would surely be at the top of the list.[20] Robert and Edward occasionally moved back and forth from the farm in Marshall to Baton Rouge to live with their parents.

Arthur, Mary, Edward, Robert   Anna, Edward, Robert

---

19   1930 US Census, Pine Bluff, Jefferson Co., Arkansas, ED 43, sheet 20A, National Archives Microfilm, T626, roll 79.
20   Letter from Edward Lee Hazlewood to his niece Cissy, May 4, 1997.

Mary, Anna, Elizabeth
Edward and Robert

In May of 1939, Anna, Mary, and Arthur, together with sons Robert and Edward, went to Kosciusko, Mississippi, for the Ratliff family reunion with the extended Ratliff family, many of whom had not seen each other in years.

Edward, who was eight years old at the time, remembered going to the Ratliff Family Reunion and wrote that "they had to serve lunch in a pasture to get all the people around."[21] The reunion was held on the farm of Anna's younger brother Zack Mitchell Ratliff near Sallis.

Among the many family photographs taken that day were "four-generation" photos, in which great-grandmother Cornelia posed with each one of her children, his/her child, and the oldest great grandchild. Anna and daughter Mary had their photo taken with Cornelia and Mary's older son Robert.

---

21   Ibid.

Arthur Robert Hazelwood, Anna Ratliff Donoho,
Cornelia Mitchell Ratliff, Mary Lee Donoho Hazlewood

After the reunion, Anna wrote in a letter from her home in Marshall to her brother Tom in Corsicana, Texas: "My boys were glad to get home. Robert came home sick and has not been well since he got home."[22]

At the time of the 1940 census, Anna was staying temporarily with her sister Sudie in Kosciusko.[23]

---

22 Letter from Anna to her brother Tom, June 11, 1939.
23 1940 US Census, Kosciusko, Attala Co., Mississippi, ED 4-3, sheet 7A, National Archives Microfilm, T627, roll 2008.

Anna

Anna died at home in Marshall, Texas, on November 14, 1950, after a lengthy illness. She was seventy-seven years old. She was buried next to her husband, Robert, in the family plot at Greenwood Cemetery.

THE CHILDREN OF ANNA AND ROBERT DONOHO

Mary Lee Donoho

As earlier noted, Mary Lee and her identical twin sister, Sarah Elizabeth, were born on June 28, 1910, on the family farm in Harrison County, Texas.

Mary married Arthur Lee Hazlewood on October 13, 1928, when she was only eighteen. They were married in Marshall, but it is not known how they met.

Arthur was born on November 26, 1907. Arthur Lee's grandparents, Lee and Jodie Hazlewood, were from Tennessee. According to Arthur and Mary's son Edward, Lee and Jodie decided to head west in a wagon train. Their wagon broke down around what would become Winfield, Texas, and they settled there. They had two sons born there—Joseph, born in 1886, and Walter, born in 1889. Both were farmers and also peace officers at one time.

Joseph married Belle Tollefson from Arkansas around 1905. They had three children: Arthur Lee, Fred, and Maude. Arthur's son Edward recalled his grandparents Joseph and Belle in a letter to his niece Cissy. He wrote as follows:

> Grandpa was a very capable man around the farm. He raised all his own food, from beef, to pork, to vegetables. I remember going to Winfield many times when I was just a little fellow.
>
> Grandpa ground his own wheat into flour, made his own syrup, and I can remember he had a little house out in the yard that was screened in where he kept the good stuff, even his dried meats. Every now and then we could hear a loud "pop" when one of his jugs of corn whiskey or home-made wine would blow the corncob stopper out.
>
> So there we have my paternal grandparents, Poppa Joe and Momma Belle. That's what everyone called them except my

father. They were Poppa and Momma to him. Momma Belle was a housewife. Poppa Joe was a jack-of-all-trades kind of a fellow. He was a big burly fellow, while Momma Belle was a trim, slender-built woman. He was a County Sheriff, a night watchman, and even a barber. He cut my hair many times. In fact, my father also did a short stint as a barber before he married my mother.[24]

Arthur Lee and Mary Lee Donoho Hazlewood had two sons: Arthur Robert, born on June 27, 1929, and Edward Lee, born on December 1, 1931. According to Edward, both sons were born at home on the family farm in Harrison County, Texas, and were delivered by a country doctor. But due to an "oversight" by the doctor completing the official birth certificates, the two sons ended up with differently spelled last names.

When the doctor completed the birth certificate for Arthur Robert Hazlewood, he mistakenly spelled it "Haz*el*wood." No one noticed the mistake, so that's the way it was filed and it became Arthur Robert's legal name. On record, his younger brother's legal name was Edward Lee Haz*le*wood. When Arthur and Mary sent Robert's birth announcement out to friends and family, they spelled the last name like his father Arthur's—"Haz*le*wood."[25] Presumably they did not discover the mistaken spelling of Robert's family name by the doctor until later.

In 1930, Mary and Arthur Lee Haz*le*wood and their son Arthur Robert Haz*el*wood (note the different spelling) were in Pine Bluff, Arkansas.[26]

As indicated earlier, Robert and Edward lived with their grandmother Anna for many of their younger years, while their parents worked in the candy manufacturing business in Louisiana. In 1935, Mary and Arthur

---

24 Letter from Edward Lee Hazlewood to his niece Cissy, May 18, 1997.
25 Robert's birth announcement sent to his Aunt Elizabeth Donoho Kimberlin, courtesy of Susan and Barbara Mingee.
26 1930 US Census, Pine Bluff, Jefferson Co., Arkansas, ED 43, sheet 20A, National Archives Microfilm, T626, roll 79.

Lee were in Alexandria, Louisiana. Their two sons, Robert and Edward, were with their grandmother Anna in Marshall.[27]

Edward and Robert in 1935

Mary and Arthur's son Ed wrote about his childhood experiences, both with their grandmother Anna and with his parents when he and his brother Robert were living with them. About living in the country with their grandmother, Ed wrote the following:

> We both attended Knight School. This was a two-room school house. Room one, row one was first grade; row two was second grade; row three was third grade; row four was fourth grade; and then you were promoted to the other room…That room also had four rows, and of course, you could tell what grade a person was in by which row he/she sat in. Knight School was almost directly across the road from the house. In fact, Robert and I used to make sure we could get into the building during the summer. We would borrow a spelling book, and have all our homework assignments

---

27 1940 US Census, Baton Rouge, East Baton Rouge Parish, Louisiana, ED 17-3, sheet 61A, National Archives Microfilm, T627, roll 1396.

for the next year finished before summer was over, then we would return the speller.

As kids, we used to pick cotton for neighboring farms for less than a penny a pound, as I recall. Our grandmother used to lease out the fields, and we would be up at the crack of dawn to head for the field to chop cotton/pick corn/or collect potatoes. We also had a large peach orchard which Momma (our grandmother) would faithfully can every year. I can still taste those sweet peach pickles! Then of course, every country boy worth his salt has been known to be in on raiding a neighbor's watermelon or cantaloupe patch by moonlight.

Yes, we were typical country boys. We each had a pair of brogans and two pairs of overalls—one blue and one striped. You wore the blue ones all week. Come Saturday night, you had to take a bath, because on Sunday, you put on the striped pair and went to church, which was about ¼ mile up the road toward town.[28]

---

28   Letter from Edward Lee Hazlewood to his niece Cissy, April 26, 1997.

School Days 19 44   School Days 19 44
Robert   Edward

When Robert and Edward were with their parents in Baton Rouge, they attended Istrouma High School, a Catholic school. They both were in US Army Junior ROTC. By this time, their father Arthur had decided he didn't want to make candy anymore, and he became a salesman on a candy route for the same company. Mary also left the candy factory to stay home. Later she took over the candy route from Arthur when he briefly became a deputy sheriff in Baton Rouge. Ed remembered that he and Robert sometimes were permitted to tag along on the candy route with their mother to help carry the candy and cookie boxes into the stores. Arthur later was a city bus driver for a while.

In the 1940 census, Mary and Arthur and their two sons were in Baton Rouge, Louisiana. Arthur Lee was listed as a candy maker and Mary was a candy maker's helper.[29]

When World War II began, rationing and shortages spelled the end of the candy business and times got hard for the Hazlewoods. Arthur went to California and became a brakeman for the Santa Fe

---

29   1940 US Census, Baton Rouge, East Baton Rouge Parish, Louisiana, ED 17-3, sheet 61A, National Archives Microfilm, T627, roll 1396.

Railroad, working out of Needles, California. Edward remembered living in Needles, as well as Prescott, Arizona, San Bernardino, and Los Angeles, California, where he graduated from high school. Edward wrote that his brother Robert didn't like Needles, so he returned to Marshall to live with their grandmother Anna. Around 1946 or 1947, Robert dropped out of school and joined the US Army Air Corps, which later became the US Air Force. He got his GED (high school-equivalency diploma) in the air corps.[30]

Robert with his mother, Mary

On October 13, 1948—her twentieth wedding anniversary—Robert and Edward's mother, Mary Lee Donoho Hazlewood, died of a brain aneurysm at her mother's home in Marshall.[31] Family members pointed to a malfunctioning hairdryer in a beauty shop that either overheated or shorted out as the precipitating cause. The chemicals used for a permanent

---

30 Letter from Edward Hazlewood to his niece Cissy, April 25, 1997.
31 Letter from Edward Hazlewood to his niece Cissy, May 4, 1997; Mary Lee Donoho Hazlewood obituary, *Marshall (TX) News Messenger*, October 14, 1948; Texas Death Index 1903-2000.

wave combined with the intense heat could have been a contributing factor. She was only thirty-eight.

Mary Donoho Hazlewood

Robert was with the US Army Air Corps on Guam, and Edward was still at home in Marshall. Mary was buried in the family plot in Greenwood Cemetery, where her father was already interred. Mary's husband, Arthur, would eventually remarry and live in San Reno, Oklahoma, until his death in January 1981.

On July 14, 1949, a year after his mother's death, Edward joined the US Navy. When grandmother Anna died on November 14, 1950, Edward was stationed in New London, Connecticut. Brother Robert was by then a corporal in the US Air Force in Albuquerque, New Mexico.[32]

---

32   Anna Ratliff Donoho obituary, *Marshall (TX) News Messenger,* November 15, 1950.

Arthur Robert Hazelwood

Arthur Robert was born on June 27, 1929, in Marshall, Texas. On March 2, 1950, while he was in the air force, Robert married Mary Katherine Shaw, born in 1934.

He and Katherine had eight children, born between 1951 and 1969:

Robert Charles Hazelwood, born 1951
Kenneth Clyde Hazelwood, born 1953
Joe Walter Hazelwood, born December 18, 1956
(died of a heart attack November 19, 2001)
Kathryn Anne Hazelwood, born 1958
Pamela Joyce Hazelwood, born 1961
Martin Keith Hazelwood, born 1964
Connie Elaine Hazelwood, born 1965
Mary Elizabeth Hazelwood, born 1969

Robert with children in 1958
From left, Bobby, Kathy, Joe, Ken

Robert was wounded in the Korean War and received a Purple Heart. After seventeen years in the air force and attaining the rank of staff sergeant, Robert left the service around 1965.

After being discharged, Robert drove long-haul tractor-trailer trucks. While in Houston, Texas, on October 13, 1972, Robert was standing between the loading dock and a trailer when the trailer rolled back and pinned him against the loading dock. The doctors said he would be crippled for a year or so but with therapy he would be fine. However, the doctors and hospital staff failed to notice that gangrene had set in. Tragically, Robert passed away on October 17, just four days after the tragic accident.[33]

---

33 Email message from Robert's daughter Cissy to the author, March 2008.

Edward Lee Hazlewood

Edward Lee was born on December 1, 1931, in Marshall, Texas. In 1950, Edward married Doreen Faye Potter, born May 31, 1933, in Los Angeles, California. Ed and Doreen had one son, Darrell Austin, born September 26, 1951, in Los Angeles.

Ed with son Darrell

Ed and Doreen later divorced, and Doreen remarried in April 1954 to Bobby Horace McDaniel. Bobby adopted Darrell, whose name was changed to Darrell Austin McDaniel. Darrell maintained contact with his Hazlewood relatives in his early years. Tragically, Darrell was killed in a construction accident on August 15, 1989, in Chatham, Georgia, at age thirty-eight. He was buried in the McDaniel family plot in Cloverdale Memorial Park in Boise, Idaho.

Edward spent twenty-five years in the US Navy. While stationed in Hawaii, he remarried. Retiring about 1974 as a yeoman chief petty officer, Ed's naval service spanned both the Korean and Vietnam Wars. After retirement, Ed had a second career with the US Postal Service in Honolulu, Hawaii, and "was instrumental in opening the Philatelic Center in Honolulu."[34]

Ed passed away on June 27, 2004, in Honolulu. He left a wife, a son, three daughters, and nine grandchildren. He was buried in the National Memorial Cemetery of the Pacific in Honolulu.

---

34   Edward Lee Hazlewood obituary, *Honolulu Advertiser*, July 8, 2004.

Sarah Elizabeth Donoho

Sarah Elizabeth Donoho, Mary Lee's identical twin sister, was also born June 28, 1910, and was probably named for her mother's "Aunt Bettie," Sarah Elizabeth Ratliff, who enjoyed a long career as a school teacher in her hometown of Kosciusko.

Sarah Elizabeth, called "Elizabeth" or "Betty" within the family, remained at home in Marshall with her mother until at least 1930, when the census reports her occupation as "telephone operator."[35] It is surmised that, at some point, she worked in nearby Shreveport, Louisiana, since her social security card was issued in Louisiana rather than Texas.

January 1, 1932, found Elizabeth and Marvin Bechtold in Washington, Arkansas, accompanied by two friends, to get married.[36] The marriage did not last. In 1933, Elizabeth took a job with Southwestern Bell Telephone Company in Tyler, Texas. It is not known if Marvin accompanied her. But it is likely that he didn't since the couple divorced shortly thereafter. The exact date of the divorce is unknown. From a scrapbook that Elizabeth kept, it appears that she attended Tyler Community College at some point while living there.

As previously mentioned, in 1930 Elizabeth's twin sister, Mary, was in Pine Bluff, Arkansas, with her husband, Arthur Lee Hazlewood, and son Robert. A nineteen-year-old man named William Henry Kimberlin Jr. was a lodger in the candy factory owner's home, which was next door to the Hazlewoods. He also worked as a candy maker in the same factory where they were employed.[37] One can imagine that when Elizabeth visited Mary in Pine Bluff, she would have met the young Henry Kimberlin. Around 1932, Henry left Pine Bluff to go to work for the Tyler Candy Company in Tyler, Texas.

That would place both Elizabeth and Henry in Tyler by 1933. According to an article in the *Tyler Morning Telegraph*, estimated to

---

35   1930 US Census, Precinct 3, District 13, Harrison County, Texas, ED 13, sheet 3B, National Archives Microfilm, T626, roll 2354.

36   Newspaper clipping, presumably from the *Marshall (TX) News Messenger*, early January 1932.

37   1930 US Census, Pine Bluff, Jefferson Co., Arkansas, ED 43, sheet 20A, National Archives Microfilm, T626, roll 79.

have been published sometime in 1934, Elizabeth and Henry married in Marshall at her mother Anna's home.[38]

William Henry Kimberlin Jr. was born on August 5, 1911, in Missouri. His father, William Henry Kimberlin Sr., was from Virginia, and his mother was a German immigrant. William Henry Sr. was also a candy maker, according to the 1910[39] census in St. Joseph, Missouri, and the 1920[40] census in Little Rock, Arkansas. Moving from Little Rock, Henry wound up in the candy factory in Pine Bluff, probably not that much earlier than 1930 since he was only nineteen then.

Henry and Elizabeth

Henry eventually left the candy business and became a painter of highway billboard signs. He traveled all over the country, wherever the work took him. Elizabeth usually went with him, and the work sometimes was protracted enough locally that they could rent a house and stay settled

---

38　*Tyler (TX) Morning Telegraph,* sometime in 1934.
39　1910 US Census, St. Joseph, Ward 6, Buchanan, Missouri, ED 81, sheet 5A, National Archives Microfilm, T624, roll 772.
40　1920 US Census, Little Rock, Ward 8, Pulaski Co., Arkansas, ED 146, sheet 2B, National Archives Microfilm, T625, roll 79.

for a while. At one point, they had a house from which one could see Pike's Peak in Colorado.

Sign by Henry Kimberlin in Desoto Parish, Louisiana

Henry's nickname was "Hank" and their nieces and nephews called them "Aunt Betty" and "Uncle Hank."

Elizabeth and Henry were dog lovers. According to Henry's great niece Susan Mingee:

> He and Aunt Elizabeth always had a dog, sometimes more than one. They loved dachshunds, which all had German names (The Kimberlins are of German descent). The dogs were Lena, Adolph, and Gretchen. Lena was Henry's mother's nickname; Adolph was his uncle's name; and we don't know where the name Gretchen came from.

Hank's niece Barbara Ann McNeil Mingee (Susan Mingee's mother) shared other memories of Uncle Hank and Aunt Betty:

> Reflections of Barbara Ann McNeil Mingee
> Niece of William Henry Kimberlin Jr.
>
> Elizabeth and Henry Kimberlin were a part of my life from my birth until their deaths. They lived in many places including Texas, Mississippi, Louisiana, Arkansas, North Carolina, Washington State, Oregon, and New Mexico. My parents, John and Wilma Kimberlin McNeil, and my siblings and I lived in Fayetteville, NC, Raleigh, NC, and Natchez, MS at the same time that Henry and Elizabeth lived in those places. Mary "Lena" Kimberlin, Henry and Wilma's mother, lived with the McNeil family from 1932 until her death in 1951.
>
> Aunt Elizabeth was very careful when cooking, baking, sewing, and also in her housekeeping. When I was about eight years old, she would let me "help" her. As she got older, she lost her ability to take care of those things. Elizabeth and Grandma Donoho, her mother, pieced quilt

tops together for years. Upon Aunt Elizabeth's death, I was given some of those quilt tops. I...shared them with my daughters, my sister, and the remaining two with the children of Elizabeth's nephew Robert. A wool quilt top sent to the Hazelwood children was said to have been made from cloth from suits that belonged to men in Elizabeth's and Anna's family.

Aunt Elizabeth and I baked our last cake together in 1965. It was a three layer, fresh coconut cake. She grated all of the coconut and my "helping" was only done as she directed me to do. Uncle Henry and Aunt Elizabeth always bought school clothes for the five McNeil children. Since they had no children of their own, they were very close to my siblings and me.

Uncle Henry and Aunt Elizabeth moved whenever there was a better job opportunity for Henry to paint signs and billboards. There were times when he worked with his brothers, Tom and James. He also hired my brothers, John and Henry, to work for him for a short time when they were teenagers.

Uncle Henry played the bass violin in night clubs to supplement his income. He also played the regular violin and often played for weddings including both my wedding and my sister's in the mid-1950's. Aunt Elizabeth eventually became jealous of the time he spent in the clubs, so he stopped working in them.

I recall that Henry and Elizabeth came to Natchez for my sister's wedding in 1952. Elizabeth fell ill during that visit and had to be admitted to the hospital. She was unresponsive and was in what I remember as a coma for almost three weeks. I do not remember the diagnosis, but she was never quite the same after that illness.

Henry and Elizabeth were always in love. It is so sad that they had no children of their own, as they both loved children. I often heard her talk about my two Kimberlin cousins, her nephews, Robert and Edward, and my siblings and me with love.[41]

Elizabeth was close to her Aunt Bessie Ratliff Causey. After Henry passed away, Barbara Ann Mingee found letters from Aunt Bessie to Elizabeth during the period of 1964 to 1967. These letters show a loving relationship and frequent correspondence over a period of years. In one letter, Bessie made reference to Elizabeth's acquaintance with Lady Bird Johnson:

It must give you a thrill to remember your association with Lady Bird. I can't say that I admire Pres. Johnson's stand on the Civil Rights Bill. Seems to me we are, some of us, having our rights taken away from us. But of course that is just my opinion.[42]

In another letter, obviously in response to a letter from Elizabeth, Aunt Bessie noted Elizabeth's interest in having Aunt Bessie's "little gun" after Bessie's eventual passing, and she asked what other items Elizabeth might be interested in. Aunt Bessie outlived Elizabeth by sixteen years.

At some point, Elizabeth began to have breathing problems. Presumably it was emphysema as a result of many years of heavy smoking. A doctor recommended that they move to New Mexico where the air

---

41 Email from Susan Mingee containing her mother Barbara's recollections, November 22, 2011.
42 Letter from Bessie to Elizabeth, July 2, 1964.

quality might help her condition. So they packed up and moved to a small rented house in Deming, New Mexico.[43]

Henry was able to continue working as a sign painter in New Mexico. Although the drier climate may have eased Elizabeth's breathing problem to some extent, she began to show signs of dementia. Henry did not feel he could safely leave her home alone because she might forget to put clothes on and/or wander around the neighborhood, confused about where she was.

According to Susan Mingee, Henry asked his sister, Wilma Kimberlin McNeil, to come out to New Mexico to stay with Elizabeth so he could go to work without worrying about Elizabeth's being home alone. Wilma took the train from Natchez to New Mexico twice, staying about two weeks each time.

In a candid and poignant letter to her daughter Barbara Ann back home in Natchez, Wilma described the situation at Henry and Elizabeth's house:

> Thursday, June 15th, '72
>
> Dear B.A. and Family,
> Glad to hear from you. It's like a tomb here—sitting and burning up all day while Aunt Libba sleeps (and Gretchen, too). Uncle Henry comes home so tired he eats and gets on the sofa and goes right to sleep (if she will let him, for making him jump up and down). He doesn't even undress at night and stays right on the sofa in the living room. (TV as loud as it will go. If you turn it off or down, it wakes him up.)
>
> I wanted to be home for Father's Day, but he keeps hinting about going back to El Paso to the doctor. I don't

---

43   Email from Susan Mingee to the author, November 15, 2011.

know if he wants me to go or not. And the other day she asked him if I wasn't going to be here indefinitely. Oh, boy!

They are both in such a shape and haven't made arrangements with anyone (no burial insurance, no lots, no money, no anything). They haven't even talked with the minister here, and now she says she doesn't want to be buried with the family, and he doesn't want to either. He might get some lots here, he just doesn't know.

She will call me and I go to see what she wants and she wants her mama (but still she doesn't want her back here on earth.) It's pitiful. Yet she can turn around and carry on a real nice conversation with Theresa in Washington State without a bobble.

She wants to see you. She talks all the time about it. You sent some pictures and the negatives. Were they all Uncle Henry's? I put them in the little holder and Aunt Libba liked them.

I am melting here. I mean no fans or air conditioner. She wouldn't have them on anyway. I am glad your Daddy is doing alright. I worry about him, too. I want to call but the phone is so expensive. Tell my little girls to take care of him for me. How is Susan and her poison oak, and my little hot shot, Peggy Ann? I know my big girl is fine and thinking about her trip to Denver soon.

We went to Rock City Sunday and saw the largest copper mine. Couldn't take any pictures because it was cloudy. Your Uncle Henry said I could get a post card of it to send you. This is the only time I've been away from the house since I've been here.

> The lady that comes to the house is here about 2 and a half hours. She changes Aunt Elizabeth's bed, and washes the clothes, dusts and wet mops. This is a small house, and she is fast. She is past 70 and looks about 40. Well I guess I'll stop. Love, Mother[44]

Elizabeth passed away in a nursing home in Deming on March 2, 1973. Her body was transported back to Marshall, Texas, and she was buried on March 6 at Greenwood Cemetery in the family plot where her mother, father, and twin sister, Mary, were already interred.[45]

Henry Kimberlin eventually moved to Natchez, Mississippi, where his sister Wilma lived. He passed away on May 6, 1987, and was buried in the Natchez City Cemetery.

---

44 Letter from Wilma Kimberlin McNeil in Deming, New Mexico, to her daughter Barbara Ann, in Natchez, Mississippi, June 15, 1972.

45 Elizabeth Donoho Kimberlin obituary, *Marshall (TX) News Messenger*, March 5, 1973.

2

MARY BELLE RATLIFF

San Antonio, Texas – January 24, 1932

Around 1928, Belle's husband, O.W. Wilson, had left her in San Antonio while he went to Phoenix to open another furniture store, taking their oldest son, O.W. Jr., as well as Belle's sister Florence, who was a bookkeeper. Now four years later, they were still in Phoenix while Belle, her daughter Sudie, and youngest son, Jeff, were still living in San Antonio. Presumably O.W. sent money every month for the family's expenses. But it was apparent from later events that Belle might not have been in the best mental state by then. Her son, Jeff, must have had problems as well.

Belle may have been considering all of these troubling circumstances when a gunshot suddenly rang out from upstairs!

THE LIFE OF MARY BELLE RATLIFF

Mary Belle Ratliff was the second child and second daughter of William Pinkney and Cornelia Mitchell Ratliff. Born June 22, 1875, on the family farm near Ethel, her family called her "Belle." In 1880, she and her parents and her siblings Anna, John B., and Sudie were living on the farm in Ethel.[1]

The family had moved to Kosciusko in the early 1890s but by the late 1890s had returned to a family farm near Zilpha. In 1900, Belle and her eight younger siblings were on the farm in Zilpha. By that time, her elder sister Anna and brother John B. had left home to be on their own.[2]

Belle was a pretty girl. Early photos show a dark-haired beauty, with a touch of melancholy.

Mary Belle Ratliff

On October 10, 1901, in Attala County where she resided with her family, she married Overton Welch "O.W." Wilson, a successful furniture

---

1   1880 US Census, Township 14, Range 6, Attala Co., Mississippi, ED 18, sheet 17, National Archives Microfilm, T9, roll 641.

2   1900 US Census, Zilpha, Attala Co., Mississippi, ED 7, sheet 6B, National Archives Microfilm, T623, roll 800.

store owner. Wilson was born on November 28, 1874, reportedly in Vaiden, Carroll County, Mississippi, northwest of Kosciusko. No information could be found about how the couple met and fell in love. Belle was by then twenty-six and was probably a schoolteacher.[3] Perhaps she was teaching somewhere when she met her future husband. The 1940 census indicated that she had attended college.[4]

The earliest record found for Wilson was in 1900, when he owned a furniture store with two partners in Bessemer, Alabama.[5] One partner was Tom Wilson, but it could not be determined if Tom was a brother or another relative. According to this census record, Overton Welch Wilson's parents were also born in Mississippi. O.W. and his two partners lived together in a rented house on Alabama Avenue in Bessemer. O.W.'s obituary listed a sister, Emma Wilson Harvey, and a brother, Frank H. Wilson, but no other records with their names have been found.[6]

Presumably the newly married couple settled in Bessemer initially. However, they moved around quite a bit over the next thirty years, as O.W. was establishing furniture stores in other cities.

On November 29, 1902, the couple's first child, Overton Welch Wilson Jr., was born in Bessemer, Alabama.[7]

---

3   Occupation indicated on death certificate for Mary Belle Wilson.
4   1940 US Census, Justice Precinct 7, Bexar County, Texas, ED 15-44, sheet 13A, National Archives Microfilm, T627, roll 3987.
5   1900 US Census, Bessemer, Ward 2, Jefferson Co., Alabama, ED 121, sheet 1B, National Archives Microfilm, T623, roll 23.
6   Death notice of O. W. Wilson, *San Antonio Express-News*, March 21, 1940.
7   Death certificate of Overton Welch Wilson Jr., July 31, 1984.

Belle and O.W. Wilson with O.W. Jr.[8]

May 24, 1906, saw the arrival of a daughter, Sudie Wilson, born in Meridian, Mississippi.[9] Meridian is the largest town in Lauderdale County, so it is likely that O.W. had established a furniture store there.[10]

---

8   Photos of Belle and O.W. and their children are courtesy of Ellen Oakes Pettit, great-granddaughter of W.P.'s brother John Whitfield Ratliff. Family photos were found in the effects of a Ratliff relation after her death in Jackson, Mississippi.

9   Delayed certificate of birth, September 7, 1960. The author is particularly indebted to Mrs. Patricia Jenkins Hartman, wife of Sudie Wilson Hartman's step-grandson Alan Hartman, who went out of her way to research court records, newspaper archives, and cemeteries in San Antonio in order to document the lives of Belle Ratliff Wilson and her family.

10   Death notice of O. W. Wilson, *San Antonio Express-News*, March 21, 1940.

Sudie Wilson

April 21, 1910, finds O.W., Belle, son O.W. Jr., and daughter Sudie in Shawnee, Oklahoma.[11] Presumably, O.W. had established yet another furniture store in Shawnee. On September 1, 1910, O. W. and Belle welcomed a second son, Jefferson Clay Wilson, born in Shawnee.

Sometime before 1915, the family moved to Sealy, Texas, where it is likely that O.W. established yet another furniture store. Within two years or so, it appears that the family was planning to move to San Antonio, Texas. Bexar County records indicate that on October 20, 1917, O.W. Wilson purchased two lots in the Mission View addition to the city of San Antonio.[12] The purchase price was $6,060, with a down payment of $1,000 and monthly payments of $500 at 8 percent interest.[13] On May 31, 1918, having made the necessary payments, O.W. filed for a release of lien,

---

11 1910 US Census, Shawnee Ward 6, Pottawatomie Co., Oklahoma, ED 227, sheet 3B, National Archives Microfilm, T624, roll 1271.

12 Deed of trust, Deed Records of Bexar County, no. 109125, 469-470.

13 Purchase agreement, Deed Records of Bexar County, no. 109124, 409-410.

giving him title to the property.¹⁴ On May 21, 1919, O.W. paid $6,500 in cash for two more lots in the Alamosa addition to the city of San Antonio.

At some point, Belle's sister Florence—younger than Belle by more than ten years—began living with the Wilson family and working as a bookkeeper in the Wilson Furniture Store.

In a letter dated September 22, 1918, Belle's brother Albert wrote that

> Mr. Wilson,¹⁵ Mama, and Florence are at Jacksonville, Texas now. Mr. Wilson bought a farm there. He is making lots of money now, as is everyone over here.¹⁶

Moreover, O.W. registered for the military draft in Jacksonville on September 11, 1918. He gave Belle's name as his wife with a residence of Jacksonville, Texas.¹⁷

In a May 28, 1919, letter to their younger brother Tom in Bangalore, India, Belle's sister Sudie wrote the following:

> Mr. Wilson and family and Mama will move to San Antonio soon. Mama and Florence will live to themselves.¹⁸

On December 2, 1919, from the Wilson family home at 2803 S. Presa Street in San Antonio, Mama herself (Cornelia) wrote to her son Tom. So presumably the family moved to San Antonio between May and December of 1919.¹⁹

In the 1920 census, O.W. and Belle, their three children, and Belle's sister Florence were all living together in the South Presa Street home in

---

14 Release of lien, Deed Records of Bexar County, no. 7405, 114-115.
15 When writing about O.W. Wilson, all of Belle's family referred to him as "Mr. Wilson" rather than "O.W." or "Overton."
16 Letter from Albert Wade Ratliff, September 22, 1918, to his brother Tom Watson Ratliff, who was with the British army in Bangalore, India.
17 WWI draft registration for Overton Welch Wilson, September 11, 1918.
18 Letter from Sudie Ratliff Spain to her brother Tom, May 28, 1919.
19 Letter from Cornelia Mitchell Ratliff to her son Tom in Ft. Worth, Texas, December 3, 1919.

San Antonio. O.W. was the owner of a furniture store, while Florence was "bookkeeper" in a furniture store.[20]

On January 22, 1918, O.W. Wilson executed a will in which he instructed that, upon his death, his estate be divided five ways, as f0llows:

> I bequeath, devise, and give unto my beloved wife Mary Belle Wilson, an undivided one-fifth (1/5) of my estate…
>
> I bequeath, devise, and give unto my beloved children O.W. Wilson, Junior; Sudie Wilson; and Jeff Clay Wilson; each an undivided one-fifth (1/5) of my estate…
>
> I bequeath, devise, and give unto my beloved sister-in-law Florence Ratliff, an undivided one-fifth (1/5) of my entire estate…[21]

It is not known whether any family members were aware of this will at the time it was executed. Although not unprecedented, it was odd in the first place that he did not leave his entire estate to his wife. Had he wanted specifically to name the children, he could have left half his estate to his wife and the remaining half to his children. It is of course conceivable that he was sufficiently wealthy that one-fifth of his estate would have been a tidy sum in itself, sufficient for each of his heirs.

Additionally, one could assume that O.W. thought of Belle's younger sister Florence as "one of the family." While Belle was home raising the children, O.W. and Florence were together all day at the furniture store. At some point—it came out later—O.W. and Florence must have begun having an affair. It could have gone on for years without Belle's knowledge. One odd note: a newspaper article reporting the funeral of Belle's father, William Pinkney Ratliff, in Kosciusko in 1927 listed Florence and O. W.

---

20   1920 US Census, Ward 8, San Antonio, Bexar Co., Texas, ED 98, sheet 9A, National Archives Microfilm, T636, roll 1780.
21   Last will and testament of Overton Welch Wilson, January 22, 1918.

among the relatives coming from out of town. W.P.'s daughter Belle did not attend.[22]

However, an affair was by no means the end of it. Around 1928–1929, O.W. left Belle, Sudie, and Jeff in San Antonio and moved to Phoenix, Arizona, with Florence. Perhaps the fact that his son O.W. Jr. had married an Arizona girl, Jessie T., in 1922 or 1923 and was living in Phoenix influenced O.W.'s decision to move there. His decision to take Florence with him seems self-explanatory.

The 1930 census records show Belle, her daughter Sudie, and younger son Jefferson Clay at home with her at 2803 S. Presa Street in San Antonio.[23] O.W. was reported as living there as well. However, he was also included in a completely separate census record, where he was listed as living at 605 N. Fifth Avenue in Phoenix, Arizona, with his sister-in-law Florence, his son O.W. Jr., and O.W. Jr.'s wife, Jessie.[24] There was also an O.W. Wilson Furniture store at 320 W. Washington Street.[25] One can't be in two places at once, so presumably Belle told the census taker her husband was living with her in San Antonio out of embarrassment or awkwardness or in order to conceal the fact that her husband had left her to live with her sister Florence. So O.W. got counted in two places, though he was obviously living in Phoenix.

This was not to be the last of Belle's troubles by far. The rest of her life was even more tragic. On January 24, 1932, Belle's youngest son, Jefferson Clay Wilson, shot himself in the right temple with a rifle in his bedroom. When Belle heard the shot and found him dead, she notified a neighbor, who called the police.[26] The cause of death written on his death certificate was "Gun-shot wound self-inflicted (suicide)."[27] He was buried in Mission Burial Park (South) in San Antonio on January 27, 1932.

22   *Kosciusko Star-Herald,* sometime after the death of W.P. Ratliff in May 1927.
23   1930 US Census, District 144, San Antonio, Bexar Co., Texas, ED 144-15, sheet 19A, National Archives Microfilm, T626, roll 2298.
24   1930 US Census, Phoenix, Maricopa Co., Arizona, ED 8, sheet 14A, National Archives Microfilm, T626, roll 57.
25   1930 Arizona directory of Phoenix and surrounding towns.
26   *San Antonio Express,* January 25, 1932.
27   Death certificate for Jefferson Clay Wilson, January 27, 1932.

No one knows what drove him to commit suicide, but the effect on Belle must have been horrendous. With Jeff gone and her estranged husband living in Phoenix with her sister Florence and her son O.W. Jr., she was all alone except for her daughter Sudie. The pain must have been unbearable for her.

Sometime after her son's suicide in 1932, Belle was committed to the San Antonio State Hospital, a mental institution.[28] The 1940 census indicates that she was already in the state hospital by 1935. Belle's brother Tom told his daughter Bessie Ratliff Herrin that he had visited Belle in the hospital and that she was "perfectly sane." He said that at that time, a husband could have his wife committed and no one could do anything about it and that Belle's husband O.W. had had her committed so he could marry Florence.[29] However, Alan Hartman, step-grandson to Belle's daughter Sudie remembered Sudie being upset because "she had been the one who had her mother committed to the state mental institution…"[30] The exact circumstances of her commitment remain unknown.

Belle's estranged husband, O.W. Wilson, died March 19, 1940, in Little Rock, Arkansas, where he was living with Belle's sister Florence. The newspaper announcement of his burial noted his surviving family members but made no mention of his estranged wife, Belle.[31] He was buried in San Antonio in Mission Burial Park (South).

At some point after her commitment, responsibility for Belle's affairs was assumed by Alamo National Bank of San Antonio as "Guardian of the Estate of Mary Belle Wilson, N.C.M."[32]

---

28 The author sought information from the San Antonio State Hospital about Belle's confinement there. Unofficially, it was acknowledged that she had been a patient there, but Texas state privacy laws prevented the hospital from releasing any information, even though Belle had by then been deceased for more than forty years. However, her death certificate stated that she died in the San Antonio State Hospital.
29 Email from Tommie Jane Ratliff Allen to the author, August 10, 2007.
30 Letter to the author from Patricia Jenkins Hartman, wife of Belle's daughter Sudie Wilson Hartman's step-grandson Alan Hartman, June 9, 2008.
31 *San Antonio Express-News*, March 21, 1940.
32 N.C.M. is the abbreviation of the legal term from the Latin *Non Compos Mentis*, meaning "not of sound mind."

In 1952, Belle's house on South Presa Street, as well as another property in San Antonio identified as Lots Five (5) Six (6) and Seven (7), Block Two hundred two (202), Alamo Heights, San Antonio, were sold. Down payments for both properties, as well as mortgage payments under deeds of trust, were made to the Estate of Mary Belle Wilson, Alamo National Bank of San Antonio.[33]

Belle remained in the San Antonio State Hospital until her death of bronchopneumonia on August 6, 1964, at age eighty-nine. She had been confined in the mental institution for at least thirty years. Her estate, under the guardianship of Alamo National Bank, would have gone to her two surviving children.

Bill Hartman, another step-grandson of Belle's daughter Sudie, remembers that shortly after Sudie married his grandfather Robert William Hartman, Sudie's mother Belle Ratliff Wilson died. He recalls attending the funeral at age six or seven, along with his grandfather, Sudie Wilson Hartman, and other Hartman family members. Bill said he remembered it well because it was the first funeral he had ever attended. The services were held at a funeral home,[34] and "she was buried in a silver, metal casket with a pink frilly lining."[35] She was buried in the family cemetery plot at Mission Burial Park (South) - Section 18, which is called Woodland Estates, block 554, next to her estranged husband O.W. Wilson, who predeceased her.

---

33 Various legal papers regarded the property sales, dated in July and October of 1952.
34 Death certificate filed August 10, 1964, identified it as Riebe Funeral Home.
35 Letter to the author from Patricia Jenkins Hartman, wife of Alan Hartman (Bill Hartman's brother), June 9, 2008.

THE CHILDREN OF MARY BELLE RATLIFF WILSON

Overton Welch Wilson Jr.

Overton Welch Wilson Jr. was born on November 29, 1902, in Bessemer, Alabama,[36] where his father had a furniture store. In 1910, he was in Shawnee, Oklahoma with his family,[37] and he was in San Antonio by 1920.[38]

Around 1922 or 1923, O.W. Jr. married a woman from Arizona identified as Jessie T. Wilson.[39] In 1930, the couple was living with O.W. Sr. and Florence in Phoenix. At some point, they obtained a divorce.[40]

By 1935, O.W. Jr., presumably divorced at this point, returned to San Antonio and was living in the family home on South Presa Street.[41] In 1940, he was working as a self-employed boat builder in San Antonio.

O.W. Jr. enlisted in the US Coast Guard in New Orleans, Louisiana, on September 9, 1942. It was not entirely clear where he was living at the time, but his discharge certificate referenced Fort Worth, Texas. He was in New Orleans until October 15, 1942, presumably in processing. He was transferred to St. Augustine, Florida, on October 17, 1942, and served there until May 31, 1945. He received an honorable discharge from the US Coast Guard—Discharge Center #8, CG Receiving Station, New Orleans, Louisiana—on June 9, 1945. He achieved the rank of carpenter's mate first class, service number 587-199.[42]

O.W. Jr. returned to San Antonio at some point and opened up a watch repair shop in his home at the intersection of Hackberry Street and

---

36 US Coast Guard Honorable Discharge Certificate of June 9, 1945.
37 1910 US Census, Shawnee Ward 6, Pottawatomie Co., Oklahoma, ED 227, sheet 3B, National Archives Microfilm, T624, roll 1271.
38 1920 US Census, Ward 8, San Antonio, Bexar Co., Texas, ED 98, sheet 9A, National Archives Microfilm, T636, roll 1780.
39 1930 US Census, Phoenix, Maricopa Co., Arizona, ED 8, sheet 14A, National Archives Microfilm, T626, roll 57.
40 O. W. Wilson Jr. death certificate, filed on August 2, 1984, gave his marital status as "divorced."
41 1940 US Census, San Antonio, Bexar Co., Texas, ED 259-201, sheet 18A, National Archives Microfilm, T627, roll 4208.
42 US Coast Guard honorable discharge certificate, June 9, 1945.

Highland Boulevard. Bill Hartman remembers going into the watch repair shop with his father, Ted Hartman, who had a keen interest in repairing things. Bill remembers his father taking him to the shop on a Saturday to "watch the repair of a watch or clock, or whatever." By that time, O.W. Jr. was an old man. Bill said he liked hanging around in the musty, dark workroom. He said his family had a 400-day clock that his father Ted was constantly trying to have fixed. It never ran more than twenty-eight days at a time! Bill's brother Alan remembers buying a typewriter from O. W. Jr.'s shop.[43]

Overton Welch Wilson Jr. passed away on July 31, 1984, at the Audie L. Murphy Veterans Administration Hospital of San Antonio, Texas, of a "cardiovascular collapse, caused by a massive intracerebral hemorrhage."[44] He was eighty-one at the time of his death. His residence was listed as 1042 Steves Avenue, San Antonio. His remains were cremated, and his ashes were buried at the foot of his mother Mary Belle Ratliff Wilson's grave at Mission Burial Park (South). There is no gravestone, though cemetery records indicate the location of his ashes.[45]

Sudie Wilson

Sudie Wilson was born in Meridian, Mississippi, on May 24, 1906. Like her older brother Overton Welch Wilson Jr., she was with the family in Oklahoma in 1910. In 1920, she was with her mother and father and brothers O.W. Jr. and Jefferson Clay Wilson, as well as her aunt Florence Ratliff, all at the same address—2803 S. Presa Street, San Antonio.

In the 1930 census, Sudie's occupation was listed as "Teacher—Public School." She could have graduated from Brackenridge High School, the only high school near her home on South Presa Street. At one point, she taught at Smith Elementary School in San Antonio. According to her obituary, she taught elementary school for forty years.[46]

---

43 Letter to the author from Patricia Jenkins Hartman, wife of Alan Hartman, June 9, 2008.
44 Death certificate, August 2, 1984.
45 Again, courtesy of the thorough research efforts of Patricia Jenkins Hartman.
46 *San Antonio News-Express*, February 20, 1999.

No records were found documenting her college attendance or graduation. In those days, one didn't necessarily need a college degree to teach school, though many teachers were graduates of "normal schools," the two-year teachers colleges of their day. Sudie's step-grandson Bill Hartman remembered Sudie telling him—late in her teaching career—that she had to take some classes at Incarnate Word, a college in San Antonio, presumably to maintain or update her teacher certification.[47]

Sudie Wilson

Late in life—at age 57—Sudie married a widower, Robert William Hartman. He was a career military officer, retiring from the US Army as a lieutenant colonel with thirty-four years of service. Robert Hartman was married to his first wife, Miriam, for more than forty-five years until she passed away in 1963. He married Sudie in 1964.

---

47 Letter to the author from Patricia Jenkins Hartman, wife of Alan Hartman, June 9, 2008.

Robert William Hartman   Sudie Wilson Hartman

Robert and Sudie were married for almost thirty years, until he passed away on March 16, 1993, at the age of ninety-six.[48] He had two sons by his first wife, who both predeceased him. He had five grandchildren and nine great-grandchildren.[49]

Robert William Hartman's grandson Alan's wife Patricia Jenkins Hartman wrote about the difficulties that Sudie had as a new wife, stepmother, and step-grandmother:

> It was a difficult thing for the family. Alan's grandfather (Robert William Hartman—called "Pop" by his grandchildren) had been married for many years to a wonderful, loving woman who died suddenly at age 64 in April of 1963. They were all in shock. Alan's grandparents had been part of the backbone of their lives and lived only blocks away. They visited and talked daily on the telephone, sometimes more than once. His grandmother had been warm and sweet. Barely a

---

48 *San Antonio Express-News*, sometime around March 17/18, 1993.

49 Two of his grandchildren were Alan and Bill Hartman—sons of Ted Hartman—whose recollections about members of the Wilson family are contained in this chapter, thanks to Alan's wife, Patricia Jenkins Hartman.

year had passed when Alan's grandfather married Sudie. It was too soon for Alan's mom and dad. They didn't want to accept it.

Of course, Sudie could never take the place of their favorite grandmother. She wanted to though. She was set up for failure from the beginning, even if she had been the sweetest of persons. But she wasn't. She was overbearing and expected too much too soon. She wanted to tell everyone what was what. One of her biggest mistakes was telling Alan's mother how to rear her children. She had never had children of her own but thought that teaching children in a classroom made her an expert on them. She wasn't. Alan's mother had her feathers ruffled regularly by the things Sudie said or did, or didn't say or do.

When I joined the family, Sudie and Pop had been married almost 10 years. I determined to like Sudie. She was overly kind to me, trying her hardest to be accepted. It became unnatural and overwhelming. We visited them occasionally, especially when we were in town from out of state. Sudie was very sweet to us, too much so, I'm afraid.

If you had known Sudie, you would have recognized that something was not quite right about her. She talked very loudly. She kept her house hot, about 85 all the time. The house was kept very dark. She wanted to give you things to make you like her. For example, she sewed…strange, outdated, over-sized-buttoned type clothes. She thought we shared this hobby. I tried to be kind and compliment her tries. It was difficult. She also constantly gave me old, outdated magazines, strange fabric, and odd recipes. She thought she was a great cook, but no one wanted to eat dinner at their house.

After Pop died in 1993, Sudie kind of locked herself up in her own little world. She hired people to do her handiwork—the yard, the house, and such. She said she didn't want to lean on anyone. She got a lawyer she liked and depended on him for everything, until he did something she didn't like. She wanted to be left alone! Eventually, she got a little sick and needed medical attention. Alan's youngest sister (Carole) and her husband, a trained EMT, were able to help her out. She wouldn't let Alan near her.

To me, she seemed to become somewhat paranoid. She shut out Alan's brother Bill as well. One Christmas she gave us some old, used Christmas cards all stuck together and asked us if we could use them in our ministry—actually send them out. We thanked her and took them. During the next year, she accused us of stealing them and said she never wanted to see us again. I sent her the usual birthday gift which she returned by mail, the box all crumpled up. I asked her some questions on the phone about our families—hers and Pops—for genealogy purposes, I told her. She yelled at me that I was interfering and called me an ugly name, then told me to "butt out." I never talked to her again.[50]

It is entirely possible the mental problems of Sudie's mother Belle were inherited by both her daughter Sudie and her son Jeff, who shot himself to death at age twenty-one. Sudie was able to function in society, both in marriage and professionally, but obviously with some difficulty. She was also estranged from her older brother, O.W. Jr., for reasons that were not entirely clear. And it is not surprising that, given the family history, she was not very forthcoming with any information about her family background.

---

50   Email from Patricia Jenkins Hartman to the author, June 9, 2008.

Sudie Wilson Hartman passed away on February 19, 1999, at the age of ninety-two.[51] Her step-grandson the Reverend Alan Hartman officiated at her funeral. She was buried at Mission Burial Park (South) in the plot with her mother, father, and her two brothers.

Jefferson Clay Wilson

Jefferson Clay Wilson, O.W. and Belle's second son and youngest child, was born on September 1, 1910, in Shawnee, Oklahoma.

Tragically, on January 24, 1932, he shot himself in his upstairs bedroom at the family home on South Presa Street in San Antonio.[52] He was only twenty-one years old. Could it have been a type of mental illness like his mother had? The real story cannot be known.

Jeff was buried in Mission Park (South) Cemetery in San Antonio, in the family plot where his mother, father, brother O.W. Jr., and sister Sudie would also be buried.

Sadly, none of O.W. and Belle's children had offspring of their own, so the line stopped with the death of the three children.

---

51 Texas Death Index 1903-2000.
52 *San Antonio Express*, January 25, 1932.

3

JOHN BARTON RATLIFF

Cotton Crisis - Mid-1920s

John B. had many acres planted in cotton, the family's major source of income. Cotton prices hit their peak during WWI, and everyone was making good money. But the price was rapidly dropping and no one knew how low it would go. Would all of John B.'s hard work go for naught? With the bank holding the mortgages on all three farms, as well as having advanced money to keep things going until the cotton could be sold, would John B. survive?

THE LIFE OF JOHN BARTON RATLIFF

John Barton Ratliff[1] was born in Ethel on May 14, 1878, the first son and third child of W. P. and Cornelia. The family called him "John B." and "John Barton."

In 1880, John B., age two, was living with his parents and his two older sisters in Ethel.[2]

The June 8, 1892, edition of the *Kosciusko Star* reported on the closing exercises at the Kosciusko Male and Female Institute, located in the old Baptist Church building on North Huntington Street. Among the medals awarded was one for elocution to fourteen-year-old John B. Ratliff. John B.'s cousin Mary Eddie Wasson (daughter of W.P.'s sister Mary Jane Ratliff Wasson) was also awarded a medal.[3] According to Sally Wasson, widow of Eddie's nephew William "Billie" Eugene Wasson, Aunt Eddie was still proudly displaying her medal when Sally knew her many years later.

A short item in the "Town and Country" section of the Friday, September 11, 1896, edition of W.P.'s newspaper, the *Alliance Vindicator*, reported, "J.B. Ratliff left Tuesday for The A&M College at Starkville."[4] He was eighteen years old and went on to complete two years of college.[5] In 1900, John B. was living in a boarding house in Liberty Chapel with a family named Jenkins.[6] The head of household was Ben J. Jenkins, age fifty-four, and his wife was Elois L. Jenkins, age sixty-one. John B. was identified

---

1 John Barton Ratliff was the author's grandfather.
2 1880 US Census, Township 14, Range 6, Attala Co., Mississippi, ED 18, sheet 17, National Archives Microfilm, T9, roll 641.
3 Copy of reprint from *Kosciusko Star-Herald* (date unknown) kindly provided by Sally Wasson, who copied it from a scrapbook belonging to Rosalind Smith Shelley, a descendant of Eddie Wasson Mitchell. Sally Wasson is the widow of William "Billie" Eugene Wasson, whose grandmother Mary Jane Ratliff Wasson was William Pinkney Ratliff's sister. With permission.
4 *Alliance Vindicator*, August 28, 1896. John B.'s father, William Pinkney Ratliff, was the publisher and associate editor of the *Vindicator*. A&M College in Starkville, Mississippi, is the present-day Mississippi State University.
5 1940 US Census, Drew, Sunflower Co., Mississippi, ED 67-35, sheet 3B, National Archives Microfilm, T627, roll 2067.
6 1900 US Census, Liberty Chapel, Attala Co., Mississippi, ED 5, sheet 10A, National Archives Microfilm, T623, roll 800.

as a boarder and his occupation was "miller." According to J.B.'s daughter Martha, her father showed a great interest in all things mechanical from an early age, so perhaps he was doing some sort of mechanical work in a mill.

The following year, on October 31, 1901, John B. married Emma Roxana Jenkins in Kosciusko.

John Barton Ratliff   Emma Roxana Jenkins

Emma Roxana Jenkins was born February 11, 1880, in Attala County. Her parents were James L. Jenkins, born in 1843 in Tennessee, and Eliza Light Jenkins, born in 1848 in Alabama. Emma, four months old at the time of the 1880 census, was listed with her parents and four older siblings—Alice, age eleven; Thomas (later to be called "Uncle T" by his nieces and nephews), age eight; Fannie, age four; and Danah, age two.[7] John B.'s daughter Martha remembered that when her family would visit their relatives in Attala County, they stayed at Uncle T's, where she and her siblings would sleep on the floor on pallets.[8]

---

[7] 1880 US Census, Township 14, Range 6 E, Attala Co., Mississippi, ED 48, sheet 14, National Archives Microfilm, T9, roll 641.

[8] Many conversations over a period of years about family history between the author and Martha Ratliff Whetzel, John B. and Emma's younger daughter.

No family connection can be found between Emma Jenkins's family and that of Ben J. and Elois L. Jenkins, where John B. was a boarder in 1900. Ben J. was born in Georgia, whereas Emma's father James was born in Tennessee.

One interesting note: the 1880 census showed Emma's family living in Township 14, Range 6 E, the very same area as John B. and his family. So it is likely that Emma and John B. knew each other from an early age.

In the 1900 census, Emma, whose occupation was listed as "teacher," was living in Sallis, west of Kosciusko. By that time, her older sisters Alice and Danah had left home. Thomas, age twenty-eight, was working as farm labor, presumably on the family farm. In the twenty years since the 1880 census, three more daughters had been born: Wessie, age nineteen; Netta, age seventeen; and Hattie, age fourteen.[9]

Emma Roxana Jenkins *(right, front)* with her sister Fannie and probably her brother Thomas and father, James L. Jenkins

---

9   1900 US Census, Beat 4, Attala County, Mississippi, ED 8, sheet 6A, National Archives Microfilm, T623, roll 800.

It is not known where the newly married couple lived after their 1901 wedding, but presumably it was somewhere in Attala County. Sometime between 1901 and 1905, they moved to Silver City, in Humphreys County, where their first two children were born. A period photo of John B. in front of Silver City Furniture Company, along with four women who might have been part of a sales force, leads one to the conclusion that he might have owned and/or managed the store.[10] John B.'s sister Belle's husband, O. W. Wilson, owned a furniture store in Bessemer, Alabama, and in the coming years would open furniture stores in a number of other cities around the country. So perhaps having a brother-in-law in the furniture store business resulted in the move to Silver City so John B. could manage a store there.

John B. Ratliff (*standing, right*)
with employees of furniture store

---

10 Found in a collection of photos belonging to John B. and Emma Jenkins Ratliff at the home of their daughter Martha Ratliff Whetzel in Nokesville, Virginia, thanks to Martha's daughter Marlyn Wilkinson.

While John B. and Emma were living in Silver City, the young couple's first child, John Barton Jr., arrived on February 28, 1905.[11] Family and friends called him by his middle name, "Barton."

Second son, Pinkney Brooks, born May 27, 1907, was named after his grandfather William Pinkney. He too was called by his middle name, "Brooks."

By late 1908 or early 1909, the family moved to Sunflower County, outside of Drew, in the Mississippi Delta. And on February 23, 1909, Anna Belle (Anabel) was born. Anabel is believed to have been named after her father's two older sisters, Sarah Anna Lee and Mary Belle.

John B. and Emma bought a farm that, according to the 1910 census, was located in Township 28, Range 3 W, Beat 5. John B. Ratliff is listed as head of household with the occupation of farmer and as the owner of the farm, with a mortgage. The size of the farm was not indicated. Wife Emma and the three children born between 1905 and 1909 were listed in the household.[12]

The following year, Clarence Harold was born, on September 3, 1911.

Another son, James Grady Ratliff, was born on November 18, 1912. He was called "Jimmy."

---

11   John Barton Ratliff Jr. was the author's father.
12   1910 US Census, Township 28, Range 3 W, Beat 5, Sunflower Co., Mississippi, ED 95, sheet 14A, National Archives Microfilm, T624, roll 759.

John B. and Emma Jenkins Ratliff about 1912-1913
From left, front, Brooks, Barton, Anabel, Clarence, Jimmy

After Jimmy, three more children were born into the household before the 1920 census.

They were:

- Paul Adams Ratliff, born in 1914

- William Rodgers Ratliff, born in 1916

- Martha Cornelia Ratliff, born in 1917

Sadly, Clarence died on August 29, 1917, just before his sixth birthday. John B. Ratliff registered for the World War I draft on September 12, 1918. His registration listed a permanent home address in the town of Drew. His next of kin was listed as Emma Ratliff, also of Drew. He registered as

John Barton Ratliff but signed his name as "J.B. Ratliff." There is no other record of the family having a house in town by this date.[13]

In 1920, the family was living on a farm in "Beat 5, Sunflower County,"[14] presumably the same farm they'd bought around 1909 or 1910. The family prospered, with John B. acquiring a total of three farms. Daughter Martha said that after they bought a second and third farm, the original farm was referred to as "the old place." She said their father had a swimming pool built in the back yard. According to *Fevers, Floods, and Faith – A History of Sunflower County: 1844-1976*, "a pool built by J.B. Ratliff of Drew in 1923 is believed to have been the first in the county..."[15]

Local children enjoying the Ratliff pool

The family later moved to one of the other farms, called "Fitzhugh Plantation," although according to John B.'s daughter Martha, it was more farm than plantation.

---

13   US World War I draft registration card, 1917-1918, September 12, 1918.
14   1920 US Census, Beat 5, Sunflower Co., ED 126, sheet 20B, National Archives Microfilm, T625, roll 894.
15   Marie M. Hemphill, *Fevers, Floods, and Faith – A History of Sunflower County: 1844-1976* (Indianola, Mississippi, 1980). 584.

On December 6, 1921, John B. and Emma's youngest child, Albert Wade, was born. Albert Wade (called "Bevo") was named for his uncle Albert Wade, John B.'s younger brother, who by this time had moved with their mother, Cornelia, to Sunflower County from Texas. According to the elder Albert Wade's son, Barton Wade, John B. named his youngest son after his brother because "Uncle" Albert Wade was already thirty-five years old and still a bachelor. No one expected him to marry and have children, so John B. wanted to honor his brother by naming his new son for him.[16]

In 1922, the year after his namesake Albert Wade ("Bevo") was born, the original Albert Wade married Ruth Bullock. When the couple had a son, they returned the favor by naming him Barton Wade, after Albert Wade's brother John B. (John Barton).

As a cotton farmer, John B.'s fortunes were susceptible to the rise and fall of the price of cotton. Many farmers borrowed money during the year with the expectation of repaying the loans after their cotton crops were sold. Beginning in 1920 after WWI, overseas demand for agricultural products declined and the price of cotton dropped to a devastatingly low level. Unquestionably, the cotton crisis had a terrible effect on cotton farmers in the Mississippi Delta. The John B. Ratliff family was no exception. As a result, John B. lost all of his farms. According to John B.'s daughter Martha, when they lost the farms, the family moved into a rental house in Drew. Martha remembered that this was just as she was about to begin school—about 1923–1924.

Martha recalled that, in about 1926–1927, when she was in the fourth grade, a fire destroyed the house in which they were living in Drew, and they had to move into another house on the same property. Until the fire, as noted previously, that house had been occupied by Martha's grandmother Cornelia, who was then sent to live with her daughter Sudie Spain in Kosciusko.

---

16   Email from Barton Wade Ratliff to the author, 2007.

In 1930, John B. and Emma and the seven younger children were living on First Street in Drew.[17] Having lost the farms, John B. had to find other employment. His daughter Martha said that because of his knowledge of farming, he was able to secure work as an overseer at Parchman Farm, a prison farm in Sunflower County with 20,000 acres of farmland planted primarily in cotton. It was later called the Mississippi State Prison at Parchman, and inmates worked the cotton fields. John B.'s nephew, Robert, son of John B.'s younger brother, Zack, recalled visiting his uncle John B. and his family when he was young:

> I visited your granddad when he was the warden at Parchman and lived on prison grounds in a large home with a screen porch on three sides.[18]

By 1940, John B. and Emma were living in Drew, together with sons Paul and Bevo (Albert Wade).[19]

In 1942, after the outbreak of World War II, John B. and Emma moved to Pascagoula, Mississippi, when daughter Martha's husband Hilbert Wilkinson was drafted into the navy and sent to Pascagoula. The grandparents assumed the daily care of granddaughter Marlyn. Around 1943, the families moved to Mobile, Alabama.

In 1946, John B. and Emma, along with Martha and Marlyn, moved to Nokesville, Virginia, settling into a house on a farm purchased for them by son Billie, who was stationed at nearby Quantico Marine Base. Martha took a job in Washington, DC, leaving Marlyn under the loving care of her grandparents during the day.

With the job market in the Washington, DC, area vastly superior to that of the Mississippi Delta, son Paul also moved to Virginia, as did

---

17 1930 US Census, Beat 5, Drew, Sunflower Co., Mississippi, ED 67-22, sheet 1B, National Archives Microfilm, T626, roll 1166.

18 Letter from Robert Ratliff to the author, March 13, 2012.

19 1940 US Census, Drew, Sunflower Co., Mississippi, ED 67-35, sheet 3B, National Archives Microfilm, T627, roll 2067.

Brooks and his family. Brooks and Paul both took jobs at Union Station in Washington.

John B. and Emma farmed, raised chickens and milk cows, grew vegetables for the family and hay for the cows, and, except for the cotton, lived a life on the farm similar to their early days in Mississippi. The farmhouse initially had no indoor plumbing. About 1948, the author remembers the second trip he and his family took to Nokesville, just in time to find an indoor bathroom under construction, much to the delight of all of the visiting children and grandchildren.

He also remembers helping to "get in the hay" and riding the draft horses bareback. The horses were resistant to any guidance by a rider and generally went wherever they wanted. When a calf was born, Emma named the calf "Joy," in honor of her granddaughter Sidney Joy Ratliff.[20]

John B. and Emma continued to farm and enjoy the nearby presence of Martha and Marlyn, as well as sons Brooks, Billie, Paul, and their families. Their other children, along with their families, visited on a regular basis at Christmas time and particularly in the summers.

On October 31, 1951, John B. and Emma celebrated their fiftieth wedding anniversary.

---

20 Younger sister of the author.

Seated, from left, Mary Hoffman Ratliff (Billie's wife), Emma, Marlyn (Martha's daughter), John B., Billie (John B.'s son); *standing, from left,* Martha (John B.'s daughter), Paul (John B.'s son), Roxana (Brooks's daughter), Maye (Brooks's wife)

As John B. and Emma became older, they moved in with their daughter Martha so she could take care of them. The farmhouse remained furnished but unoccupied.

On May 22, 1960, John B., who had been sick for some time, was stricken with bad stomach pains and transported by ambulance to Sibley Hospital in Washington, DC. Surgery was undertaken quickly and revealed inoperable stomach cancer. Sometime early the next morning—around 2:00 am May 23, 1960—he passed away without regaining consciousness. He was eighty-two years old. John B. Ratliff was buried at Valley View Cemetery in Nokesville, Virginia. All eight of his children came for the funeral and to honor their father and lend support to their mother.

After John B.'s Funeral
Front, Paul, Emma, Anabel; *middle,* Jimmy, Martha, Brooks, Barton; *back,* Billie, Bevo

After John B.'s death, Emma lived with her daughter Martha for some time longer and then stayed with each of her children in Mississippi, Louisiana, Texas, and Florida on a rotational basis. All the children learned that when Emma came to stay, family members would be enlisted to assist with her quilt making, an endeavor she continued until the end of her life.

While staying with her daughter Anabel Ratliff Thomas in Hattiesburg, Mississippi, Emma passed away on January 21, 1970. She was just six months short of her ninetieth birthday. At the time of her death, she had eight children, fifteen grandchildren, and many great-grandchildren. She was buried next to her husband John B. in the Valley View Cemetery in Nokesville, Virginia.

THE CHILDREN OF JOHN B. AND EMMA RATLIFF

John Barton Ratliff Jr.

John B. and Emma's oldest son John Barton Jr. was born on February 28, 1905, in Silver City, Mississippi. He was called "Barton." About the time he began high school, he moved in with his Uncle Albert and family on their dairy farm near Wade, outside of Drew.

Barton as a young man

Albert Wade's daughter Cornelia remembers Barton driving her to school every day. Albert's son Tom said that his father helped Barton with his math, and when Barton wanted to finish high school early, Albert taught Barton enough Latin so that he could pass the test and graduate a year sooner. Albert's sons Barton Wade and Tom both said that their father spoke of Barton with great affection.

Barton also lived with his Uncle Albert and his family in the summers during college and when he began teaching in Drew. He was with the family at the time of the 1930 census, after he had graduated from college.[21] Barton felt close to and maintained regular lifetime contact with his cousins, Cornelia, Barton Wade, and Tom.[22]

Barton graduated from Mississippi A&M College (now Mississippi State University) in 1927, majoring in agriculture. He played cornet in the "Famous Forty Maroon Band." The 1927 Reveille Yearbook had this to say about Barton:

> "Rat" came to A&M typically endowed with the best qualities of the Delta folk. He adapted himself to his surroundings, and entered into nearly every phase of college life with a spirit of enthusiasm and determination. His spirit was victorious; his ambitions were richly rewarded.
>
> Alpha Phi Epsilon; Varsity Band; Philotechnic Literary Society; Demosthenean Club; Baraca Sunday School Class; Promotion Force; Bugler; Sunflower County Club; Alumni of 1492; Charter Member Glee Club.

---

21   1930 US Census, Beat 5, Sunflower Co., Mississippi, ED 67-26, sheet 13B, Archives Microfilm, T626, roll 1166.
22   Through personal observation by the author, and as told to the author by his father, J. Barton Ratliff Jr.

Barton's graduation photo

In 1928, Barton traveled to cities around the United States as a guest member of the State Teachers College Band on the "Know Mississippi Better" train. The State Teachers College is now the University of Southern Mississippi in Hattiesburg. At each stop on the train tour, the band would play a concert, representatives of Mississippi would give informative speeches about the state, and residents of the town could tour the railroad cars containing exhibits of products grown and produced in Mississippi.[23] Barton toured as a band member more than once and said he had travelled through more than forty states on the train.

Barton also served in the Civilian Conservation Corps (CCC) for a time during the Depression. With a college degree in agriculture, he could have supervised workers on one project or another.[24]

At some point, Barton began teaching math and science in the public schools in Drew, where he was also coach for the Drew High School girls' basketball team that included his sister Martha.

---

23   *Helena (MT) Independent*, August 13, 1928, courtesy of Rose Diamond, Calhoun County, MS, Historical & Genealogical Society, Inc.
24   Memories of the author as a child, hearing from his father about his life.

Drew High School Girls' Basketball Team with Coach Barton
and Martha, second girl on the left

Around 1932, a new chorus director and speech/drama teacher—Elsie Vera Mixon—began teaching at Drew High School, and Barton and Vera began dating. On one occasion Barton took Vera to a basketball game where he was coaching. He got so engrossed in the game that when it was over, he forgot he had brought a date and drove home without Vera![25]

Vera Mixon was born October 20, 1907, in Amite, Louisiana. Her father was parish tax assessor. She earned a diploma in piano and a certificate in speech arts from Mississippi Woman's College in Hattiesburg in 1929. The yearbook for her senior year contained this prediction:

> Who can predict what Vera will accomplish in her lifetime? Knowing her many talents, especially in music, we certainly can expect that she will be recognized as a great musician. She is a jolly, good-natured sort of person who will always be

---

25 As told to the author by his mother, Vera.

welcome in any group because of her extraordinary ability to entertain.

After graduation, Vera taught first at Mt. Olive High School, Mt. Olive, Mississippi, then moved to Drew High School, where she met her future husband. In 1933, she joined the faculty at her alma mater, Mississippi Woman's College.

Barton and Vera married in Amite, Louisiana, on August 23, 1934. She was called "Mickey" by members of the Ratliff family.

Vera   Barton and Vera's Wedding

At some point early in their marriage, Barton received his MA in education, believed to be from the University of Chicago. Throughout her professional career, Vera was a public school music teacher and choral director and gave private piano lessons as well.

As schoolteachers, Barton and Vera had no employment or income in the summer, so they sometimes spent summers with Vera's parents in

Amite. It was during the summer after their marriage that their first son, John Barton III, was born in Baton Rouge, Louisiana, in 1935.[26]

That fall, Barton began teaching at a school in or near Greenville, Mississippi. It was there, on August 22, 1936, that a second son, Neil Mixon, named after Vera's brother Neil Holton Mixon, was born.

John and Neil   Neil and John

By 1938–1939, Barton and Vera were teaching at the Marie Consolidated School, outside of Indianola, in Sunflower County.

---

26 The author.

Vera Mixon Ratliff and her class at Marie School
Smallest children in front, Neil and John

When the family attended the 1939 Ratliff Reunion in Attala County, the photographer took four-generation photos with Cornelia Mitchell Ratliff and her child, grandchild, and oldest great-grandchild of each eligible family. The following photo was one of those taken that day.

John B. Ratliff Family four-generation photo
John B. Ratliff, John Barton Ratliff III,
Cornelia Mitchell Ratliff, J. Barton Ratliff Jr.

In the fall of 1939, the family moved to the Four Mile Lake community, outside Belzoni, in Humphreys County. Both Barton and Vera taught at the Four Mile Lake School, named after the nearby lake, which looks more like a river because it is very narrow and extends for four miles. One day, Barton decided to take John and Neil, along with a friend and his son, on a boat ride on Four Mile Lake. Barton's friend, who was quite heavy, was the last one to get in the boat, and when he did, it sank! Barton was the only one who could swim, but fortunately they were near the shoreline where the water was not deep and Barton was able to get everyone back safely to land.[27]

In 1940, the family was still in the Four Mile Lake community. Both Barton and Vera were teaching in Four Mile Lake School. Sons John III and Neil were listed as being in the household.[28]

In 1941, the family moved to McComb, in Pike County. After the school year was over, Barton took a job for the summer of 1942 as a carpenter in Kentucky, where the family lived in a boarding house.

Sometime during that summer, six-year old Neil contracted polio. There was such a fear of polio at that time that the landlady immediately evicted the family and burned the mattress on which Neil and John had slept. The family was forced to move to a motel.[29]

The Kentucky Department of Health quarantined Neil in the motel and refused to permit his family to take him out of the state. Finally Barton was able to persuade a state government official to permit the family to drive with Neil to Warm Springs, Georgia,[30] where Barton was successful in getting the Georgia Warm Springs Foundation (now known as the Roosevelt Warm Springs Institute for Rehabilitation) to accept Neil as a patient. President Franklin Delano Roosevelt had started the foundation in 1927, after contracting polio and finding that bathing in the warm springs of that area in Georgia was therapeutic.

Thanks to the recommendation of Barton's college roommate L.D. Stacy, who was teaching at Riverside Military Academy in Gainesville, Georgia, Barton was able to get a job teaching at Riverside for the fall of 1942 so that the family could be near Neil. Neil missed his first year of school because he was in the hospital.

---

27 Recollections of the author, supported by his cousin Barton Wade Ratliff, who was staying with the family at the time and recalled the incident years later.

28 1940 U.S Census, Beat 1, Humphreys Co., Mississippi, ED 27-3, sheet 10B, National Archives Microfilm, T627, roll 2030.

29 Called a "tourist court" in those days; the author has strong memories of the whole incident, though only seven years old at the time.

30 The author recalls the trip vividly, with brother Neil crying in pain all the way.

Neil and Vera at Warm Springs

Neil began first grade in 1943, at the age of seven. Each summer until about age twelve, he would go to Warm Springs for more surgery on his legs. He was fitted for leg braces and used crutches all of his life.

In 1945, Barton and Vera welcomed a daughter, Sidney Joy, named after Vera's youngest brother James Sidney Mixon.

Barton and Joy

Neil, Barton, John, Joy, Vera at Warm Springs

In 1946, Barton took a faculty position at Brenau College, a girls' school in Gainesville. In the summers, he was also a recruiter for the college, traveling all over the South paying visits to recent high school graduates who had expressed an interest in Brenau.

In 1949, the family moved to Hammond, Louisiana. Barton took a faculty position at Southeastern Louisiana College (now University) and Vera taught music and directed choruses in public schools nearby, eventually ending up at Ponchatoula High School. After a few years, Barton left teaching and worked in the treasurer's office at Southeastern. He would eventually return to education, teaching math and science at various high schools in Louisiana.

Both Barton and Vera sang in the choir in the Baptist church, and Vera regularly sang solos. Barton played the trumpet all his life. All three children inherited their parents' love for and talent in music, playing instruments and singing around the piano at home from early childhood.

John, Joy, Neil, Vera, Barton

Joy, Neil, John

Vera had a very successful career as a high school chorus director. On the occasion of her retirement in 1973 after twenty-two years directing the high school chorus at Ponchatoula High School, chorus members presented her with a trophy of appreciation and held a surprise reception for her in the school lobby. The newspaper account of the presentation described her as "a lovely lady, whose ever-present smile reflects the joy of giving herself to the youth of Ponchatoula for the past 22 years..."[31] A former student, reminiscing more than forty years after Vera's retirement, had this to say:

> Anyone who can get high school jocks to sing and like it and behave in class was special in my book and she could make them behave like gentlemen...never any threats, just a certain look and they would come to attention and kind of wiggle in their seats and sing...I was always in awe of her turning her back to play when their spit balls were flying all over the place especially in the first few classes...then it got better when they started learning and liking to sing...Just good old country boys with delinquent tendencies.[32]

Barton was an active tennis player all his life and was president of the Hammond Tennis Club at one time. In retirement, he was active in the seniors tennis circuit in the South, and in 1974, at age sixty-nine, was ranked number nine among players in the sixty-five–sixty-nine bracket. In 1975, shortly after entering the seventy–seventy-four bracket, he won second place trophies in tournaments in Sarasota and Cape Coral, Florida.[33] Even at the advanced age of eighty, he played tennis with son John[34] in the summer of 1985.

After a long illness Vera passed away of congestive heart failure on July 9, 1982, in Hammond, Louisiana. On November 26, 1985, at his home in Hammond, Barton died suddenly of an aneurysm. Both were buried in the Mixon family plot in the Amite Cemetery, Amite, Louisiana.

---

31 *Ponchatoula (LA) Enterprise*, April 22, 1973.

32 Recollections of Lydia Cosgrove, Ponchatoula High School, Class of 1967.

33 *Hammond (LA) Daily Star*, about March/April 1975.

34 The author.

THE CHILDREN OF BARTON AND VERA MIXON RATLIFF

John Barton Ratliff III

John graduated from high school in Hammond, Louisiana, in 1953. After a year as a voice major at Southeastern Louisiana College (now University), John joined the army, where he studied intensive Korean for a year at the Army Language School (the current Defense Language Institute) in Monterey, California. John was then assigned to duty in Japan.

John on a trip to Korea - Kimpo Air Base, 1957

After a three-year tour of service, John entered Georgetown University in Washington, DC, in 1957, majoring in Japanese. His uncles Brooks and Paul Ratliff, who shared an apartment in Washington, DC, invited him to stay with them until he got settled. It turned out to be for two full semesters, which provided a great opportunity not only to get to know his two uncles better but also to hear about Ratliff family history from his Uncle Brooks.

While at Georgetown, John was also fortunate to spend time with other Ratliff relatives in Virginia, including his grandparents; Uncle Paul;

Aunt Martha, Uncle Harry, and Cousin Marlyn; as well as his Uncle Billie, Aunt Mary, and their daughter Mava.

In 1958 John married his sweetheart Mary Diane Moffat, who was born in Amite, Louisiana, in 1938.[35] She majored in English at Louisiana State University in Baton Rouge for one year, followed by a second year at the University of Southwestern Louisiana, in Lafayette.

John and Diane after their wedding

John brought his bride back to Washington, where the couple spent many weekends at the homes of his grandparents, his Uncle Billie's, and his Aunt Martha's. Diane recalls that each time they arrived for a weekend visit with the grandparents, John B. would call out, "Mama, get the dominos!" He and Diane would play dominos for hours on end, with little said

---

35 John and Diane had dated in the early 1950s. John went to see her on his first day home after discharge from the army in 1957, in hopes of renewing their relationship.

by John B., who was fairly deaf. When he did speak to her, he called Diane "Girlie." Perhaps he knew her name or perhaps he didn't.

When John and Diane and their son John IV attended John's grandfather's funeral in Nokesville, Virginia, in 1960, this four-generation photo was taken:

John III, Emma, Barton, John IV

After receiving his undergraduate degree in Japanese, John continued in graduate school at Georgetown on a National Defense Education Act Fellowship. Although he completed all the course work for an MS in linguistics, he left school before receiving his graduate degree to take a position with the US Department of State's Foreign Service Institute, the division that trains US diplomats for service abroad. His first assignment abroad was assistant director of the State Department's Japanese Language and Area Training Center in Japan in 1963. First located in Tokyo, the training center moved to the US consulate building in Yokohama in 1964.

By 1964, John and Diane had four sons: John IV, born in 1959; Brent, born in 1961; Andrew, born in 1963; and Timothy, born in 1964.

Ratliff family in Japan about 1966
From left, Andrew, Tim, John IV, Brent

A four-year tour in Japan was followed by an assignment to the US Embassy in Bangkok, Thailand, in 1967 where, as regional language supervisor, John oversaw language programs at US embassies and consulates throughout Southeast Asia.

John, Tim, Andrew, Brent in Bangkok, Thailand

In mid-1969, John returned to Yokohama as director of the Japanese Language Training Center.

Yokohama, Japan - 1971
Front, Andrew, Tim; *back,* John, Brent

In 1974, the family returned to Washington, DC, after eleven straight years in Asia. John supervised various language programs at the Foreign Service Institute between 1974 and 1976, including Japanese, Vietnamese, Cambodian, and German. In 1976, he was promoted to assistant dean for overseas programs, which included supervising advanced language schools in Yokohama, Taipei, Tunis, and Seoul.

In 1980 John was promoted to associate dean of the School of Language Studies, overseeing all language training in the Foreign Service Institute and abroad. In 1985, he was awarded the State Department's Superior Honor Award "for improving language training programs for foreign service personnel." He served as acting dean of the School of Language Studies for six months before his retirement in August 1985.

After retiring from the Department of State, John founded Diplomatic Language Services (DLS), a commercial language school/translation services company, and saw it prosper. In 1992, DLS was selected by *Inc. Magazine*™ to the *Inc. 500*™ list of America's Fastest Growing Private Companies.

At one point, John, his wife, Diane, three of their four sons, and two of their daughters-in-law were employed at DLS, providing expertise in administration, language training supervision, finance, marketing, and government relations. To that extent, DLS could certainly be called a family business.

Family members of the Ratliff family business
John, Diane, John IV, Yoshiko (wife of John IV),
Debbie (wife of Andrew), Andrew, Tim[36]

---

36 Photo taken for an article written by the author in the Winter 2006 issue of *Family Business*™ magazine entitled "Why We Sold Our Family Business."

By that time, the company had sixty language classrooms and occupied 30,000 square feet in an office building in Arlington, Virginia. At its peak, DLS had branch offices in Columbia, Maryland; Atlanta, Georgia; Miami, Florida; and Tokyo, Japan. The family sold DLS in 2001 after sixteen years in business.

John then worked for the mergers and acquisitions company that handled the sale of DLS. As director of business development, he wrote a series of newsletters entitled "Getting the Best Price for Your Business," directed at business owners. He retired a third time in 2009 in order to devote more time to writing this book about his great grandparents W.P. and Cornelia Ratliff and their eleven children.

Below is information about the four Ratliff sons and their families:

John Barton IV, born in 1959 in Washington, DC, is married to Yoshiko Imai. They have two children: Bennett Justin, born in 1992, and Maris Jewel, born in 1998.

Brent Edward, born in 1961 in Washington, DC, is married to Candy Hawthorne. They have two daughters: Hailey Marjorie, born in 1991, and Hillary Diane, born in 1993. Hillary married Jeffrey Thelin in 2013.

Andrew Michael, born in 1963 in Baton Rouge, Louisiana, is married to Deborah McDade. They have two sons: Eric McDade, born in 2000, and William Patrick, born in 2002.

Timothy Moffat, born in 1964 in Tokyo, Japan, is married to Laura Peterson. They have two children: Emily Catherine, born in 1996, and Charles Peterson, born in 1998.

John and Diane live in Northern Virginia, and are fortunate to have their four sons and their families nearby.

The Ratliff sons
Still "cracking up" into their fifties
John, Brent, Andrew, Tim

John and Diane and the family at their
50th wedding anniversary celebration in 2008

Neil Mixon Ratliff

Neil never thought of himself as handicapped, though he wore leg braces and walked on crutches as a result of having polio as a young child. He never let his physical impairment deter him from achieving his goals in life.

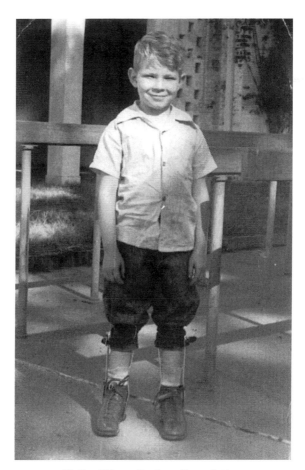

Neil at Warm Springs Foundation

Neil received an undergraduate degree in piano from Southeastern Louisiana College and completed all requirements except dissertation for a PhD in musicology at Indiana University. In 1963, after moving to New York City to accept a position in the New York Public Library for the

Performing Arts, he enrolled in graduate school at Columbia University, where he earned an MA in Library Science.

Neil at Lincoln Center in New York City

In 1980, he left the library in New York to accept a position at the University of Maryland, College Park, as head of both the Music Library and the International Piano Archives at Maryland (IPAM).

Neil was active in both the American Library Association and the International Association of Music Librarians (IAML), where he served as secretary-general for four years.

At the University of Maryland, Neil was directly responsible for the revitalization and expansion of the International Piano Archives at Maryland, attracting the personal papers of many famous piano artists and issuing rare recordings never before available to the public. He also spoke fluent Greek and lectured on Greek popular music to groups in New York and Washington.

Neil passed away on September 17, 1994, after a long illness. In his memory, the University of Maryland created the Neil Ratliff Fund—an endowment for the International Piano Archives at Maryland (IPAM).

Also in his memory, The Music Library Association and International Association of Music Librarians created the Neil Ratliff Outreach Grant to assist in the expense of the shipping of donated music collections to libraries.

John, Joy, Diane, honoring Neil's memory
This photo of Neil was hung in the Piano Room of the
Performing Arts Library at the University of Maryland.

Sidney Joy Ratliff

Joy earned a BM in voice from Southeastern Louisiana College (now University) in Hammond. After graduation, she enrolled in graduate school at Northwestern University in Evanston, Illinois, earning an MM in vocal performance.

In 1973 she moved to Germany, where she performed leading mezzo-soprano roles in opera houses there for over a decade. She specialized in trouser roles such as Octavian, Cherubino, Hansel, and Orlofsky but also performed such roles as Carmen, Suzuki, and Cenerentola. She was on one/two-year contracts with the opera companies of Cologne, Krefeld, and Saarbrücken and had guest contracts in Aachen, Hannover, Lubeck, and Kiel.

Joy as Octavian in *Der Rosenkavalier*

Joy plays the title role of Octavian, a seventeen-year old pageboy, in *Der Rosenkavalier* ("The Rose-Bearer") by Richard Strauss. *On the left,* Octavian, disguised as the Marschallin's chambermaid, flirts with Baron Ochs in Act I; *on the right,* Octavian has fallen in love with Sofie in Act II.

After Germany, Joy enrolled in the graduate music program at the University of Maryland in College Park, earning a DMA in vocal performance in 1997.

Joy receiving her doctorate

She then accepted a position on the music faculty at Marshall University in Huntington, West Virginia. In 2002, she left Marshall for a position with her alma mater, Southeastern Louisiana University in Hammond, where she is an associate professor of voice.

She married a German national while living in Germany. From this marriage she has a son, Oskar Barton Hillebrandt, born in 1978, and a daughter, Vera Vanessa Hillebrandt, born in 1980, and five grandchildren.

Oskar and Vanessa

Pinkney Brooks Ratliff

Pinkney Brooks was born in Silver City, Mississippi, on May 27, 1907. In 1935, he married Hattie Maye Sanders. They had one daughter, Frances Roxana (named for her grandmother Emma Roxana Jenkins Ratliff), born on February 26, 1937. Roxana and her parents were at the Ratliff Family Reunion in Attala County in 1939.

Four-generation photo: Roxana, John B. Cornelia, Brooks

In 1940, Brooks, Maye, and Roxana were living in Ruleville, a few miles from John B. and Emma in Drew. Brooks was a timekeeper in a road construction company.[37]

After moving north in 1946, Brooks worked at Union Station in Washington, DC, for many years and for a few years also drove a cab on his off hours. Maye was employed by the US Department of the Interior.

---

37 1940 US Census, Ruleville, Sunflower Co., Mississippi, ED 67-37, sheet 7B, T627, roll 2067.

Maye and Roxana Brooks and Roxana

Brooks died at age fifty-eight on September 29, 1965, in Nokesville, Virginia. He was buried in Valley View Cemetery in Nokesville. Maye, from whom Brooks was divorced, died on June 10, 1987, in Batesville, Mississippi.

Roxana married Lloyd Wright Green, born in 1933, on July 17, 1954. They had six children:

Peggy Elizabeth and her husband, Stephen Brooks, have two children, Stephen Jr. and Alicia, and live in Catlett, Virginia.

William Brooks "Buddy" and his wife, Wanda (Stanley), have three children—Heather, Jessica, and William "Billy"—and live in Ashland, Virginia.

David Barton and his wife, Debbie Ree (Shifflett), have a daughter, Samantha, and live in Caroline County, Virginia.

Maye Lynne and her husband, Ronald "Ronnie" Whitfield, live in South Boston, Virginia.

Herbert Lee and his wife, Tina (Hitt), live in Fauquier County, Virginia. Lee has two sons by a previous marriage: Brandon and Travis.

Lloyd Alan and his wife, Dianna Dawn (Weakley), have two children, Candice and Cody, and live in Spotsylvania County, Virginia.

Lloyd and Roxana also have six great-grandchildren.

At John B.'s funeral in Nokesville, Virginia, in 1960, Brooks and Roxana and her three children were photographed with Emma for a four-generation photo.

Roxana, Emma, Brooks, David, Peggy, Buddy

Roxana and Lloyd *(front, seated)* and their family, Christmas 2013

Tragically, Roxana died suddenly from a stroke on February 24, 2014.

Anna Belle (Anabel) Ratliff

Anabel Ratliff was born in Sunflower County, Mississippi, on February 23, 1909. Around 1928, she enrolled in the newly established Arlington Hall Junior College for Women in Arlington, Virginia.

After graduation, she returned to Drew to teach school. At one point, her parents sent her and her sister Martha to Texas to study dance, after which they taught dance in the public schools.[38]

Anabel met her future husband, Harry Milton Thomas, while teaching in Cleveland, Mississippi. He was born in Mississippi on September 12, 1908. They married on June 30, 1939, in Drew. Harry received his BS in education from Mississippi Normal College (now the University of Southern Mississippi) in 1930.

Anabel   Harry

In 1940, Anabel and Harry were living in a boarding house that seemed to be affiliated with the Cleveland Consolidated School. Harry

---

38   Conversation between Martha and the author, 2008.

was a trade and industrial arts teacher, and Anabel was a private dance teacher.[39]

During WWII, Harry worked as a carpenter at the Mobile Shipyard and then for the army air corps in Leland and Greenville, Mississippi, and Stuttgart, Arkansas. After the war, he earned a master's degree in guidance from Mississippi Southern College (the former Mississippi Normal College, now the University of Southern Mississippi). He was a veterans' advisor at Southern after WWII and later moved to the position of director of buildings and grounds.

Harry and Anabel

---

39 1940 US Census, Ward 3, Cleveland City, Bolivar Co., Mississippi, ED 6-41, sheet 2A, National Archives Microfilm, T627, roll 2010.

Harry Thomas Sr. died on February 7, 1978, in Hattiesburg, Mississippi. He was buried in the Highland Cemetery in Hattiesburg. Anabel passed away in Hattiesburg on July 15, 1987, and was buried next to Harry.

THE CHILDREN OF
HARRY AND ANABEL RATLIFF THOMAS

Anabel and Harry had two sons, Harry Milton Thomas Jr., born in 1942, and Jack Ratliff Thomas, born in 1946.

Harry Jr. and Jack

Dr. Harry Thomas Jr. married Beverly Grace Johnson on August 31, 1962. He had a successful career as a cardiologist in the US Army, alternating between assignments in Honolulu and Denver. Upon retirement from the army, he and Beverly moved to Las Vegas, Nevada, where Harry went into private practice. In March 2011, after twenty-three years in practice in Las Vegas, Harry retired once again, and he and Beverly moved to San Antonio, Texas, to be near their grandchildren.

Harry and Beverly have two sons: Harry Milton III, born in 1964, and Christopher William, born in 1969. Harry III, who is married to Emily Johnson, has two daughters: Molly, born in 2006, and Kally, born in 2007.

Beverly, Harry III, Chris, Harry Jr., July 1977

Jack Ratliff Thomas married Dru Irving in 1980. They had a daughter, Rachel. Rachel is married to Sam Owens, and they have a daughter, Frances. Jack and Dru later divorced, and Jack married Jenny Jennings on November 7, 1996. He works for Mississippi Public TV in Jackson, designing and building sets for their award-winning children's programs. His sets have been nominated for Emmy awards twice.

Jack and Jenny 2011

James (Jimmy) Grady Ratliff

James Grady was born November 18, 1912, in Sunflower County and was presumably named for his father's brother, Paul Grady Ratliff. He was called "Jimmy." Jimmy attended Delta State College in Cleveland, for two years[40] and married Mary Garrott Gray on October 28, 1939, in Greenville. Mary was born in Mississippi on January 11, 1921.

---

40 1940 US Census, Cleveland, Bolivar Co., Mississippi, ED 6-42, sheet 10A, National Archives Microfilm, T627, roll 2010.

Jimmy   Mary

Jimmy and Mary had three sons:

James Grady Jr., born in 1943,
William Hubert, born in 1946,
John Gray, born in 1948.

In 1940, Jimmy and Mary were living in Cleveland as boarders in a private home. Jimmy was a salesman for an auto parts store.[41]

Jimmy enlisted in the US Air Force on March 7, 1944, and was discharged on April 20, 1946. He founded a chain of auto parts stores in the Mississippi Delta. He passed away on October 30, 1988, in Cleveland. Mary died on January 12, 1999, also in Cleveland. Jimmy and Mary were buried in Memorial Gardens Cemetery in Cleveland.

---

41 Ibid.

JOHN BARTON RATLIFF

THE CHILDREN OF
JAMES AND MARY GRAY RATLIFF

After graduating from Mississippi State University, son James Jr. was a pilot in the US Air Force. Upon his discharge, he became a commercial airline pilot. He and his wife, Nancy, live in the Atlanta, Georgia, area. They have two daughters. Mary Christine, born in 1964, has a son, Garrett Hurt, and a daughter, Chloe Teague, and lives in Atlanta. Jenifer Irene, born in 1972, is married to Chris Shahda, has two daughters, Lillian and Evelyn, and lives in Decatur, Georgia.

William (Billy) ran the family auto parts business in Mississippi for many years and later was a long-distance truck driver. He is partner/manager of a body shop in Cleveland. He was married and subsequently divorced. He is now married to Sallye, and they live in Cleveland.

Billy has three daughters and one stepson:

Lisa Vann lives in Huntsville, Alabama. She is married to Jimmy Downs and has two daughters, Callie Crawford and Susan Harrison (married to Wilks Wood);

Emily Eugene lives in Cleveland, Mississippi. She is married to Allen Lee Havens Jr. and has three children: William Allen, Elizabeth Gray, and Anna Patrick;

Pamala Roxana lives in Omaha, Nebraska. She is married to Patrick Thomas Tvrdik;

David Mullen lives in Cleveland, Mississippi.

John Gray, James and Mary's youngest son, is a retired federal government employee and lives in Georgia. He is divorced and has two children.

From left, John, Jimmy, Billy

Paul Adams Ratliff

Paul Adams Ratliff was born on October 29, 1914, in Sunflower County. He may have been named for his Uncle Paul Grady. The name "Adams" probably came from his great-grandmother Sarah Lucretia Adams Ratliff. Paul was of slight stature and walked with a limp—a birth defect. His older brother Brooks gave him the nickname "Flea."

In 1940, Paul was living in Drew with his parents and brother Bevo. In high school, he was the manager of the football team. After graduation, he was a clerk in a drug store in Drew.[42] Paul played drums and had his own dance band.

Paul *(left)* at City Drugstore in Drew

---

42   1940 US Census, Drew, Sunflower Co., Mississippi, ED 67-35, sheet 3B, National Archives Microfilm, T627, roll 2067.

Paul's dance band - Paul on drums

After Paul moved from Drew to the Washington, DC, area in 1946, he worked in administration at Union Station in Washington. He married Shirley Richards in the early 1960s. Shirley had one son from a previous marriage. After Paul's retirement, he and Shirley moved to Indian Head, Maryland. Paul died in Indian Head on October 19, 1978, at the age of sixty-three.

William Rodgers Ratliff

William Rodgers Ratliff was born on March 24, 1916, in Sunflower County and was called "Billie." He joined the National Guard in 1936 and transferred to the US Marine Corps in 1938.

Billie as a child   Billie as a marine

Billie had a long and distinguished career in the US Marine Corps and saw action in the Pacific in World War II. He earned the World War II Victory Medal, American Defense Medal, American Theater Medal, The Asiatic-Pacific Theater Medal, and the China Theater Medal. After the war, among other tours, he served on the battleship *Missouri* and at the Quantico Marine Base in Virginia.

At some point after World War II, while assigned to the Quantico Marine Base, Billie began purchasing farmland in Northern Virginia, eventually owning three farms. As previously mentioned, he bought one of those farms for his parents.

Billie married Mary Eva Hoffman in 1955. Mary was born on February 11, 1910, in Springfield, Massachusetts. They met at the Pentagon, where Mary was a secretary. In 1956, they adopted a two-week-old daughter—born in Westfield, Massachusetts. Her adoptive parents named her "Mava," after the states her parents called home: Massachusetts and Virginia.

Billie retired from the marine corps as a chief master sergeant in 1960, the same year that his father, John B., passed away. Among the many photographs taken after John B.'s funeral was one of Billie, Mary, and Mava.

Billie, Mava, Mary

Around 1964, the family bought an estate near Front Royal, Virginia, which included cattle, apple orchards, and a mansion with a ballroom large enough for 200 people.

In 1966, Billie and Mary sold the estate and moved to Marathon, Florida, where they owned and operated a motel for some years. Billie's Aunt Bessie noted in a letter dated May 3, 1966, that Billie, Mary, and their daughter, Mava, along with Billie's mother, Emma, stopped by to see Bessie at her home in New Smyrna Beach.

Billie and Mary divorced in 1977, and Billy moved to Miami. A kindhearted and generous man,[43] on his first Thanksgiving away from his family, he cooked two turkeys with all the trimmings and offered servings to

---

43 In 1959, his Uncle Billie cosigned a bank loan so that the author and his new bride could purchase a new washing machine.

passersby in front of a grocery store that was frequented by senior citizens of modest means in North Miami. Having spent about seventy-five dollars on the feast, which he cooked himself, Billie said, "I'm getting more pleasure from this seventy-five dollars than I would having a thousand dollars stuffed in the casket beside me."[44]

Billie died on April 19, 1996, in Miami. His ashes were interred in the Ratliff family plot at Valley View Cemetery in Nokesville, Virginia. Mary died at the age of ninety-four on November 5, 2004, in Marathon.

Daughter Mava was married and subsequently divorced. She has two sons and lives in Tennessee.

---

44 *Miami Herald*, November 26, 1977.

Martha Cornelia Ratliff

Martha Cornelia Ratliff was born on December 1, 1917, in Sunflower County. She was named for her grandmother Cornelia.

Martha with her Jenkins grandparents

Martha as a young lady

As mentioned earlier, about 1937-1938, Martha's parents sent her and her sister Anabel to Texas to study with a noted dance instructor. When they returned home, they began teaching dance together at the public schools in Drew. Later, they were sent to separate schools—Martha to Shelby and Anabel to Cleveland, towns in Bolivar County, Mississippi, where they both met their future husbands.

Martha married Hilbert Wilkinson on May 7, 1937, in Drew. Hilbert was born on March 5, 1917, in Mississippi. They had one daughter, Marlyn Frances Wilkinson, born in 1940. In 1940, Martha, Hilbert, and Marlyn were living in Shelby, Mississippi, where Hilbert was manager of a farm.[45]

Martha and Hilbert

The family moved to Pascagoula, Mississippi, when Hilbert went into the navy during World War II. Martha took a bookkeeping course and began working as a bookkeeper for a department store. Martha's parents moved with them to provide care for Marlyn while her parents were working.

---

45 1940 US Census, Beat 3, Shelby, Bolivar Co., Mississippi, ED 6-27, sheet 9B, National Archives Microfilm, T627, roll 2009.

About 1943, the family moved to Mobile, Alabama, where Martha began working in an aircraft factory. Initially she was building aircraft engines. After most of the men in the area were drafted into military service, her duties changed to installing engines into aircraft. Martha and Hilbert divorced in 1943, with Martha, her parents, and her daughter, Marlyn, remaining in Mobile, where Martha bought a house.[46]

In 1946, Martha, Marlyn, and Martha's parents moved to Nokesville, Virginia, to the farm that her brother Billie had purchased for them. On the day they arrived, Billie introduced Martha to Harry Whetzel, a Nokesville man. Martha and Harry married on June 10, 1949. The newlyweds bought a two-story brick house on Fitzwater Drive, the main street of Nokesville, and moved out of the farmhouse where they had lived with her parents. In 1958, Martha and Harry had a son, Harry Allen Whetzel Jr.

Harry Whetzel with Marlyn

---

46   Conversations between the author and his aunt Martha Ratliff Whetzel, around 2009.

Martha, Emma, Marlyn 1960

Harry and Martha owned a successful livestock auction company in Nokesville, Virginia, for many years until Harry passed away on February 29, 1996. Martha passed away in her sleep at home in Nokesville on February 25, 2012, at the age of ninety-four. Her great-grand niece Hillary Ratliff[47] sang "You'll Never Walk Alone" at her funeral.

---

47   The author's granddaughter.

Martha's "Glamour Shot" in her nineties

Daughter Marlyn worked on Capitol Hill and for nonprofit organizations in Washington, DC. Son Allen Jr. is a computer consultant. He and his wife, Sheila, had two sons, Christopher, born in 1993, and Matthew, born in 1995. Sheila passed away on October 31, 2013, after a long illness.

Christopher, Sheila, Allen, and Matthew 1996

Albert Wade "Bevo" Ratliff

Albert Wade Ratliff was born on December 6, 1921, in Sunflower County. His older brother Brooks gave him his nickname, and he was called "Bevo" all his life. Bevo was an army air corps pilot near the end of WWII. He married Elaine Bengel on April 27, 1944.

Bevo in the army air corps

Bevo and Elaine

Bevo and Elaine at their wedding

Bevo and Elaine had three children: Susan Elaine, born in 1949, Jack William, 1951, and Brooks Allan, 1954.

After military service, Bevo graduated from the University of Texas. He and Elaine lived in Austin, Texas, where Bevo worked as an engineer with the Texas Highway Department and Elaine was employed by the Internal Revenue Service.

Bevo, Elaine, Jack, Susan, Brooks

Upon retirement, they built a house on the golf course in Horseshoe Bay, Texas, where Bevo enjoyed golfing every day. They were active in their church and did volunteer work at the food bank and local theater. They enjoyed making friends in the new community as well as traveling during their more than twenty years of retirement.

Bevo passed away in his sleep on November 7, 2010, at the age of eighty-eight. Elaine died the following week on November 14, 2010, at the age of eighty-seven. They were buried side by side at the Cook-Walden Capital Parks Cemetery near Austin, Texas.

Bevo and Elaine's daughter Susan married W. Murray Thompson Jr. Susan works with her husband at W. Murray Thompson Construction

Co., Inc., established in 1946 in San Benito, Texas. They have two children: son Joshua Murray and daughter Rebecca Susan.

Joshua married Alison Jane Cole. They have a daughter, Violet May, and reside in San Benito, Texas. Rebecca married Keith Lee Smith, and they live in Corpus Christi, Texas. Rebecca and Keith have a daughter, Charlotte, born in 2014.

Bevo and Elaine's son Jack works in farming in Lebanon, Missouri.

Their son Brooks works in energy-efficient lighting in Bastrop, Texas. His children, Elise Marie Ratliff and Wade Allan Ratliff, live nearby in Austin, Texas.

4

SUDIE RATLIFF

Kosciusko - About 1926

Shunted from one adult child's home to another for over ten years, Sudie's mother, Cornelia, was on her way from Drew to live with Sudie in Kosciusko. Cornelia was not happy about the move so it would be up to Sudie to make the most loving home for her that she could.

THE LIFE OF SUDIE RATLIFF

Sudie Ratliff was born in Ethel on January 31, 1880. The fourth child and third daughter, she was probably named for her aunt Susannah Tatum (Sudie) Ratliff. In 1900, at age twenty, she was still at home with the family in Zilpha.[1]

When the family moved north to Winona, Sudie presumably went along. On December 27, 1906, she married Ernest Claude Spain there. Claude, who was born in Attala County on July 3, 1883, came from a line of long-time Attala County residents. The couple immediately settled in Kosciusko where Claude was a "merchant" in a "grocery store."[2]

About 1913–1914, Sudie and Claude had a studio photo made with Sudie's sister Bessie and brother Grady.

Claude, Sudie, Bessie, Grady

---

1   1900 US Census, Zilpha, Attala Co., Mississippi, ED 7, sheet 6B, National Archives Microfilm, T623, roll 800.
2   1910 US Census, Beat 1, Kosciusko, Attala Co., Mississippi, ED 3, sheet 43A, National Archives Microfilm, T624, roll 722.

In 1900, according to *Kosciusko-Attala History*, Claude's father, Major Johnson Spain, purchased a grocery store located on West Washington Street on the courthouse square from L. B. Rosenthal.³ Claude Spain and two of his brothers entered the business with their father sometime later on. A photograph in the referenced book, taken in 1920, shows Major Spain and sons Claude and David in front of Spain Brothers Grocery Store.⁴

Claude Spain *(in truck)*, M.J. Spain, Dave Spain *(sitting on feed)*, Man Miller *(sitting on feed)*, Ike Thompson *(owner of store next door)*

Kosciusko-Attala History describes the contents of Spain Brothers Grocery as follows:

> Spain's was well known for the large variety of stock sold, from Mrs. Sudie Spain's home-made candies to Ferndale goods, salt mackerel, souse meat, Meadow Grove cheese,

---

3   Kosciusko-Attala Historical Society, *Kosciusko-Attala History* (Walsworth Publishing Company, 1976), 179.

4   And a special thanks to Thomas Craft, of Kosciusko, who provided the author with a good copy of the original photo of the Spain Brothers grocery store; caption below photo is from *Kosciusko-Attala History*.

guns, pistols, saddles, bridles, and harness. Usually feed, garden seed, and plants were displayed outside the store on the sidewalk to draw the interest of passersby. Trusty porters, two of whom were Man Miller and Sam Wingo, delivered purchases all over the county in wagons, and later in trucks.

Sudie's nephew Robert Edmond Ratliff (youngest son of Sudie's brother Zack Mitchell Ratliff) said he went into the store regularly. He remembered that his Uncle Claude "could stand on the front sidewalk in a brown suit, white shirt, and bow tie for hours and hours. I never saw him sit." He said that Aunt Sudie sat upstairs at a desk on the mezzanine and kept the books in addition to making candy for sale in the store.[5]

Robert offered this description of Spain Brothers Grocery Store:

> There were wash tubs of onion and cabbage sets and also tubs of turnips and greens when in season. Open sacks of seeds were also on the sidewalk. There was also a card on the counter with pocket knives—I think the name on the card was "Bar D", and they sold for 20 cents. There was always a stack of bananas just inside the door to the left. Next was a rolled front glass candy case with candy sold by the ounce. Then the only refrigeration was a freezer for four cylinder wells, 10" × 18." They kept ice cream—Dixie™ Cups. A wooden barrel with smoked mackerel, large hoop of cheese, burlap bags of seeds, and feed stacked in the back. High up on the ceiling was hung with horse collars, hames,[6] and britches. There was a high desk (draftsman style) and a wooden stool where Aunt Sudie kept the ledgers. Customers would buy seeds, groceries all

---

5   Letter from Robert Edmond Ratliff to the author, July 16, 2008.
6   Curved metal pieces attached to the collars.

year and when the cotton was ginned in the fall, they came in to pay their bills. The main items farmers bought were flour, sugar, coffee. When we had extra fryer chickens, Mother would tie the legs of two together and take them to Aunt Sudie. She had customers she would call to come buy them.[7]

Inside Spain Grocery Store

Sudie and Claude lived in a house on North Street. They had no children. When Claude registered for the draft in 1918, he listed his occupation as "Merchant, Spain Brothers."[8]

On May 28, 1919, Sudie wrote a letter to her brother Tom, who was in the British army in Tiflis, Russia (present-day Tbilisi, Georgia). The letter was written on company letterhead:

---

7   Letter from Robert Edmond Ratliff to the author, July 16, 2008.
8   WWI draft registration for Ernest Claude Spain, September 12, 1918.

THE WILLIAM PINKNEY RATLIFF FAMILY SAGA 1847-1988

SPAIN BROTHERS
STAPLE AND FANCY GROCERIES

Sole Agents for Fernell Products   Sole Agents for Postel's Elegant Flour

In the same letter, Sudie wrote that their brother Albert, who was selling candy with a carnival, was in Memphis the previous week and Sudie and Claude had gone to see him.

Sudie, Claude, and Cornelia appeared in the 1930 census in the house on North Street.[9]

Sudie, Claude, and Cornelia attended the 1939 Ratliff Family Reunion on Sudie's brother Zack's farm near Sallis, west of Kosciusko.

Claude and Sudie 1939

In 1940, Sudie, Claude, and Cornelia were still living in the same house on North Street. Sudie's sister Anna was visiting at the time the census was taken.[10]

When Cornelia passed away on June 18, 1942, she had been living with Sudie and Claude for more than fifteen years.

---

9   1930 US Census, Kosciusko, Attala Co., Mississippi, ED 2, sheet 22A, National Archives Microfilm, T626, roll 1138.

10 1940 US Census, Kosciusko, Attala Co., Mississippi, ED 4-3, sheet 7A, National Archives Microfilm, T627, roll 2008.

SUDIE RATLIFF

Sometime before 1964, Sudie began to have serious health problems. Her younger sister Bessie wrote in a February 4, 1964, letter to niece Sarah Elizabeth Donoho Kimberlin that Sudie was in the hospital in Jackson, Mississippi, with pneumonia, kidney infection, enlarged liver, and a very bad heart.[11]

Bessie visited Sudie in early April and wrote to Elizabeth on April 9, 1964, that Sudie was back home—attended by a nurse. But by May 10, she was admitted to Montfort Jones Memorial Hospital in Kosciusko. Her poor health problems continued, and on October 1, 1965, she passed away at age eighty-five. Upon her death, her husband, Claude, closed Spain's Grocery. He passed away less than two years later on July 4, 1967, at age eighty-four. They were buried in Kosciusko City Cemetery with a shared tombstone.

---

11 Letters from Bessie to her niece Elizabeth were kindly provided by Barbara and Susan Mingee, niece and great-niece respectively of Elizabeth's husband, Henry Kimberlin.

5

ZACK MITCHELL RATLIFF

Victoria, Texas - November 23, 1909

That morning while supervising a railroad crew of Mexican workers just north of Victoria, Zack had a dispute with one of the workers that got physical. Zack was carrying brass knuckles, but the worker somehow got them away from him in the fight. Perhaps brooding about this and worried that his authority over the workers would be compromised, Zack decided to take back his brass knuckles and teach the worker a lesson. That decision changed the fates of both men in the blink of an eye!

THE LIFE OF ZACK MITCHELL RATLIFF

Zack Mitchell was born December 7, 1881, in Ethel, the fifth child and second son of W.P. and Cornelia.

Zack was with his family on their move into Kosciusko and back to the farm in Zilpha about 1896.

In the 1900 census, Zack and his parents and siblings were living on a farm in Zilpha and Zack was approaching his nineteenth birthday. His occupation was listed as "farm labor."[1]

Once, Zack and his sister Kate, while still living with their parents, "borrowed" a visiting minister's carriage and team of two white horses for an afternoon of fun and likely received a fairly severe punishment from their father.[2]

Zack Mitchell Ratliff

---

1 1900 US Census, Zilpha, Attala Co., Mississippi, ED 7, sheet 6B, National Archives Microfilm, T623, roll 800.
2 Email message from Zack's son Robert to author, June 19, 2009.

As a young man, while Zack was taking a rifle out of a buggy, it discharged, shattering his forearm. Although the arm became deformed, Zack was able to work, farm, and hunt.[3]

Around 1907, Zack moved west to Texas and began working on railroad crews for the Missouri-Kansas-Texas Railroad, known as the "K-T" or "The Katy." He eventually was promoted to section foreman.

On November 23, 1909, events took a sudden and tragic turn that would impact Zack's fate severely and lead to the death of another man.

That morning, Zack was working with a railroad crew a short distance north of Victoria, Texas, near the old oil mill grounds. He was timekeeper, or "second boss," of an extra railroad crew composed mostly of Mexicans. At some point that morning, a dispute occurred between Zack and a young Mexican man named Enrique Gonzales. During the dispute, Gonzales took a pair of brass knuckles from Zack, who probably carried them because of the need to maintain control of the rowdy railroad work gangs.[4]

As Zack testified later (there were no other eye witnesses), about noon he approached Gonzales for the purpose of "giving him a strapping." When Gonzales resisted, Zack struck him over the head with a pistol and then shot him dead.[5]

Zack was arrested and held for trial. The case was entered onto the criminal docket sheet in Victoria County Court on November 30, 1909, as follows:

<blockquote>
Case #3628 State of Texas vs. Z.M. Ratliff
Offense: Murder"[6]
</blockquote>

---

[3] Letter from Zack's son Robert to author, July 16, 2008.

[4] *(Victoria) Daily Advocate*, December 20, 1909.

[5] *(Victoria) Daily Advocate*, December 17, 1909. The author is grateful to Zack's granddaughter Judith Ratliff Evans, who unearthed two articles regarding the incident at the local library in Victoria.

[6] Victoria District Court criminal docket for Z.M. Ratliff case, from filing on November 30, 1909, to completion of trial on December 21, 1909. The criminal docket was also found and provided by Zack's granddaughter Judith Ratliff Evans.

It was only fifteen years earlier that Zack's father had been charged with the murder of Sam Jackson at the Attala County Courthouse, and now his son was facing the same charge.

Seventy-five men were summoned for jury duty at 2:00 pm on Monday, December 13. Twelve men were selected and the case was set for trial to begin at 9:00 am on Wednesday, December 15.[7]

On the morning of the trial, the jury was impaneled and the defendant arraigned. His plea was not guilty.

The December 17 *Daily Advocate* reported the progress of the trial in the following article:

In the District Court

> The Z.M. Ratliff case is still occupying the District Court, and will probably go to the jury tomorrow. Ratliff is charged with killing Enrique Gonzales, a member of an extra railroad gang, of which he was the second boss. The other members of the gang were eating dinner when the killing occurred. Martin Jackson, an old Negro, who was cooking for the gang, was a witness in the case yesterday, and caused considerable amusement by his comical statements. "Where were the rest of the Mexicans when the shot was fired?" asked District Attorney Mitchell of Jackson. "In the dining car eating dinner," replied the Negro. "Did they go back and finish the dinner after the shooting?" inquired the district attorney. "No, suh," answered Johnson, "an' dat dinner ain't never been finished."

In spite of this brief moment of levity in the trial, after deliberating for almost twenty-four hours, at 3:00 pm on Sunday, December 19, the jury

---

7   Ibid.

found Zack guilty of manslaughter. He was sentenced to two years in the penitentiary.[8]

On January 4, 1910, Zack was taken to the Texas State Penitentiary in Huntsville, between Dallas and Houston. He was incarcerated as prisoner number 30228. His prison record indicates that he was 28 years old, 5 feet 7 inches tall, weighed 141 pounds, and had a "very large shattered forearm."[9] He had gold fillings in two upper front teeth and wore size-six shoes. He had fourteen years of schooling,[10] and his place of residence was listed as "Wharton, Texas."

Zack stayed at Huntsville only one month, after which he was transferred to Convict Camp Goree on January 4, 1910.[11] The 1910 census for Convict Camp Goree showed a Zack M. Ratliff as "prisoner" and occupation as "Section Foreman, Railroad."[12] During that period, Texas prisoners were often "leased out" to businesses and individuals. It is not known if Zack was sent to work on the railroad while at Camp Goree.

Zack was back at the penitentiary in Huntsville after ten months at Camp Goree. He was a model prisoner, with no punishments appearing on his record. His two-year sentence was to expire December 21, 1911, but he was released two months early on October 21.

Since Zack's residence of record was listed in the prison records as Wharton, he must have been staying there earlier in 1909 while working on the railroad crew. He may have stayed at the Riverside Hotel, a boarding house owned and run by a widow, Mrs. Georgia Abernathy. Two of Georgia's daughters, Laura and Frances, were sweet on Zack.[13]

---

8 *Daily Advocate*, December 20, 1909.
9 See incident earlier in this chapter that describes an accident with a rifle as a young man while getting out of a buggy.
10 Fourteen years of schooling could be an error since the 1940 census reports Zack as having eight years of education. Presumably, he was the source of the 1940 information.
11 Prison record for Z.M. Ratliff, Texas State Library and Archives Commission.
12 1910 US Census Justice Precinct 1, Walker Co., Texas, ED 157, sheet 16A, National Archives Microfilm, T624, roll 1597.
13 Letter from Judith Ratliff Evans to author, June 26, 2008.

Frances won Zack's heart, and just two months after being released from prison, Zack married Frances B. Abernathy on December 20, 1911, in Wharton, Texas.

Frances Abernathy was born in Texas on September 20, 1888. In 1900, the family was living in Ganado, Texas. Her parents were Joseph Luther Abernathy, born in 1848 in North Carolina, and Sophia Georgia (Georgie) Carruth, born in 1854 in Mississippi. Frances had five older siblings—Anna S., Baird, Robert, Brownie, and Laura—and one younger brother, Mercer.[14]

Zack and Frances's youngest son, Robert, recalled his grandmother Georgie coming to visit when he was about six years old. She wore her hair up in a bun, and when she let it down it reached the floor.[15] Zack's son Joe told his daughter Judith that Georgie "had very long red hair, and after she washed it, she sat on the front porch of the hotel and hung her hair over the porch railing to dry." Joe further shared that "everyone in town would walk by to see Miss Georgia's beautiful hair." Her hair stayed red until shortly before she died, when it began turning gray from the roots, indicating that it probably had been dyed.[16]

Son Robert said his parents lived in a railroad car, which enabled them to move at any time in connection with Zack's work as a section foreman. Robert's mother, Frances, told him about the day she went to the grocery store and came back to the railroad car to find that it was gone, the railroad work having moved to a new location![17]

Zack's work also took the newly married couple to Arkansas where their first child, Joseph Pinckney,[18] was born in Washington County in 1912. A second son, Mitchell Carruth, was born in Sealy, Texas, in 1916.

In 1918, Zack registered for the draft on December 12 in Royce City, Texas. Question no. 29—"Has person lost arm, leg, hand, eye, or is he

---

14   1900 US Census, Ganado Jackson Co., Texas, ED 59, sheet 10A, National Archives Microfilm, T623, roll 1648.
15   Email from Robert Ratliff to the author, June 22, 2009.
16   Email from Judith Ratliff Evans to the author, April 6, 2009.
17   Letter from Robert Ratliff to the author, July 16, 2008.
18   Note the different spelling from that of his grandfather, William Pinkney.

obviously physically disqualified?" was answered with a "No." However, as noted above, Zack had a deformed arm from the accident with a rifle while getting out of a buggy some years earlier.

In a September 22, 1918, letter to his brother Tom, who was with the British army in India, Zack's brother Albert wrote while at Camp Travis in San Antonio, "Zack is still with the Katy. He is at Royce City...Don't think they will take Zack as he is working for the R.R. and on account of his hand too. He wants to get into the service, however."[19] Zack was never drafted into the military in WWI, probably because the war ended shortly after this letter was written.

The 1920 census finds the family in Melville, Louisiana, with Zack's occupation listed as section foreman with the railroad.[20]

Perhaps as early as 1923 Zack left the railroad and moved his family to Sunflower County, where two of his brothers, John B. and Albert, lived with their families.

Zack and Frances with one of their four sons, probably Joe

---

19   Letter from Zack's brother Albert to his brother Tom, September 22, 1918.
20   1920 US Census, Melville, St. Landry Parish, Louisiana, ED 9, sheet 2B, National Archives Microfilm, T625, roll 630.

Around 1924, Joe was sent to live with his aunt Laura "Lolly" Abernathy Landry in Wharton, Texas, so that he could get braces from an orthodontist in nearby Houston.

A third son, Zack Abernathy, arrived in Sunflower County, Mississippi, in 1926. A fourth son, Robert Edmond, was also born in Sunflower County in 1927.

About a year later, Zack and his family moved back to Attala County where he had been born and raised. They bought a farm near Sallis, a community west of Kosciusko. The farm was across the creek from Zack's Uncle Edmond's farm (a brother of William Pinkney).[21]

With oldest son Joe now living with Frances's sister Laura in Wharton, the 1930 census recorded Zack and Frances with sons Mitchell, Zack Abernathy, and Robert on the farm at Beat 4, Attala County.[22]

Around 1933, Mitchell also went to live with his Aunt Lolly in order to attend the University of Texas in Austin. Zack and Robert, born more than ten years after their two older brothers, remained at home with their parents.

Robert and Zack with dog Hobosh
at the potato house on the farm in Sallis

---

21   Letter from Robert to the author, July 16, 2008.
22   1930 US Census, Beat 4, Attala Co., Mississippi, ED 12, sheet 16B, National Archives Microfilm, T626, roll 1138.

Reminded by some pictures that were recently discovered, Zack's son Robert shared some memories of his childhood on the farm:

> I remember well (the photo of) Zack and me with Hobosh the dog, named from one of Tarzan's monkeys. The horse's name was Pat—the only horse we had. All the rest were mules. The small house behind us & Hobosh was a potato house. Dad used to cure sweet potatoes. It had double walls filled with sawdust between them. The small door was about 3 ft. 5 in. sq. with shelves down both sides. A coal oil or kerosene heater was used to maintain a constant temperature.[23]

Zack's granddaughter Judith recalled a 1950 visit to her grandfather's farm when she was about six years old. She wrote that the house had a corral built adjacent to it where they kept a bull named Major. She remembers there was a door in the room where they were sleeping that opened out to the corral.[24]

As noted earlier, the Ratliff Family Reunion was held in May of 1939 on Zack's farm near Sallis. Descendants of W.P. and Cornelia came from all over the country.[25]

The Zack Ratliff house in Sallis
on Ratliff Reunion Day 1939

---

23 Letter from Robert to author, 2009.
24 Email from Judith Evans to the author, 2008.
25 Photos taken at the reunion can be seen in part two, chapter three of this book.

Zack and Frances 1939

Tragically, on December 4, 1942, Zack's wife, Frances, died after a loss of blood resulting from a nosebleed that lasted three days and which was aggravated by high blood pressure. She was fifty-four years old. Frances was buried at Springdale Cemetery, west of Kosciusko, where William Pinkney Ratliff and other family members were buried.

Zack Abernathy moved to Texas in 1944, just after high school. Robert left Sallis in 1946 to join the army air corps and was sent to Germany. He was discharged after his enlistment was completed, but in 1950 he was recalled to active duty when the Korean War broke out.

Zack in his later years

On February 2, 1951, Zack, while returning from hunting rabbits, slipped on his icy back porch, and his shotgun went off, resulting in his death.[26] Annie Ryan, his neighbor across the road, who often went over to play dominos with Zack, found him that day on the back porch, dead of a gunshot wound with his shotgun lying beside him. She reported his death immediately and was questioned for some time by the police to confirm there had been no foul play. The conclusion was that he slipped on the icy porch and shot himself accidentally.[27] He was sixty-nine years old.

His son Robert said the air force refused his request for compassionate leave from his base in Korea to travel to his father's funeral. Zack Mitchell Ratliff was buried in Springdale Cemetery next to his wife, Frances.

---

26 *Kosciusko Star-Herald*, February 8, 1951. With permission.
27 Told to the author by Joan (Snookie) McMillan Weatherly, Annie Ryan's granddaughter, on April 23, 2009, at her cabin near Arnold Mountain in Attala County, Mississippi. She also kindly provided copies of the photos of young Zack and Robert at the farm.

THE CHILDREN OF ZACK MITCHELL AND FRANCES ABERNATHY RATLIFF

Joseph Pinckney Ratliff

Joseph Pinckney[28] was born November 20, 1912, in Washington County, Arkansas.[29] He was with his family as they moved from one place to another.

Joe's daughter Judith Ratliff Evans recalled that when she was twelve, she was stricken with Bright's disease and bedridden for about four months. At that time, her father taught her to knit. When she asked how he learned to knit, he said that as a boy he did not have anyone his age to play with (his brother Mitchell was too young and his other brothers had not been born yet), so he would sit on the porch with his mother and she taught him to knit. He would knit scarves with her.

About 1924, when Joe was twelve and the family was still in Sunflower County, he needed braces, and Frances's sister Laura (Aunt Lolly), who was operating the family-owned Riverside Hotel in Wharton, Texas, suggested they send Joe to live with her. She could arrange for him to see an orthodontist and also ease the family's financial burden.[30] From that time on, Joe lived apart from his parents, only visiting them during vacations.

---

28 As noted earlier, though his namesake W.P. spelled his name "Pinkney," his grandson Joseph Pinckney's name was spelled with a "c."

29 The author is grateful to Joseph Pinckney Ratliff's daughter Judith Ratliff Evans for most of the information about her father and family in this section.

30 Letter from Joe's brother, Robert to the author, July 16, 2008.

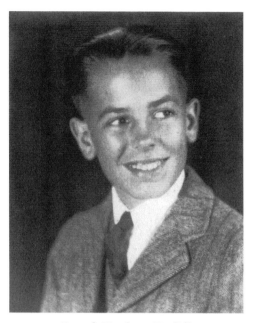

Joseph Pinckney Ratliff

On a trip to Sunflower County with his daughter Judith in 1970, Joe reminisced about working at a service station called "Tree Frog Service Station - Service with a Hop." He told Judith that while working there he saw a car with an engine that had eight cylinders, but no one at that time would believe that such a thing existed.[31]

Joe graduated from Wharton High School in 1929 at age sixteen. The 1930 census records Joe living at the hotel in Wharton, Texas, with Aunt Lolly, her husband Robert A. Landry, and Joe's maternal grandmother, Georgie Abernathy.

Joe was offered an appointment to the US Military Academy (West Point) but turned it down. Instead, he enrolled in the University of Texas in Austin where he studied engineering for two years. Later Joe changed his major to accounting and business. Although he attended college for five years, he did not graduate.[32]

---

31 Email from Joe's daughter Judith to the author, June 25, 2008.
32 Brown and Root job application, found by his daughter Judith.

The University of Texas yearbook, *The Cactus*, lists Joe as a student in the years 1933–1936. He is also listed as a member of the Tejas Club.

Information on a job application to Brown and Root indicated that Joe was working as a secretary at Patrick Transfer and Storage in Houston in May 1935.

The 1940 census found him in Wharton, Texas, working as an agent for a brewery.[33] His son Joe Jr. said his father drove a beer truck for Regal Brewery. Regal may have had a distribution center in Houston, which was about an hour from Wharton. However, Joe was also listed in the 1940 Corpus Christi telephone directory as an assistant cashier (which may have meant accountant) at the CC Cottonseed Oil Mill in Corpus Christi. Perhaps his Aunt Lolly reported him as residing in Wharton because she wanted to be certain he was counted in the census or perhaps he moved from Wharton to Corpus Christi after the census was taken. He worked at the cottonseed oil mill until sometime in 1943.

Joseph Pinckney Ratliff

---

33   1940 US Census, Wharton, Wharton Co., Texas, ED 241-2, sheet 4B, National Archives Microfilm, T627, roll 4161.

On September 6, 1940, Joe married Virginia Mae Wollesen, who was born September 23, 1922, in McAllen, Texas. Virginia's father, a farmer, was born in Germany, and her mother was born in Illinois of German parents.

Daughter Judith related the story told to her by her mother about her childhood years:

> She grew up in the Rio Grande Valley, graduating from Donna High School in 1938, when she was 16. She was the fourth "Indian Sweetheart" selected by the high school.
>
> Mother was one of 11 surviving children out of 13. When she was six, she was "hired out" as a companion to a "little rich girl." She told me she cried herself to sleep every night because she was so homesick. She was paid a nickel a week, which she gave to her parents. Then she was a maid or something. I remember that she hated navy beans because she always had to cook navy beans on the day she had to (hand) wash diapers. Later, she had a paper route in high school.[34]

Joe and Virginia had a son, Joseph Pinckney Jr., in 1941 and a daughter, Judith Camille, in 1944.

---

34 Email from Virginia's daughter Judith to the author, July 18, 2009.

Virginia and Joe

By 1947, Joe Sr. was working for Consumers Lumber & Supply Company (CLASCO) in Corpus Christi. Judith recalled that her father coached women's softball and Little League. CLASCO sponsored one of his teams.

Joe was one of the people responsible for bringing Little League to Corpus Christi in the early 1950s. According to Judith:

> He was very proud of that. We worked on building the first Little League Ball Park (Longhorn) in Corpus Christi, then another one later on. This must have been in 1953, because I remember not being able to read the scoreboard and I had to get glasses—I was in the 3rd grade. Mother worked the concession stand and I helped her some and cleaned the restrooms! Daddy was the game announcer, and later I kept official score in the "press box" where we were behind home

plate. This was all around 1956 to 1959. Hard to believe I could keep "official score" when I was a 6th grader! Daddy also coached the Braves, his little league team in the National Little League.[35]

Around 1950, Joe went to work for a company called Robinson & McCall. Again, according to Judith:

> Robinson & McCall were home builders and, in fact, built the subdivision where Joe's youngest brother Robert later lived. In 1951, he built a strip shopping center—the Suburban Shopping Center on Norton Street in Corpus Christi, Texas—one of the first, if not the first. He had a hardware store there and he and mother ran it.[36]

According to Judith, Joe also built the family home:

> He designed a fantastic house (still relatively modern by today's standards [except for no air conditioning]), and we moved into it the summer of 1951. The house was covered with a material he sold at his lumber yard called "Besto-Rock." It was in a shingle form, but made from some form of solid asbestos. It would not burn. That was before asbestos was found to be harmful.
>
> He designed the house so that it faced predominately South/North because our prevailing winds here are from the South. It had windows almost floor to ceiling and they had glass louvers about 5" wide that were frosted. So we did not need curtains and could leave the windows open at whatever angle we wanted at night. He also built a "shop" for

---

35   Email from daughter Judith to the author, July 16, 2009.
36   Email from daughter Judith to the author, July 18, 2009.

his woodworking off the garage and a little "potting room" with sink for mother to work with plants.

The kitchen was one of the greatest features. A living room fireplace was built such that the "fire box" part was about waist high. This was so he could cook on it. But this backed up to the kitchen. The back of the chimney was also the back of the stove. It had two electric burners on each side of a commercial-type griddle. The griddle had a top part (with independent temperature control) that you could lower and smash grilled-cheese sandwiches, hamburgers, steak, etc. On the back wall (common to the back of the chimney) was a huge ceramic-tiled copy of the picture from "Snow White and the Seven Dwarfs" where the wicked witch is cooking the poison apple. It showed her stirring her cauldron, the crow sitting on the skull, and she was holding up the apple. It was amazing![37]

Further, Judith wrote the following:

In 1958, he built the Suburban Siesta Apartments behind the shopping center. It included a 3-bedroom home for us and we moved there in the summer of 1958. He "retired" and operated the apartments and shopping center.[38]

On November 1, 1974, Joe and Virginia divorced after almost thirty-four years of marriage. In 1977, he went to New Smyrna Beach, Florida, to visit his Aunt Bessie, his father Zack's youngest sister, who was eighty-five years old. He said he wanted to see her one more time before she died.

Judith said that while Joe was visiting his Aunt Bessie, Judith's mother, Virginia, called her and the two of them met for lunch. Her mother revealed

---

37 Email from Judith to the author, June 23, 2009.
38 Email from daughter Judith to the author, July 16, 2009.

that she had made a terrible mistake in leaving Joe. With the expectation they could work things out, Judith told her mother she knew her father still loved her and Virginia should contact him. Sadly, shortly after he came back to Corpus Christi from visiting his Aunt Bessie and before Virginia had a chance to speak with him and tell him how she felt, Joe had a fatal heart attack on April 4, 1977.[39] His ashes were scattered in the Nueces River, near the boat dock of the family's place on the river.

Virginia Mae Wollesen died on February 16, 2005, of a "mystery" illness that was thought to be some form of Lou Gehrig's disease. She donated her body to the University of Texas Medical Branch. Her ashes were scattered over the Gulf of Mexico.[40]

Joe and Virginia's son Joe Jr. married Sandra Deal. Joe had three children: Joseph III, Sean Dee, and Miki Jo. Joseph III passed away on September 23, 1995. Sandra passed away on April 11, 2013.

Joe and Virginia's daughter Judith married Larry Trcka. They had no children together. Larry passed away on September 1, 2013.

---

[39] Email from daughter Judith to the author, January 9, 2013.
[40] Email from daughter Judith to the author, December 15, 2013.

Mitchell Carruth Ratliff

A second son, Mitchell Carruth, was born on April 4, 1916, in Sealy, Texas. He presumably was named after his grandmothers, Cornelia Mitchell and Georgia Carruth.

By the time the family moved from Sunflower County to a farm in Sallis around 1929, Mitchell was about thirteen years old.

After finishing high school in about 1934, Mitchell enrolled in the University of Texas in Austin and lived with his Aunt Laura "Lolly" in Wharton. He attended college for about two years. In the 1940 census, he was still living in Wharton at the Riverside Hotel but was working as a helper in a beer company. Perhaps it was the same company where his brother Joe was employed. The census record indicates that Mitchell had resided in the same residence five years earlier, in 1935.[41]

At some point, Mitchell went to work for Brown and Root as a surveyor. When WWII broke out, he joined the Seabees and was stationed at Dutch Harbor in the Aleutian Islands. When he was discharged at the end of the war, he had achieved the rank of carpenter first class.

About 1946, he married a widow, Runie Bevly Cole, in Corpus Christi, Texas. Runie Bevly was born on November 18, 1909, in Clarkwood, Texas. Her first husband, Trenton Cecil Cole, was killed in the crash of a private plane on August 22, 1941, in Jim Wells County, Texas. She had one son, Trenton Cecil Cole Jr., born in 1926.

Trenton Jr. recounted the following story of the plane crash to the author.[42] Trenton Jr. and his father were at the airfield, preparing to fly in a private plane to another city in Texas on business. His father discovered that some papers they needed had been left in their car. He sent his son to get them. However, through some misunderstanding, the pilot took off without Trenton Jr. The plane crashed shortly afterward, and his father was killed.

By the time Mitchell and Runie married, Trenton Jr. was out on his own. Mitchell and Runie were living in Corpus Christi, Texas.

---

41 1940 US Census, Wharton, Wharton Co., Texas, ED 241-2, sheet 61A, National Archives Microfilm, T627, roll 4161.

42 Telephone conversation between Trenton Cole Jr. and the author, 2009.

Sometime after Mitchell's father, Zack, died in 1951, Mitchell and Runie moved to the old family farm in Sallis, and Mitchell built a new house where the old house had stood. He tried raising hogs but couldn't make a go of it. After about five years, the couple decided to move back to Corpus Christi. They sold the farm in Sallis to Sam Ryan, a longtime neighbor from across the road.

Mitchell also built his own house in Corpus Christi, and he and Runie lived there for many years. For a time, he worked in maintenance at the rental apartments owned by his brother Joe. According to his stepson, Trenton Cole Jr., Mitchell was the scoutmaster of Trenton's son Trenton III's Boy Scout troop.

Later, Mitchell went to work for Texas A&M in Kingsville as an electrician. When he retired from A&M, he and Runie moved to Orange Grove, Texas, where they played golf and raised birds. Mitchell's niece Judith said they had a fox terrier named Tony.

Mitchell, *left,* and Robert in front of brother Zack's painting about 1998

Runie passed away on December 12, 1998. Mitchell died on December 20, 2004, at the age of eighty-eight.

Zack Abernathy Ratliff

Zack Abernathy, third son of Zack and Frances, was born on April 19, 1926, in Sunflower County. After finishing high school in Attala County, he moved to Texas where he worked at a number of jobs over the years.

Zack Abernathy

Zack suffered from schizophrenia all his life. With medication he could function fairly well, but there were periods when he relapsed. Niece Judith wrote, "He was talented in the arts. I remember he also liked working with plants and flowers—a gentle soul." He was called "Uncle Abby" by his niece Judith and nephew Joe Jr. in Corpus Christi.[43]

---

43   Email to the author from Judith, April 6, 2009.

His younger brother Robert wrote this about Zack:

> The mental problems started at a young age. He was working at Wilson Supply, an oil field supply company at Texas City when a hurricane came thru and he was the only one at the warehouse. There was considerable damage to the building. He continued to have some relapses over the years.
>
> He was good with plants and worked for a nursery in Corpus Christi. After that, he moved to Houston, where he did map drafting for Superior Oil and Atlantic Richfield for some 12 to 14 years. He spent a summer in Arizona at the Frank Lloyd Wright School of Architecture, came back to Houston and got a degree in architecture, but never used it. The last job he had was 3 to 4 years with a nursery in Houston.[44]

His brother Robert also wrote that Zack liked art and painting and sang with the Houston symphony orchestra. He painted what he liked, whether it would sell or not. A painting of his in the Houston Art Exhibition at the Blaffer Gallery in 1996 received this favorable comment in an art magazine:

> Pleasantly surprising. Zack Ratliff gives us a painting of a big rock, all jagged and brilliant like flint, against a ground of bare plywood. Two saguaros and two yuccas are intently real.[45]

---

44   Letter to the author from Robert, sometime in 2009.
45   *Houston Artletter*, February 15, 1996. With thanks to Bill Davenport.

From left, Zack Abernathy with brother Robert

Zack Abernathy passed away July 1, 2000, in Houston at the age of seventy-four.

Robert Edmond Ratliff

A fourth son, Robert Edmond, was born in 1927 in Sunflower County. He was named after his great-uncle Zachariah Edmond Ratliff.

Robert and his mother, Frances,
with horse Pat and dog Hobosh

From left, Zack, Robert, with horse Pat

On March 6, 1946, after completing high school, Robert enlisted in the army air corps at Fort McClellan, Alabama.[46] He was initially assigned to a P-61 Night Fighter Squadron. Later he was sent to the Earding Air Depot Signals Division, in Munich, Germany.

Robert in the army air corps

After discharge in 1949, Robert went to Corpus Christi and decided to make his home there. He went to work at CLASCO (Consumers Lumber and Supply Company), where his older brother Joseph worked.

At that time, Robert's enlistment conditions required him to serve three years in the inactive reserve after being discharged from active duty. When the Korean War broke out in 1950, Robert was recalled to active duty where he served until December 1951 in Korea in a mobile teletype unit relaying information from air reconnaissance to ground forces.

As mentioned earlier, when Robert's father died in 1951, Robert was denied leave to Mississippi for his father's funeral.

---

46 US World War II Army Enlistment Records, 1938–1946.

In his two tours of military service, Robert was awarded the World War II Victory Medal, Korean Service Medal with three Bronze Stars, and the Army of Occupation Medal.

After returning from Korea, Robert went back to work for CLASCO as yard superintendent, the position he had held before being called back to active duty. In 1955, he began working for Southwestern Oil and Refining, later to become Kerr McGee Corp. He retired in 1990.

Robert married Joyce Ann Whidden, who was born on July 20, 1933, in Sequin, Texas. They had four children:

Daniel David Mead Ratliff, born in 1953. Dan was married but later divorced. He has no children. He lives in New Braunfels, Texas.

Rebecca Ann Ratliff, born in 1957. Rebecca married Allan P. Johnson IV. Rebecca had two children by an earlier marriage: Brandon Lee Whitworth (deceased 2005) and Bridget Kelly Whitworth. Bridget has twin daughters, Victoria and Jazmine Smith. Rebecca and Bridget and her family all live in Corpus Christi, Texas.

Christopher Barton Ratliff, born in 1959. Chris married Tracy Diane Love. They have a son, Wesley Garrett Ratliff, and live near Corpus Christi, Texas.

Melissa Frances Ratliff, born in 1962. Melissa married Gary Lavell Marcum Sr. They have no children together. Gary had five children by previous marriages: Gary Lavell Marcum Jr. (deceased), Michelle Lynn Marcum (deceased), Martin Lee Marcum, Kary Denise Marcum, and Jason Donavan Marcum. Melissa and Gary live in Round Rock, Texas.

Easter 1963
Christopher, Rebecca, Daniel, Joyce, Melissa

Easter 1963
Rebecca, Melissa, Robert, Daniel, Christopher

Robert in Guadalajara, Mexico, late 1950s

Ultimately, Robert and Joyce divorced. Sometime after retirement, Robert moved to Wimberley, Texas, and, in 2010, he moved to Round Rock, Texas to be near his daughter Melissa. Joyce passed away on February 12, 2011, in Corpus Christi, Texas. Her ashes were scattered in the Bay of Corpus Christi.

Robert in his grandmother Cornelia's rocking chair 2013

6

KATHERINE ELAINE RATLIFF

At Home in Chicago - September 3, 1926

Kate must have been terribly worried. Her husband, Peter, had suffered from ulcers for some months now and this latest attack seemed especially severe. The doctor had visited that morning but must have offered very little encouragement. Having lost her daughter to the Spanish Flu at age four, would she also lose Peter, leaving her to raise their son, Fred, all alone?

THE WILLIAM PINKNEY RATLIFF FAMILY SAGA 1847-1988

THE LIFE OF KATHERINE ELAINE RATLIFF

Katherine Elaine was born January 20, 1884, in Ethel and was called "Kate."

Kate at thirteen

When the family moved to Winona around 1906, Kate may not have made the move, since she was twenty-two years old by then. Census records for 1940 indicate that she attended college for two years, so perhaps it was sometime between 1902 and 1906 that Kate left home.[1]

In the 1910 census, the only Kate Ratliff of approximately Kate's age to be found was living in the Convent of the Good Shepherd in Shelby, Memphis County, Mississippi. It would seem unlikely that this is our Kate Ratliff.

A undated letter from Kate's older sister Anna to her brother Tom in Hope, Arkansas, estimated to have been written around 1911 or 1912, references the fact that Kate and her sister Florence were in Hope with Tom and their parents.

When she left the family in Hope, Arkansas, Kate possibly went to Chicago, Illinois, since it was there she met her future husband, Peter Francis Naylor. Peter, born in New Hampshire of French Canadian

---

1   1940 US Census, Villa Park, DuPage Co., Illinois, ED 22-13, sheet 9B, National Archives Microfilm, T627, roll 796.

parents, was living in Chicago at the time of the 1910 census. Family records reveal that Kate and Peter married on September 11, 1913, and made their home in Chicago. Kate was twenty-nine, and Peter was twenty-six. Kate's brother Grady was living in the Chicago area about this time, attending Northwestern University. However, letters written in 1910 and 1911 from Grady to his brother Tom make no mention of Kate.

Kate and Peter welcomed a daughter, Frances Christine, born May 27, 1914, in Chicago.[2] A year later, on July 17, 1915, their son, Peter Frederick (Fred), arrived.[3] At the time of Fred's birth, the family resided at 201 Hill Street in Chicago. Fred's birth certificate listed father Peter's occupation as "Bartender." Fred told his son Michael that his father owned two bars in Chicago.[4]

Peter's WWI draft registration card listed his occupation as "Machinist," so perhaps he was a machinist by day and a bartender/bar owner at night. He indicated that his dependents were "mother, wife, and two children."[5]

Tragically, the deadly strain of influenza that ran rampant toward the end of World War I struck the Naylor family. Daughter Frances Christine died of bronchial pneumonia October 1, 1918, at age four and was buried at St. Adalbert's Cemetery.[6] The family was living at 2450 Southport Avenue.

So, from age three, Fred was effectively an only child. When he got older, Fred took dancing lessons and recalls tap dancing on the bar at his father's drinking establishment and receiving coins from customers.[7] At

---

2   Illinois Deaths and Stillbirths Index, 1916–1947.
3   Birth certificate, Cook County, Illinois, July 23, 1915.
4   Videotaped interview of Fred by his son Michael Robert Naylor in 2004. Much of the information about Fred and his family comes from that interview. The author is grateful to Michael for sharing the videotape, as well as to Fred's daughter Kathryn Naylor Prenevost, who provided much family information and encouragement.
5   US World War I Draft Registration cards: 1917-1918, June 5, 1917.
6   Frances Christine Naylor death certificate, October 2, 1918.
7   Videotaped interview of Fred by his son, Michael Robert Naylor, 2004.

some point, his father was also a salesman of millinery at Susman and Goldstein.[8]

Fred recalled that they lived in an apartment directly across the street from Wrigley Field, the home of the Chicago Cubs baseball team. Today, many such buildings, including 1032 Waveland Avenue where Fred and his family lived, have bleachers on their roofs, charge admission for home baseball games, and have a revenue-sharing plan with the Cubs.

There is no record of the family in the 1920 census in Chicago, though other records indicate they were living there. As a bartender and bar owner, Kate's husband fell victim to what might be considered an occupational hazard—heavy drinking—and, by 1926, had become seriously ill. He died at home on September 4, 1926, at age thirty-nine of an ulcerated stomach and hepatitis. According to the attending physician, as indicated on his death certificate, every three months for a period of about ten days each time, he would suffer a gastric hemorrhage. Peter was buried at St. Adalbert's Cemetery. His death certificate stated he had lived in Chicago for fifteen years.[9]

After her husband's death, Kate sent son Fred to boarding school in Oak Park, Illinois. When he reached the eighth-grade level, he transferred to Jasper Academy in Jasper, Indiana.

At the same time—about 1929—Kate met Robert "Bob" Henry Bopp, born in Chicago October 27, 1899, into a family of Swiss German immigrants. Kate and Bob soon married, and Bob, Kate, and Fred moved to Des Plaines, Illinois, where Fred attended Maine (East) High School. About the time Fred finished high school in 1932–1933, the family returned to Chicago.

At this point in the lives of Kate and Bob, the trail grows cold again. Kate's nephew Robert (son of Kate's brother Zack) said he remembered Kate living on a farm in West, Mississippi, though he could not recall the year. Neither Kate nor Bob could be found in the 1930 census.

---

8   Peter Francis Naylor death certificate, September 4, 1926.
9   Death certificate, September 4, 1926.

Both Kate and Bob attended the Ratliff Family Reunion in May of 1939.

Bob and Kate Bopp 1939

The 1940 census finds Kate and Bob living at 214 N. Michigan Avenue in Villa Park, Illinois, west of Chicago. Bob's occupation was listed as a pressman in a printing shop, and Kate was the operator of a wholesale millinery establishment. The records indicate that in 1935 they were living in Chicago.[10] Oddly, a Bob Bopp was also listed in the 1940 census at Kate's son Fred's residence in Chicago. He was identified as Fred's stepfather, age forty, with an occupation of timekeeper on a road project for the WPA (Works Project Administration).[11] In addition, this Bob Bopp attended two years of college, whereas the Bob Bopp living with Kate in Villa Park attended only one year of high school. Even if one concedes that there are two Bob Bopps, the fact that one is listed as Kate's husband and the other is listed as Kate's son Fred's stepfather defies explanation.

In 1950, Kate and Bob were living in Rawlins, Wyoming.[12] Eventually, they moved to a farm in Oregon, near La Grande, where Kate's son, Fred, and his wife, Maxine, lived.

---

10 1940 US Census, Villa Park, DuPage Co., Illinois, ED 22-13, sheet 9B, National Archives Microfilm, T627, roll 796.
11 1940 US Census, Chicago, Cook Co., Illinois, ED 103-2851, sheet 11A, National Archives Microfilm, T627, roll 1011.
12 Anna Ratliff Donoho [Kate's sister] obituary, *Marshall (TX) News-Messenger*, November 15, 1950.

Kate and Bob at home in La Grande, Oregon

Around 1957 or 1958, Kate and Bob moved to Portland, Oregon, presumably following Fred and his family, who had moved there earlier. Bob passed away in Portland on October 29, 1960.

In a May 3, 1966, letter to niece Elizabeth Donoho Kimberlin, Kate's sister Bessie wrote that Kate had sold her house and moved into an apartment. Her grandchildren remember visiting her. A November 14, 1966, letter from Bessie to Elizabeth reports that Kate had had another fall—this time resulting in a fractured vertebrae. According to her grandson Michael, Kate lived her last days in a nursing home in Portland.

Kate's granddaughter Kathryn Ann "Kathy" Naylor Prenevost recalls spending time as a child with her grandmother. She said Kate was an excellent seamstress and often made clothes for Kathy's dolls.[13]

Kate passed away on March 25, 1969, at age eighty-five. Because Bob Bopp had been a veteran of World War I, both Kate and Bob were buried at the Willamette National Cemetery in Portland.

---

13   Email from Kathryn Naylor Prenevost to author, September 17, 2011.

CHILD OF KATHERINE ELAINE RATLIFF

Peter Frederick (Fred) Naylor

Fred Naylor

Kate's son Fred's life through high school is outlined above. According to the 1940 census, he had one year of college and was working as a hotel porter in Chicago.[14] Fred married around 1938. The maiden name of his wife is not known, but her first name was Ruth. On August 1, 1939, they had a son, Peter Frederick Naylor Jr., born in Illinois. At some point after that, Fred must have moved to Missoula, Montana, because on April 20, 1942, Fred enlisted in the army air corps, indicating Missoula as his place of residence. His enlistment papers showed he was working as a hotel clerk. Even though his marital status was listed as "married,"[15] it is not known whether Ruth and Fred Jr. were in Missoula with him. In any case, at some point while he was in the army air corps, he and Ruth must have divorced.

---

14 1940 US Census, Chicago, Cook Co., Illinois, ED 103-2851, sheet 11A, National Archives Microfilm, T627, roll 1011.

15 US World War II Army Enlistment Records, 1938–1946.

Fred described his military service during World War II in a 2004 videotaped interview conducted by his son Michael. A transcript of Fred's firsthand account of his military service "in his own words" is included below, with only minor changes for clarity and to correct some recollections of the dates when certain events occurred.[16]

> I enlisted in the cadets in the army air corps shortly before I turned twenty-seven years old because you had to be under twenty-seven to get in.[17] My first base was Santa Ana (Army Air Base, California), and they gave us all kind of tests.
>
> I had a bad cold and wasn't able to pass the eye test to be a pilot. But my grades were such that they thought I would be a good navigator. So I ended up in navigation school. I spent almost nine months as a cadet, learning how to be a navigator.
>
> When I finished navigation school they made me an instructor, so they sent me to (Hondo Army Air Field) Hondo, Texas. I stayed there until they formed the air/sea rescue group.
>
> From Hondo, I went to Mississippi. They formed the crews there. The captain of my ship happened to be someone who thought I was the best navigator in the world, so I ended up as his navigator.
>
> From Mississippi, we went to Sacramento, California, where we stayed for about a month while they fixed our airplanes. The airplanes were all Canadian because the Americans

---

16 Videotaped interview of Peter Frederick Naylor about his life, by his son Michael Robert Naylor, 2004. Thanks to Michael for permission to use this.
17 According to enlistment records, Fred enlisted on April 20, 1942, about three months before his twenty-seventh birthday.

didn't have any PBY's with wheels and we needed to be able to land in water or on land.

We were then designated to go overseas, and we flew from the United States to Guadalcanal. We crossed the International Date Line just before we got to Tarawa, where the big battle was. We ended up in Australia, in Biak.

On my very first mission, we were able to pick up a crew that was shot down. Every day we had a flight going, following the bombers and the fighters. And they said that once we got there, the flights improved. The fellows weren't turning back before they got to the target. They were staying right there because they knew we would pick them up.

About the third flight I had, we were sent into New Guinea, to a lake site that the Americans were using as an outpost. We were sent there because they had been attacked by Japanese forces. We landed on this lake—there wasn't any wind at all. And we picked up this crew—they had one Japanese prisoner. Finally, they let the wheels down on the airplane so we could stop. And the wheels got tangled up with a bunch of weeds. And as we started out, they couldn't get the wheels back in the plane because of the weeds. The radio man and I jumped out and cleared the weeds from the wheels. For that, I received a Bronze Star (for bravery). And so did the radio man. The captain that I flew with was the one who put us in for the Bronze Star. We were the only two to get any medals in our squadron.

Shortly after that—on Christmas Eve—we were bombed. So I spent Christmas in a hospital bed. The Japanese loved to disturb us on holidays, and Christmas Day was just another day to them. During the bombing attacks, the medics at the hospital had to take me out of the bed and put me on the floor and put blankets and mattresses over me, because they didn't know if the Japanese would bomb the hospital or not. After the third time that they put me on the floor, I said, "Just leave me here."

After I was hit, they took me to surgery, of course. That was when my buddy passed away. We were in the same tent. There were four of us in the same tent. I don't know what happened to the other two. When the Japanese bombers were flying over, we would always be alerted with a siren. So the sirens went off and, as I finally got up and started to my foxhole, the bomb hit right in the middle of my tent and blew me into the fox hole. That's how I got all these injuries.

On Christmas Day, when I got back into my bed, a doctor came by and asked me if I could wiggle my toes (which I could). They sent me to a hospital on Biak (Australia) and performed surgery there. They got me through surgery and sent me back to the States. So I was in the hospital at Baxter General in Spokane, Washington, which is where I met your mother [Maxine Hollien, who was a nurse].

I spent six months or more there, and then they sent me over to Fort George Wright, across the river in Spokane, for rehabilitation.

When we were at Baxter, as I told you, I met your mother. And then we were married (August 11, 1945).[18]

I wanted to go back into my outfit so they did send me back overseas. And when I went back overseas, I had a wife, except

---

18 Washington State marriage record, August 14, 1945.

she wasn't allowed to come along. But this time I was with the Third Emergency Rescue Squadron and, besides the airplanes, we also had six PT boats. So when I got back there, they put me in charge of the PT outfit.

I didn't last very long overseas. My back started hurting every day. I was only able to stay there about six months before I came home. They put me on a hospital ship, coming from Hawaii, and shipped me home. And when I got back to the states, I called your mother, who was working for the Veterans Administration in Ogden, Utah. So she got on a train and met me. So we were able to spend a week together. And then she had to go back to work.

They put me in Madigan General Hospital (Tacoma, Washington), where they performed more surgery to close the gap in my back, which was covered with some transplanted skin. They cut that all out and sewed me back together.

Well, your mother came to Baxter and she got a job with the VA right away. Nurses were very much in demand. So, that is when we bought our first convertible. And we drove to La Grande (Oregon) because we had met the Hutchinsons—Dave and Eldry. And they wanted us to stop by. It was a great place, and we were looking for some kind of work to do. Finally, after all the surgery was done with at Baxter, they discharged me.[19] And we went to the Hutchinsons for a month. We decided we liked La Grande, even though there was no job. At that time, a returning soldier had to join the 52/20 club—which meant that for a whole year, you would

---

19   Discharged on July 18, 1947, per US Dept. of Veterans Affairs BIRLS Death File, 1850–2010.

get $20 a week if you weren't working. I applied for that, and within two weeks, they had me behind a desk at the employment office. I was finally discharged and put on 40% disability at that time. Since that time of course, they raised it to 80%, which is what I get now (in 2004).

After I had been working in the employment office for four or five months, Vocational Rehabilitation of Oregon wanted to put a counselor in Eastern Oregon (in La Grande). And the fellow who was doing the hiring came in the office and interviewed me. And they selected me for the job. So I worked for the Vocational Rehabilitation as a counselor, helping the handicapped find their niche in life, and providing the necessary services that they needed.

After five or six years of that, there was no place for me to go. I had had my last raise and that's when I went into life insurance, beginning with Bankers Life in 1953 or 1954.[20]

Fred was discharged from the army air corps with the rank of captain and after having been awarded the Bronze Star and the Purple Heart.

According to a Bankers Life newsletter article about Fred and his career, he spent two years in the hospital recovering from his war injuries, leaving the service when he was thirty-one. His injuries "caused some loss of muscle and nerves on the right side of his body, limiting the length of time he could sit or stand. The insurance business provided a way to control his working hours and a way to achieve his goals, both professional and personal."

---

20   According to a feature article about Fred Naylor entitled "Meet a Pro" in the Bankers Life and Casualty Company's internal newsletter sometime in 1982 or 1983, Fred began with Bankers Life in 1954, left for a year at one point, and returned in 1959. Fred sent a copy of the article to his first cousin Martha Ratliff Whetzel, who gave it to the author about 2008. Quotes and photos used with the permission of Bankers Life.

The newsletter noted that Fred started his insurance career in La Grande, using the contacts he had made as a vocational rehabilitation counselor.[21]

Fred and Maxine had two sons and one daughter while living in La Grande: Michael Robert, born 1951, Bradford Joseph, born 1955, and Kathryn Ann, born 1957. Also in 1957, Fred was transferred to the Portland, Oregon, branch of Bankers Life.

Maxine with Brad, Kathy, Michael

Tragically, Fred's son by his first marriage, Peter Frederick Naylor Jr., was killed on May 27, 1960, in an automobile accident in California while in the US Navy.[22] He was twenty-one years old and was buried at Willamette National Cemetery in Portland, Oregon.

According to the Bankers Life newsletter article, Fred was the standard against which they measured extraordinarily successful agents during his career. He received a number of top awards during his career, including earning a place in the Top Club twenty-four times, earning the

---

21   Ibid.
22   California Death Index, 1940–1997.

NQA award seventeen times, the NSAA nine times, the HIQA once, and entering the Hall of Fame in 1978.[23] Fred was in fact so successful that he and Maxine took off and vacationed for three months each winter, first in Hawaii and later in Palm Desert, California. He was also an avid golfer. He and Maxine enjoyed "bridge, music, dancing, golf, and attending basketball and baseball games."

Fred Naylor from the "Meet a Pro" article

---

23 "Meet a Pro," Bankers Life and Casualty Company internal newsletter.

Maxine and Fred from the "Meet a Pro" article

Maxine passed away October 16, 2000, at age seventy-nine. After her death, Fred wrote in a Christmas card to his first cousin Martha Ratliff Whetzel (daughter of Kate's brother John B.) that he couldn't bear to go to Palm Desert anymore without his beloved Maxine. Maxine's daughter Kathryn Ann Naylor Prenevost wrote that her mother was a very special person, loved by many people. "She had a heart of gold and an amazing sense of humor."[24]

Fred passed away on September 5, 2005, at age ninety. He and Maxine were buried next to one another at the Willamette National Cemetery in Portland, Oregon.

THE CHILDREN OF
PETER FREDERICK AND MAXINE HOLLIEN NAYLOR

Michael Robert Naylor was born in 1951. He is married, has one daughter, and lives in Maine.

---

24 Email from Kathryn Naylor Prenevost to author, September 17, 2011.

Bradford Joseph Naylor was born in 1955. He has two sons and a daughter and lives in Oregon.

Kathryn Ann Naylor was born in 1957. She married Don Prenevost. They had two sons: Mason William Prenevost, born in 1989, and Mikah Naylor Prenevost, born in 1991. Kathy and Don later divorced. Kathy, Mason, and Mikah live in Oregon.

7

FLORENCE CORNELIA RATLIFF

August 31, 1950 - Lyons, Kansas

Florence had finally gotten married, at age sixty, to a widower aged seventy-five. She and husband David had had four years of wedded bliss. But on this fateful day, the couple was on a car trip from their home in Phoenix to visit David's relatives on the family farm in Missouri. There was a terrible accident near Lyons, Kansas. David was injured seriously and was taken by ambulance to the hospital in nearby Hutchinson. Would this spell the end of Florence's short-lived happiness?

THE LIFE OF
FLORENCE CORNELIA RATLIFF

Florence Cornelia was born January 30, 1886, on the family farm in Ethel, the seventh child and fifth daughter of W.P. and Cornelia Mitchell Ratliff. She was with the family in Zilpha in the 1900 census, in Winona around 1906, and in Munson, Illinois, in the 1910 census.

Florence 1897 and 1939

Florence moved to Hope, Arkansas, in 1910 or early 1911, along with her parents and youngest siblings, Bessie and Tom. In an April 11, 1911, letter to Tom, her brother Grady mentions receiving a letter written from Florence in Hope.

Florence eventually joined her sister Belle and her family and began working as a bookkeeper in Belle's husband O.W.'s furniture business. By 1919 at the latest, Belle's family, along with Florence, had moved to San Antonio.

As described earlier, Florence and O.W. Wilson moved to Phoenix around 1928 or 1929, leaving Belle, daughter Sudie, and son Jeff in San Antonio. The 1930 census in Phoenix lists Florence and O.W. Wilson, as well as O.W. Wilson Jr. and his wife Jessie. Florence was working as a bookkeeper in a furniture store.[1]

When O.W. and Belle's son Jeff shot himself on January 24, 1932, his obituary mentioned that his father and brother were in Phoenix "where they had been for several years." One must assume that Florence was still in Phoenix with O.W. At some point, O.W. and Florence moved to Little Rock, Arkansas. Florence's Social Security death record indicates that she applied for and received her social security card in Arkansas. This could have been as early as 1936 when the Social Security Act, which had been passed in 1935, was implemented. If she had been in Phoenix at the time, she certainly would have applied there, so one can assume that she was living in Little Rock as early as 1936.

In 1939, when the Ratliff Family Reunion was held in Attala County, Florence attended alone. Martha Ratliff Whetzel, youngest daughter of Belle's brother John B., said that none of Belle's family members attended the reunion because after Florence began a relationship with Belle's husband, the Wilsons would have nothing to do with the Ratliff family.[2] Of course, Belle could not have attended anyway since she had been institutionalized after the 1932 death of her son Jeff.

Florence could not be located in the 1940 census. No records have been found that indicate Belle and O.W. Wilson ever divorced. Consequently Florence and O.W. never married. After O.W.'s 1940 death in Little Rock, his obituary in the San Antonio newspaper listed survivors as his son O.W. Jr., daughter Sudie, and a sister and brother, but it did not mention his wife Belle or sister-in-law Florence.[3]

In the probate documents submitted in Little Rock, Florence was confirmed as executrix of O. W.'s estate with her sister Belle having been previously ruled mentally incompetent. Florence was identified in the probate documents as a resident and citizen of Pulaski County, Arkansas, where Little Rock is located. The will stipulated that Florence was to inherit

---

[1] 1930 US Census, Phoenix, Maricopa Co., Arizona, ED 8, sheet 14A, National Archives Microfilm, T626, roll 57.
[2] Conversations between the author and his aunt Martha, about 2007.
[3] O. W. Wilson obituary, *San Antonio Express-News*, March 21, 1940.

one-fifth of O.W.'s assets. However, since O.W.'s son Jeff was already deceased with no wife or children, presumably Florence received one-fourth, with O.W. Jr., Sudie, and the estate of Belle (under the guardianship of the Alamo National Bank of San Antonio) also each receiving one-fourth.

Sometime after the death of O.W. Wilson, Florence returned to Phoenix. In 1946 or 1947, she married David Franklin Romine, whom she may have known when she earlier lived in Phoenix.

David Romine, born about 1871 in Missouri, married in Missouri in 1899 and divorced sometime between 1910 and 1920.[4] He was a partner in a cattle ranch with his cousin and the cousin's wife in Platte County, Wyoming. He moved to Maricopa County, Arizona, in 1928. Sometime between 1920 and 1930, he married J. Helen Romine (maiden name unknown, born in Texas about 1891).[5]

David and Helen Romine appear in the 1930 census in Phoenix[6] and also in the 1941 Phoenix city directory.

Helen Romine passed away on May 5, 1945. Florence and David were listed as husband and wife in the 1947 Phoenix city directory, living at 1522 W. Polk Street.[7]

On June 21, 1948, Florence, along with her husband, David, signed over their interest in the two San Antonio properties that she had inherited from O.W. Wilson to her niece Sudie and nephew O.W. Jr. In the document, Florence inserted the following words, (underlined here for emphasis):

> ...in consideration for the sum of one dollar in hand by the grantees hereinafter named, the receipt of which is hereby acknowledged, <u>and the natural love and affection I have for</u>

---

4   1920 US Census, Township 25, North Range 68 West, Platte Co., Wyoming, ED 76, sheet 1B, National Archives Microfilm, T625, roll 2027.
5   David F. Romine obituary, *Arizona Republic*, September 9, 1950.
6   1930 US Census, Los Olivos, Maricopa Co., Arizona, ED 93, sheet 3B, National Archives Microfilm, T626, roll 59.
7   1947 City Directory, Phoenix and Vicinity, 461.

<u>the grantees herein,</u> do by these presents grant, release, convey and forever QUITCLAIM unto my niece Sudie Wilson and my nephew O.W. Wilson Jr...[8]

Florence and David were on a trip to David's family home in Missouri in 1950 when, on August 31 near Lyons, Kansas, they were involved in an automobile accident, leaving David severely injured. He died in a hospital in Hutchinson, Kansas, on September 5, 1950.[9] His body was transported back to Phoenix and buried in the Double Butte Cemetery next to his deceased wife Helen.

Florence remained in Phoenix after David's death. She may have inherited a farm belonging to her husband's family since she appears to have travelled from time to time to a farm near Bigelow, Missouri, possibly to visit her husband's family.[10]

Florence's nephew Barton Wade, son of Florence's brother Albert, recalled visiting Florence in Phoenix in 1963 with his wife, Leah, while on their honeymoon. He said it was a pleasant visit, with no mention of the estrangement from her sister Belle or her past relationship with Belle's husband.[11]

In 1965, because of the flooding from the Salt River, Florence was forced to move her furniture up to the second floor of her Phoenix house and move to a hotel until the floodwaters subsided.[12] Eventually she moved into an apartment.

According to a brief September 12, 1972, death notice in the *Arizona Republic*, Florence Ratliff Romine passed away in her apartment in Phoenix.[13] She was eighty-six years old. The fact that no date of death was given leads one to conclude that, living alone, she was found dead in her

---

[8] Quitclaim of Florence and David Romine, Phoenix, Arizona, June 22, 1948.
[9] David F. Romine obituary, *Arizona Republic*, September 9, 1950.
[10] Letters from Florence's sister Bessie to her niece Elizabeth Donoho Kimberlin, 1964–1966.
[11] Email from Barton Wade to the author, sometime in 2007–2008.
[12] Letter from Florence's sister Bessie to her niece Elizabeth Donoho Kimberlin, April 18, 1965.
[13] Death notice, *Arizona Republic*, February 12, 1972.

apartment with no way of determining with certitude the actual date of her death. No next of kin was mentioned. The following day, September 13, 1972, the *Arizona Republic* published a second death notice—still no date of death—giving her sister Bessie Causey of New Smyrna Beach, Florida, as next of kin. Presumably, the authorities located an address book in her apartment, which led them to contact Bessie.

Florence Ratliff Romine was buried at Double Butte Cemetery in the same plot as her husband David Romine and his second wife, Helen.[14]

---

14 Death notice, *Arizona Republic*, February 13, 1972; Double Butte Cemetery records.

8

ALBERT WADE RATLIFF

Drew, Mississippi - 1942

Capitalizing on his many years of experience working in the carnival business, Albert was making a good living by making candy and selling it all over the Delta. Now he had his own candy factory and employed his own salesmen. Life was good. But the Japanese had attacked Pearl Harbor, World War II had begun, and the government had announced a rationing program, which included sugar, the lifeblood of the candy industry. What would Albert do to make a living with the candy business gone?

THE LIFE OF ALBERT WADE RATLIFF

Albert Wade, born on November 29, 1887, in Ethel, was the eighth child and third son of W.P. and Cornelia and was called "Albert."

Albert at age ten

Upon graduating from high school in 1904, Albert enrolled in Valparaiso University in Valparaiso, Indiana. His older sister Florence recalled seeing him at seventeen years old in his suit and straw hat leaving on the train to go to college.[1]

---

1 Email message from Albert's son Barton Wade to the author, recalling a conversation he had with his Aunt Florence when he and his wife, Leah, visited her in Phoenix, Arizona, on their honeymoon in 1963.

ALBERT WADE RATLIFF

Albert as a young man

After graduation in 1908, Albert began travelling around the country with a carnival, making and selling candy to carnival goers. Why he decided upon this calling is not known, but he travelled with the carnival until drafted into the army in 1917.

On his June 5, 1917, draft registration, Albert indicated that he lived in Sealy, Texas. His occupation was listed as "Showman" and his employer was "S. W. Brundage Shows."[2] His sister Belle and her family, as well as his mother, Cornelia, had been living in Sealy for some time, so perhaps Albert established a base there between trips with the carnival.

When drafted into the army, Albert was assigned to the Quartermaster Corps and stationed at Camp Travis, San Antonio, Texas. It is believed that he was drafted in late 1917 because he sent a September 18, 1918, letter to his brother Tom which said the following:

> It will be a year October 7 since I came down here. Don't know whether they will send me to France or not. Most

---

2   Albert Wade Ratliff WWI draft registration, June 5, 1917.

likely they will keep me here. I am supply sergeant in Co. 23 now. We have 27 white noncoms and about 300 Negros in the company. I have a large supply room and sleep in it. Have typewriter and desk, etc. Have it fixed up pretty nice. I am going to have stoves put in Monday. We are having a little cold spell now.³

Albert in the army

The date of his discharge from the army is not known. But since the date of the Armistice was November 11, 1918, presumably it was shortly after that date. Albert then returned to the carnival and his work of making and selling candy.

Albert's sister Bessie noted in an April 15, 1919, letter to their brother Tom that Albert probably didn't answer Tom's letter because "he is in a

---

3   Letter from Albert at Co. 23, 6th Battalion, 165 Depot Brigade, Camp Travis, Texas, to his brother Tom in the British army in Bangalore, India, September 22, 1918.

show now and it is hard to get letters to him in one place before he is gone to another."[4]

Similarly, in a May 28, 1919, letter from sister Sudie to Tom in Tbilisi, Russia, she mentioned that "Albert was in Memphis last week. [He] travels with a show. Makes and sells candy. Claude and I went up to see him. He is well. Looks well and is getting on fine."[5]

In the same letter Sudie mentioned that sister Belle, her family, and Florence were moving to San Antonio and that their mother, Cornelia, and Florence would "live to themselves."[6]

Cornelia's stay in San Antonio was brief. In a December 2, 1919, letter to Tom, who was in Fort Worth, Texas, after having been discharged from the British forces, Cornelia wrote, "Albert has gone to Jacksonville and I will go just as soon as I can get things shipped."[7] Albert had apparently quit his job with the carnival and was planning to move to Jacksonville, Texas, taking his mother with him.

The 1920 census shows Albert and his mother, Cornelia, in Cherokee County, Texas. Albert indicated his occupation as "farmer."[8] But the stay in Jacksonville was also brief. By 1921, Albert and his mother had moved to Sunflower County, Mississippi, where Albert's brother John B. lived with his family and owned three farms.

Albert met his future bride, Ruth Bullock, in Drew, where she was working in the post office. Ruth was born in Tylertown, Mississippi, on February 6, 1898. Her parents were Joseph T. and Delilah Quin Bullock.

Albert and Ruth married on Christmas Day 1922. Albert bought a dairy farm at Wade, about four or five miles northeast of Drew. Ruth continued to work in the post office, while Albert ran the dairy. Albert's

---

4 Letter from Bessie to Tom in the British army in Tbilisi, Russia (current-day Georgia), April 15, 1919.
5 Letter from Sudie to Tom in the British army in Tbilisi, Russia, May 28, 1919.
6 Ibid.
7 Letter from Cornelia to her son Tom in Ft. Worth, Texas, December 2, 1919.
8 1920 US Census, Justice Precinct 3, Cherokee Co., Texas, ED 23, sheet 4A, National Archives Microfilm, T625, roll 1786.

mother, Cornelia, moved into a house at the corner of First and Shaw Streets in Drew, behind her son John B. and his family.[9]

In 1923, Albert and Ruth's first child, Cornelia Ruth, was born. Two sons followed: Barton Wade in 1925 and Tom Jerome in 1928.

The family was still on the dairy farm in the 1930 census.

Barton Wade, Tom, and Cornelia 1935

Albert managed a domino/pool room parlor owned by Pincus Sklar in Drew for about a year. Then in 1935–1936, he traveled all over that part of Mississippi selling candy for Jackson Candy Company. Albert's nephew Barton told the author that he often "helped by driving Uncle Albert's candy route, delivering candy out in the country."[10]

About 1935, Albert sold the dairy and the family moved into the town of Drew, where Ruth still worked in the post office.

---

9   Conversations between the author and Martha Ratliff Whetzel, 2008.
10 Conversations between Barton and his son, the author.

By late 1936, Albert got together with Nathan Miller and they formed a company named Drew Candy Company. Albert had all the candy-making skills from his time spent traveling with S. W. Brundage Shows. Albert's son Barton Wade described the operation as follows:

> Drew Candy Company's factory was in a building just south of the Drew Bank (corner of Main and Shaw). When Daddy had the candy factory, Cornelia and I (and maybe Tom, too) used to wrap and box candy in the summer. Daddy had a great Negro cook who was an expert in the making of peanut brittle, caramel, and coconut into one bar of candy with white, blue and red strips. Daddy was out selling and delivering candy as well as a couple of more salesmen who went out on routes selling candy. Back then a lot of the boxes of candy were sold to black families on farms. The salesmen gave them premiums (lamps and miscellaneous things) when they would sell so many boxes of candy. The salesmen traveled throughout the farming area in the delta of Mississippi.[11]

Barton Wade's cousin Barton said that the factory also made cotton candy, but in those days they added no coloring, so it was white instead of pink.[12]

Business was good. Albert's brother John B.'s wife, Emma, worked part-time in the candy store on Main Street to make some extra money.[13] After a year or so, Albert's family bought a house at 289 Shaw Street, just cattycornered across the street from Albert's brother John B. and his family.

---

11 Email from Barton Wade Ratliff to the author, August 14, 2009.
12 Conversations between Barton and his son, the author.
13 Conversations between Martha Ratliff Whetzel and the author.

Albert and Ruth 1939

The 1940 census indicated that Albert and his family were living in Drew in the same house they had occupied in 1935. Albert's occupation was indicated as "Traveling Salesman, Wholesale Candy Factory" and Ruth was a postal clerk for the US Post Office. Daughter Cornelia was sixteen, son Barton Wade was fourteen, and son Tom was twelve.[14]

However, the outbreak of World War II dealt a fatal blow to the candy company. Barton Wade recalls the following:

> Daddy did real well with the candy factory until 1942 when the war started and they began rationing sugar. There was no way he could legally obtain sugar for making the candy so he shut down the candy factory.[15]

Then Albert went to Mobile, Alabama, and got a job as a timekeeper in the shipyards. The head of the accounting department invited him to move into accounting. According to Barton Wade, his father had taken bookkeeping after finishing college at Valparaiso University and had experience

---

14   1940 US Census, Drew, Sunflower Co., Mississippi, ED 67-35, sheet 4A, National Archives Microfilm, T627, roll 2067.
15   Email from Barton Wade Ratliff to the author, August 14, 2009.

in this type of work. He said further that his father used accounting systems that were the equivalent of the earliest form of computers. He worked in Mobile until the war ended and then returned to Drew in 1946.

Sadly, his health began deteriorating. Barton Wade reports as follows:

> Just at the time Daddy returned to Drew, he started having trouble with emphysema (he had smoked all his life) and his health began to fail. So after that, he was not really able to work and Mother continued to work in the Post Office.[16]

Albert passed away on March 31, 1957, in the Veterans Hospital in Memphis, Tennessee. Because he was only in the hospital a few hours before he died, he probably was rushed there from his home in Drew after taking a turn for the worse. The official cause of death was bronchopneumonia, pulmonary emphysema contribution.[17] He was buried in the Drew Cemetery.

The author recalls visiting "Aunt Ruth" at her home on Shaw Street in the fall of 1957 with his parents. She served delicious homemade divinity fudge, perhaps a recipe from the family's candy business.

Ruth passed away on October 16, 1975, and was buried next to Albert in the Drew Cemetery.

---

16   Email from Barton Wade to author, April 26, 2011.
17   Death certificate, March 31, 1957, from the Veterans Administration Hospital, Park and Getwell, Memphis, Shelby County, Tennessee.

THE CHILDREN OF
ALBERT WADE AND RUTH BULLOCK RATLIFF

Cornelia Ruth Ratliff

Cornelia Ruth was born in 1923. She was named after her grandmother Cornelia and her mother, Ruth. According to her brother Barton Wade, she was five years old when she finished first grade, and she graduated from Drew High School in 1940, just a few months short of her seventeenth birthday.

In the fall of 1940, she enrolled in Mississippi State College for Women in Columbus, Mississippi. In 1941 she transferred to Millsaps College in Jackson, where she earned a BA in English. At Millsaps, she met Edmann Jacob Rathke, born February 22, 1921, in Tustin, California. He was in the navy's V-12 college training program at Millsaps and later at Tulane University in New Orleans.[18] They married in New Orleans on December 9, 1944.

After discharge from the US Navy after World War II, Ed went to work for the California Company, later to become the Chevron Corporation. Early responsibilities included auditing the western fields. Their first son, Stephen Wade Rathke, was born in Laramie, Wyoming, in 1948, and their second son, Dale Lawrence Rathke, was born in 1950 in Rangely, Colorado.

---

18 The V-12 college training program selected promising enlisted men and sent them to college to become officers.

Rear from left, Tom Jerome Ratliff, Ed Rathke, Cornelia Ratliff Rathke, Barton Wade Ratliff; *front,* Dale Lawrence Rathke, Stephen Wade Rathke about 1957

The family returned to New Orleans in 1953. Cornelia received her MA from the University of New Orleans and her PhD from Tulane and taught English at a local junior college. She was dean of arts and sciences and then manager of information services for Delgado Community College. Cornelia was active in the community and the arts in New Orleans. She wrote book reviews in New Orleans, even into her eighties, and continued as a master flower-show judge. She remains active as a board member of various organizations, including Overture to the Cultural Season, the Women's Opera Guild, Fine Arts Club, the Garden Society, Raintree Services, the Orleans Club, etc.

Her husband, Ed, enjoyed a thirty-eight-year career with Chevron as a financial manager, retiring in New Orleans about 1986. With a CPA designation and an MBA from Loyola, he then chaired the accounting department for Southern University in New Orleans. He passed away on June 6, 2008, and was buried at Lake Lawn Mausoleum.

Son Wade Rathke married Marianna Elizabeth Butler, born in 1950. They have one son and one daughter: Chaco Devlin Butler Rathke, born in 1982, and Marianna Dine Rathke Butler, born in 1984. Son Dale Rathke has never married.

Barton Wade Ratliff

Barton Wade, born in 1925, played trombone in the Drew High School band and also started a small swing band. Active in the Hi-Y Men's Club as well as the Dramatic Club in high school, in his senior year he played the part of "Vin" in the play *Mrs. Miniver.*

Barton Wade graduated from Drew High School in 1943, just short of his eighteenth birthday. He then went to Mobile, Alabama, to work in the shipyards with his father. Returning to Drew in September 1943, he worked in a cotton gin for a while.

On December 29, 1943, Barton Wade enlisted in the US Army Air Forces[19] and was sent to Camp Shelby in Jackson, Mississippi. He was then transferred to Miami Beach, Florida, where he took basic training. He qualified as an aviation cadet. Upon finishing basic training, Barton Wade was sent to Furman University to an Air Force College Training Detachment for three months. He then entered preflight training at Maxwell Field at Montgomery, Alabama. In the summer of 1945, the air force shut down all flight training schools, and Barton Wade volunteered to accept training as a flight engineer on the new B-29 bombers that were to play a major role in the invasion of Japan. However, the war with Japan ended on August 14, 1945, and Barton Wade was released from the air force in November.

January of 1946 found Barton Wade enrolled in the University of Mississippi, in Oxford, where he was a student for two semesters majoring in engineering. In June of 1947, Barton Wade went to Vicksburg, Mississippi, where he worked for the US Engineering Experimental Station for the summer.

Beginning in September 1947, he moved to Norman, Oklahoma, to attend the University of Oklahoma, where he earned a BS in petroleum engineering in 1950.

In June of 1950, Barton Wade married Betty Gage and began his career in the petroleum industry working for Skelly Oil Company in Oklahoma

---

19 Though many referred to the service as the US Army Air Corps during World War II, its name was changed to the US Army Air Forces in 1941. It was not until 1947 that it became the US Air Force.

City, Oklahoma. Barton Wade and Betty adopted a baby girl, Alison, born in 1955.

Barton Wade first worked as a roustabout in the oil fields for a year while in training to become a petroleum engineer. Over the next eighteen years, he progressed up the corporate ladder with Skelly Oil with assignments in Hobbs, New Mexico; Tulsa, Oklahoma; Casper, Wyoming; Dickenson, North Dakota; and Alberta, Canada, where he was division production manager of Skelly's first drilling and production operation in Canada. Barton Wade is proud of the fact that results of tests taken at Skelly Oil encouraged him to apply and be accepted as a member of Mensa, an organization for persons with IQs in the top 2 percent.

In early 1962, Barton Wade and Betty divorced. On November 8, 1963, Barton Wade married Leah Britton Clawson. Born in Tulsa, Oklahoma, July 16, 1932, Leah had four children by a previous marriage: John, Carla, Lee, and Brian. Barton Wade adopted all four of Leah's children.

Shortly after Barton Wade and Leah were married, he was named manager of Skelly's largest production district and moved the family to Velma, Oklahoma, a short distance from Duncan, Oklahoma, where the company's offices were located. He became manager for joint operations for North America in 1967.

In 1965, Leah and Barton Wade had a son, Barton Bullock, and in 1968 they welcomed the birth of a daughter, Margaret Wade.

Barton Wade resigned from Skelly in 1968 and, with some investors, purchased Nichols Drilling Company in Duncan, Oklahoma. He became president, and the company was extremely successful. After buying out his partner in the late 1970s, he changed the name of the company to Ratliff Drilling Company and took the company public. Within a year, the company was listed on the American Stock Exchange and was valued at $60 million, with Barton Wade's share worth $42 million. The company purchased a private plane and Barton Wade was named one of three outstanding entrepreneurs in the state of Oklahoma.

Also during the late 1970s, Barton Wade was very active in community affairs and served as chairman of the Duncan Area Economic Development Corporation. He also served in several positions in the various oil industry organizations during this period. Barton Wade and Leah were very active in the church and in 1978 contributed a chapel to the church in memory of their mothers. In 1981, Barton Wade also made a contribution of $1 million to the University of Oklahoma.

Barton Bullock, Leah, Barton Wade, Margaret

The children of Barton Wade and Leah
From left, John, Carla, Lee, Brian, Barton Bullock, Margaret

The company remained active and profitable until 1984, when drilling activity severely declined. Unfortunately, in the late eighties the bottom fell out of the oil market when oil dropped to ten dollars a barrel. The stock of the company dropped to an all-time low, and because of the large debt in the company, Barton Wade had to sell Ratliff Exploration Company and liquidate the drilling company. Company operations were shut down in the summer of 1987.

Many major owners of stock in oil companies that were experiencing falling prices sold much of their stock, to the displeasure of other stockholders. However, Barton Wade never sold any of his stock during the downturn and consequently did not receive a single call of complaint from a stockholder.

Since the closing of his company and the sale of all the drilling equipment, Barton Wade has continued to be involved in the business of oil and gas exploration, as of this writing.

His wife Leah passed away on January 1, 2006. Their son Barton Bullock is divorced, has no children, and lives in Las Vegas, Nevada. Daughter Margaret Wade, who is married to Gregory John Randazzo, has two daughters—Alexandra Leah and Isabelle Angela—and a son—Jack Gregory—and lives in San Jose, California. Barton Wade also lives in San Jose.

Daughter Alison is married, has three children and seven grandchildren, and lives in Oklahoma City, Oklahoma.

Tom Jerome Ratliff

Tom Jerome, born in Drew, Mississippi, in 1928, graduated from Drew High School in 1947 and enrolled in Delta State University in Cleveland. He later earned his BS in administration from the University of Denver. In 1953 he married Charlotte Evans in Denver, Colorado. They had three children: Dawn Alane, born in 1954, Jerome Clay, born in 1957, and Lori Lynn, born in 1964.

Tom began working for Interstate Brands Corporation in Kansas as an accountant. During his career at Interstate, he was manager of the Internal Audit Department; general manager of the Emporia, Kansas cake plant; and vice president of company-wide cake plant operations, among other senior positions. He was also president of the Chamber of Commerce in Eldorado, Kansas. He retired from Interstate Brands Corporation as executive vice president of operations in 1988.

Daughter Lori Lynn married Michael John Eller. They have one daughter and two sons. Son Jerome Clay married Dawn Trese Hawks. They have two sons and one daughter. Daughter Dawn Alane has no children. Tom's wife, Charlotte, passed away on February 8, 2012.

Charlotte and Tom with their three children 1986
From left, Dawn, Jerome, Lori

9

PAUL GRADY RATLIFF

April 24, 1918

Over Austrian Territory

Lieutenant Paul Grady Ratliff was in enemy territory over the Austrian front as a forward observer in his RAF Bristol Fighter F-2 observation plane. Suddenly his engine began to fail! As he searched for a place to land, the closest place he could find was a flat spot on the top of a mountain! Would his flying skills be up to the emergency? And what of the enemy waiting below?

THE LIFE OF PAUL GRADY RATLIFF

Paul Grady was born December 31, 1890, in Ethel. Although called "Grady" by his family, he also went by "Paul" outside the immediate family.[1]

Grady at seven

Based on the eleven-grade school system then in effect, Grady should have graduated from high school in Winona around 1907 or 1908. At that point, just as his family was moving to a farm in western Illinois, Grady enrolled in Northwestern University in Chicago. Grady mentioned his studies in letters he sent to his brother Tom in 1910 and 1911.[2] Moreover, a newspaper article about his 1919 wedding stated that he graduated from Northwestern University.[3]

---

1   In letters to his younger brother Tom, he signed his name "Grady." In a letter to Judge Charles F. Amidon, Grady's brother John B. referred to his brother as "Paul."

2   Copies of letters to Tom were generously provided by Tom's daughter Tommie Jane Ratliff Allen.

3   *The Fargo (ND) Forum and Daily Republican*, February 27, 1919. By sheer coincidence, Grady's granddaughter Alison Ratliff got her degree from Northwestern as well.

He worked while going to school. In the 1910 census, Grady was listed as a lodger at 1313 Jackson Boulevard, Chicago, and his occupation was "office clerk."[4]

Grady as a young man

In his letter of June 26, 1910, to Tom on the farm near Cambridge in western Illinois, Grady wrote the following:

> …Since I started working for Siegel Cooper and Company,[5] I don't have to work but until 6:00 o'clock Saturday nights. That is "quite a bit" better than working until 10. Mr. Butler, a special friend of mine and my future roommate, is going to quit his job tonight. He had charge of the third floor there. He accepted another position at $30.00 a week. He invited me to come and take supper with him at the "Grand

---

4   1910 US Census, Ward 20, Chicago, Cook Co., Illinois, ED 880, sheet 13B, National Archives Microfilm, T624, roll 263.

5   Siegel Cooper and Company was a Chicago department store, founded in 1887.

Northern" Hotel Monday. Then, we are going down to our new room where I live now. Autos pass about fifty every minute. They don't allow wagons on the street at all. It is kept just as clean as can be. (Illegible name) sent me a large picture of the graduating class at Winona. It is 11 by 14 inches. It is certainly a good one too…

In a letter to Tom a month later, Grady wrote the following:

…Mr. Elliot, my roommate, is going back to Virginia Tuesday. I will have to get me up another one for I don't want to give up this nice room I have and 4 dollars is too much to pay alone.[6]

On April 22, 1911, almost a year after Tom and his family had moved to Hope, Arkansas, Grady wrote to Tom about his studies, using Northwestern University letterhead. He was living at 1014 Maple Avenue in Evanston, the home of the main campus. It was clear that Grady was still enrolled in the university and that money was tight:

…The people who lived here have moved out and some more have come in with lots of kids that keep up some rough-house. It is nine o'clock now and they have the talking machine going. I don't intend to try to study here. I always study at the library. It is so quiet there you could hear a pin fall. I get to studying sometimes and five hours goes away before I know it.

The Zeta (?) Literary Society letters told me the other day if I would join their society and play ball with them, they would pay all my expenses. It is such a short time until school is out and I think I will wait until next year.

---

6   July 17, 1910, letter from Grady to his brother Tom.

I am going to canvass this summer. I have already signed up the contract. I am guaranteed 178 dollars for the summer. It is a pretty good thing. A fellow here made 400 dollars clear last summer. I don't expect to make that much but think I will make "quite a bit" more than I would in Chicago…

At the time he wrote the above letter, Grady presumably had another year left at Northwestern before graduation, which could have put his date of graduation around 1912 or 1913.

Grady, perhaps at graduation

According to a Washington, Arkansas, newspaper article around June 1918, Grady went to live with his father, W.P., in Hope around 1912–1913, presumably after receiving his diploma from Northwestern. While there, he accepted a position as night clerk at the Capitol Hotel.[7] The photo below

---

7 Article about Grady, *Washington* (Arkansas) *Telegraph*, June 1918.

of Grady with his younger sister Bessie could have been taken about that time, or perhaps in his late teens.

Bessie and Grady

At least by 1917, Grady was living in Vicksburg, Mississippi, and was the assistant manager of the Carroll Hotel in Vicksburg.[8]

According to *Notes on the Ratliff Family Line*, graciously provided by Patricia Everly Ratliff, the widow of Grady's son Philip Grady Amidon Ratliff, Grady met Beulah Elizabeth Amidon while working in Vicksburg. A graduate of Barnard College in New York City, Beulah was the daughter of a federal judge in North Dakota and was active in the women's right-to-vote movement.[9] According to the newspaper account of her 1919 wedding to Grady, "she took a prominent part in the suffrage activities in

---

8   WWI draft registration, June 5, 1917.
9   Patricia Everly Ratliff, *Notes on the Ratliff Family Line*.

Washington and was in charge of the suffrage campaign in the southern states a few years ago."[10] It is likely that Beulah met Grady while staying at the Carroll Hotel in Vicksburg on suffrage business, and the flower of romance blossomed. It appears that they became engaged in 1917 because in a letter to Grady's family in 1942 about her daughter's wedding after only a two-week engagement, Beulah wrote, "...I don't believe in long engagements in war time, not after going through one myself."[11]

Patricia Everly Ratliff's *Notes on the Ratliff Family Line* also reveal that Grady joined the US Army on June 17, 1917. He was then transferred to the Canadian army air force and was commissioned at Camp Borden, Toronto, Canada.[12] According to the newspaper account of his North Dakota wedding "[Lieutenant Ratliff] enlisted in the Royal Air Service in June 1917 and went overseas in October of that year..." Presumably Grady received his flight training in Canada, was commissioned, and then sent to the European Theater. In his 1917 draft registration card, Grady outlined his military experience:

> *Rank:* Lt. MM; *Branch:* Aviation; *Years:* 1917; *Nation or State:* Pensacola, Florida; *Do you claim exemption from the draft?* No.[13]

So it is not clear whether Grady joined the US Air Corps in Pensacola, Florida, receiving a commission and learning to fly there, or whether his flight training took place in Camp Borden, Toronto, Canada. In either case, he left for the United Kingdom in October 1917. His Royal Air Force service records show that his first assignment, effective December 1, 1917, was as a forward observer in the 38th T.S. [Tactical Squadron?]. Then on February 14, 1918, he was assigned as a forward observer with the

---

10   *Fargo (ND) Forum and Daily Republican*, February 27, 1919.
11   Letter from Beulah to Grady's family, May 8, 1942.
12   Patricia Everly Ratliff, *Notes on the Ratliff Family Line*.
13   WWI draft registration, June 5, 1917.

14th Wing, 34th Squadron, RFC (Royal Flying Corps), flying the Bristol Fighter F-2 over the battlefields.[14]

Lieutenant Paul Grady Ratliff in the RAF

Grady in his RAF Bristol Fighter F-2 Observation Plane

---

14   The National Archives (UK), Air Ministry: Department of the Master-General of Personnel: Officers' Service Records; Catalogue Reference: AIR/76/418; Image Reference:490.

On an April 24, 1918, mission flying over Austrian territory, Grady's engine failed and he was forced to land. His service records listed him as "Missing." Two days later on April 26, he was reported as captured, an "unwounded" prisoner held in Salzerbad (Austria).

A May 15, 1918, letter to his brother John B. from a prison camp in Austria described Grady's capture and his conditions in captivity:

Camp Salzerbad, Austria, May 15, 1918

Dear John B.,

I wrote you a card some time ago but have reason to think it did not get off so I will write about my misfortunes from the beginning.

On April 24, while taking photographs and doing recon in Austrian territory, my engine stopped and I was forced to land. I landed on top of a mountain about 8000 [Note: line missing here from age and fold of the letter].

Fortunately, neither I nor my observer was hurt. We were taken prisoners and after being sent from place to place for eighteen days, we finally arrived at the prison camp.

The camp is in an ideal location. It is high and dry and the scenery is very pretty. We are allowed to walk outside the camp two days in the week.

The rooms are reasonably comfortable and it would not be so terrible being in prison (rest of sentence deleted by censors). The prisoners have to live entirely from the packages the Red Cross and our people send. However, they haven't nearly enough for themselves.

Please arrange or have the Red Cross there send me packages containing food that will keep – such things as bread, oatmeal, rice, canned goods - in fact, anything that will keep. My observer and I have a stove in our room and can cook on it fairly well.

Please notify Beulah Amidon. She has probably been cabled that I was missing and is worrying herself sick. Will write again when I can.

Your brother, P.G. Ratliff, Lieut., R.F.C.

P.S. I am writing Carr and Company, 16 Charing Cross, London to honor your draft on me for $100 per month. Please draw this regularly until I come home. Make the draft in dollars, not pounds.

PGR[15]

The above letter was originally handwritten. Grady's brother John B. then typed and sent it, along with other communications, to Beulah Amidon's father, Federal Judge Charles Fremont Amidon in Fargo, North Dakota. In a cover letter John B. wrote:

J.B. RATLIFF
MERCHANT AND PLANTER
DREW, MISSISSIPPI

July 4, 1918

Mr. Charles F. Amidon
Fargo, N.D.

My Dear Sir:

I am enclosing herewith Cables received from London, also copy of Paul's letter to me.

I have also received card mentioned in his to me. You will note a blank line in copy of his letter. That part was marked out by the censors.

---

15 This letter and other communications during Grady's confinement as a POW in Austria are courtesy of Curtis Deyrup, son of Beulah Curtis Ratliff Deyrup and grandson of Paul Grady Ratliff. He discovered them in a box in his attic in late 2011.

> I have sent the American Red Cross at Washington, DC Fifty ($50.00) Dollars and instructed them to buy such food as would be most beneficial to him and get to him if possible.
>
> I understand that this can be only gotten to him once a month, which I will do as long as he is there.
>
> I appreciate your willingness to do what you can for him and feel that you are in a better position to help him than I am. Will take the matter up with Senator Williams[16] and see what he can do for us.
>
> I regret very much to hear of the death of your son and offer you condolence.
>
> I am,
>
> Very Respectfully,
>
> (Signed) J.B. Ratliff
>
> P.S. Paul said in his card he is receiving good treatment from the Austrians and no need to worry.
>
> JBR[17]

Beulah Amidon also received a postcard from Grady sometime after his capture, probably in May of 1918:

> From Lt. P.G. Ratliff
> Prisoner of War in Austria

---

16   US senator from Mississippi John Sharpe Williams. Senator Williams defeated John B. and Grady's father, W.P. Ratliff, in elections for the US House of Representatives in both 1893 and 1895.

17   This letter is also courtesy of Curtis Deyrup.

To Miss Beulah Amidon
14 Jackson Place[18]
Washington, DC
USA

Dear Beulah,

(I really) hope that they haven't cabled you of my being missing, causing you such terrible anxiety, for I am quite all right and unhurt in any way. However, the British gov. do not know this and probably will not for a month. After being lost in the clouds for some time, my engine stopped and I was forced to land on enemy territory. But please do not worry more than possible for I have comfortable lodgings. (There is) no cause to be concerned. [text missing].

Paul

Grady was held prisoner until about one week before the signing of the armistice on November 11, 1918. He returned to England with the first shipment of Allied prisoners of war and was personally greeted by King George V, at which time he was awarded the British War Medal.[19]

The following letter, received by Grady from King George V, was sent to each repatriated British war prisoner:

---

18   14 Jackson Place was the headquarters of the National Woman's Party, where Beulah presumably was working at the time.
19   Patricia Everly Ratliff, *Notes on the Ratliff Family Line*.

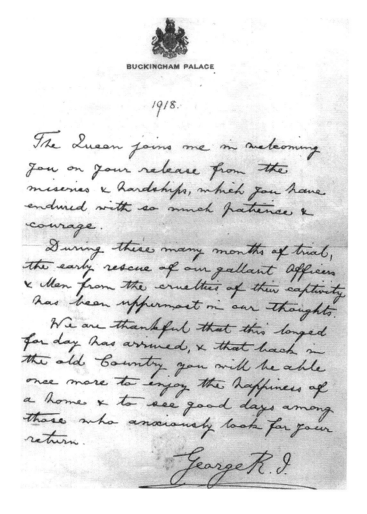

After his release, Grady remained in England until December 23, 1918. Perhaps he was receiving medical attention, and/or undergoing debriefings, pending discharge from the Royal Air Force. It is impossible to fully understand the total effect of his imprisonment upon Grady and his comrades. Grady's daughter-in-law Patricia Ratliff wrote that she heard that "though the Germans treated allied officers in the air corps very much as fellow officers and gentlemen, Germany was short of food and so fed their own first. So Grady probably lost a lot of weight on a poor diet."[20]

On December 23, 1918, Grady boarded the SS *Tunisian* in Liverpool, England, to return to the United States. The ship arrived at the Port of St. John, New Brunswick, Canada, at the mouth of the St. John River on January 4, 1919. Grady crossed the border into the United States at St. Albans, Vermont.[21] The border crossing record gave Grady's place of residence as Drew, Mississippi.

Once home, Grady visited with various family members and prepared for his wedding to Beulah that was to take place February 27, 1919, in Fargo, North Dakota.

---

20   Letter from Patricia Everly Ratliff to the author, September 10, 2011.
21   National Archives and Records Administration: Border Crossings from Canada to US, 1895–1956.

BEULAH ELIZABETH AMIDON

Beulah Elizabeth Amidon was born August 18, 1894, in Fargo, North Dakota. Her parents, Charles Fremont and Beulah McHenry Amidon, were accomplished and well known, locally and nationally.

Charles Fremont Amidon was a very impressive individual. The definitive book on Judge Amidon was written by Dr. Kenneth Smemo, Professor Emeritus, of Minnesota State University. The following summary of Judge Amidon's early life is derived from Professor Smemo's book, with his permission:

Charles Fremont Amidon, born in 1856, was the son of a circuit rider preacher in New York, and worked his way through college, receiving a degree from Hamilton College in New York State in 1882. He received many honors, including Phi Beta Kappa.

Later that year, he made his way to Fargo, Dakota Territory, where he was "the sole teacher at a new high school." After one year, "he resigned his position to begin reading the law" with a Fargo law firm and became an attorney. He married Beulah Richardson McHenry on November 15, 1892. Beulah had been one of his students in high school in Fargo in 1882 and was later named valedictorian of her senior class. She had gone on to study at the University of Minnesota for three years and assisted with taking the 1890 census, going by horseback to homes around Cass County, North Dakota. She was also very active in the movement to give women the right to vote, both in North Dakota and in neighboring states.

President Grover Cleveland appointed Charles Fremont Amidon to a federal judgeship in 1896, succeeding the first federal judge appointed after North Dakota became a state. He made many ground-breaking progressive rulings.[22]

---

22   Kenneth Smemo, *Against the Tide: The Life and Times of Federal Judge Charles F. Amidon, North Dakota Progressive* (Garland Publishing, Inc., 1986), Chapters 1–2. Out of Print.

For a complete account of Judge Amidon's professional life and accomplishments, see Professor Smemo's book *Against the Tide: The Life and Times of Federal Judge Charles F. Amidon, North Dakota Progressive*.[23]

Charles and Beulah McHenry Amidon had two daughters, Beulah Elizabeth and Eleanor F. Amidon. They also had three sons, all of whom died before age thirty-five. As parents they obviously instilled a life-long respect for education and progressivism in their children. Around 1911, at the age of seventeen, Beulah enrolled in Barnard College in New York City.

Beulah Elizabeth Amidon at age seventeen

At Barnard, Beulah became managing editor for "Social Movements" of the *Barnard Bulletin* and no doubt was already involved in activities to obtain the right to vote for women. As early as 1913, she worked on the

---

23   Ibid. The author is indebted to Professor Smemo for his helpful guidance and assistance by telephone in 2009, when in the early stages of research for this book, as well as his permission to use information from the book.

press campaign for what would eventually become the National Woman's Party.[24]

On February 7, 1915, the *New York Times* published a very long editorial opposing women's suffrage. In response, Beulah Amidon wrote a point-by-point rebuttal in a Letter to the Editor, which was published by the newspaper on February 14, 1915.

MAKE GOOD CITIZENS

> To the Editor of *The New York Times*:
> We do not ask you to support a cause with which you are not in sympathy—in a country of free speech and free opinion that would be ridiculous. We do expect, however, that the public press, even when not favorable, will be fair. There are certain statements in this editorial which are not even supported by you, and which are probably left so because you are not able to find support for them.
>
> 1. "The arguments of suffrage were long ago refuted and sent to limbo." If that is true how does it happen that this year campaigns were carried out in seven States and carried out successfully in two, a surprisingly large proportion? How does it happen that the organizations that support suffrage grow every year in membership? How does it happen that the University of Wisconsin declared suffrage no longer a debatable question for intercollegiate debate "because the matter of woman suffrage is generally recognized as a sound principle of democracy"? Finally, how does it happen that THE TIMES considers the matter of sufficient gravity to warrant an editorial the length and bitterness of that of Sunday?

---

24 Inez Haynes Gillmore, *The Story of the Woman's Party* (New York: Harcourt, Brace, and Company, 1921), 47.

2. "Without the counsel and guidance of men no woman ever ruled a State well." You speak as though you had expectations of suffragists rushing in and assuming control of the Government. No suffragist wants a matriarchate. Of course, women couldn't govern without the assistance of men—any more than men can govern without the assistance of women. Do you think the State is so perfect that it could not be improved? Did it ever occur to you that a woman's point of view would help things along? Katherine B. Davis, in bringing the woman's point of view to the question of prisons and corrections, has done nothing but benefit the State.

3. Do you not think that women, as well as men, have special training that would fit them for intelligent use of the ballot? Men and women are now acknowledged intellectually equal. They receive the same education; they have both a foundation of common sense and culture with which to attack large problems. Men, then, receive a special training in business methods and business experience. That does certainly fit them to deal with the business end of government. But women, at least some women, care for little children, they administer the complex machinery of a home, they come up against problems just as big and just as vital as the problems of bonds and capitalization, and the other problems of "business." Are not both trainings useful in making good citizens?

Also, you entirely overlook the fact that 8,000,000 women are not engaged in home industry, but are in business on the same terms of competition as men and are managing to support themselves and those dependent upon them. Men and women are both engaged in industry, either without the home or within it. This is not educative work. It is a means of earning a livelihood, not of training one's self for citizenship.

In the professions, the only place where workers may be said to be doing broadening work, there are at present in the United States 930,000 men and 730,000 women. This is not a large difference. It speaks very well for the intelligence and success of women in the intellectual pursuits.

4. "It is the privilege of men to care for women." I don't suppose you ever thought of women as rational human beings, educated, capable, and resenting this attitude that men assume, as though women were a separate, dependent, and much-to-be-pitied class of society. Women would vastly prefer justice to chivalry that allows a newspaper, edited by men, to misrepresent a cause that is so vitally important to so many hundreds of thousands of women.

5. "Women would be changed, and not for the better." Why do you say "would" be changed? If suffrage is going materially to alter the nature of women, why has it not done so? Women have voted in several States for more than twenty years. Do we hear of the "unsexed" women of Wyoming? Are the men of Colorado complaining that women are poorer housekeepers and less affectionate companions because they vote? The argument is ridiculous on the face of it.

6. "If the women were to take up man's duties who would perform woman's duties?" In the first place, is voting a man's duty? Who gave men the right to vote? Men gave it to themselves—because they wanted it. It didn't change their functions as men to take the ballot—the first citizens of the United States went on about their business as carpenters and farmers and shopkeepers after they had exercised the right of ballot for the first time. Why, then, do you think that it will take women away from their duties as women to perform the duties of citizenship? It doesn't do so in the States

where women already vote—why should it do so in New York?

BEULAH E. AMIDON

New York, Feb. 9, 1915[25]

Beulah graduated *cum laude* from Barnard College in 1915 and was also, like her father, Phi Beta Kappa. Upon graduation from Barnard, Beulah studied law at the University of Southern California.[26] Because women had the right to vote in California, Beulah registered, as a Republican, to establish her place of residence there.

In April 1915, the Women's Political Union, which was to merge with the Congressional Union to become the National Woman's Party, organized a van tour of New York City to publicize the suffrage movement. An April 25, 1915, article in the *Washington Post* entitled "Suffrage 'Shop' on Wheels to Tour New York City in Spring Campaign" reported that Beulah Amidon was to be one of the speakers "to talk about suffrage from the van platform."[27]

An October 12, 1916, article in the *Bismarck Daily Tribune* entitled "North Dakota Woman Honored" noted that Beulah was the daughter of Judge and Mrs. C.F. Amidon in Fargo and was making her home temporarily in Los Angeles, California. She was "receiving considerable commendation for her work in the recent Congressional Union campaign work in Fresno." She was appointed to work on large meetings in San Diego and Los Angeles, where the principal speaker was to be Mrs. Inez Milholland Boissevain, one of the best-known suffragists in New York City. The article went on to say that Amidon had a poem published in *Survey Magazine*,[28] where she was already working and where she continued to make her career for many years.

---

25 Beulah E. Amidon, letter to the editor, *New York Times*, February 14, 1915.
26 Beulah Amidon obituary, *New York Times*, September 25, 1958.
27 *Washington Post*, April 25, 1915.
28 *Bismarck (ND) Daily Tribune*, October 12, 1916.

As the March 5, 1917, inauguration of President Woodrow Wilson approached, organizations began demonstrating in Washington, DC, both at the Capitol and around the White House in support of a constitutional amendment to give women the right to vote. The plan was to obtain an audience with Wilson to gain his backing for women's suffrage.

The February 22, 1917, issue of the *Washington Post* carried a brief article about "The Oldest Suffragist, Rev. Olympia Brown, of Kenosha, Wisconsin," reporting that she would participate in the big demonstration of March 4. Beulah Amidon is mentioned in the same article as the youngest suffrage picket at the White House.[29]

The March 1, 1917, issue of the *Eau Claire (WI) Leader* carried a photo of Beulah Amidon above the caption "Prettiest Girl in the Picket Line." The article noted that the women in the picket line had voted Amidon "prettiest picket of all." The article also stated that Amidon was twenty-two years old "and says she has been a suffragist for practically the entire period."[30]

The March 16, 1917, issue of the *Connellsville (PA) Daily Courier* also carried Amidon's photo above the caption "To Lead Suffragists." She was not only elected "Prettiest Picket" but also was selected to be the "standard bearer in the demonstration around the White House on March 4."

The *Washington Post* carried the photo of "The Prettiest Picket" as well.[31]

According to *The History of the National Woman's Party*, by Inez Haynes Gillmore, Beulah carried the banner that suffrage pioneer Inez Milholland Boissevain had carried in the first suffrage parade[32] in New York. Boissevain collapsed while campaigning for women's suffrage in the West and died on November 25, 1916.[33] The banner read as follows:

---

29 *Washington Post*, February 22, 1917.
30 *Eau Claire (WI) Leader*, March 1, 1917.
31 *Washington Post*, March 4, 1917.
32 *New York Times*, May 5, 1912.
33 Gillmore, 183–185.

> Forward, Out Of Darkness,
> Leave Behind the Night.
> Forward Out Of Error,
> Forward Into Light.[34]

The words of this banner came from an Anglican hymn written by Canterbury Cathedral Dean Henry Alford in 1871 entitled "Forward! Be Our Watchword."[35]

W.J. Lampton, a well-known journalist and satirical poet who invented the "scream" or "yawp" free-verse style of poetry, wrote a poem about Beulah Amidon and her special role on the picket line around the White House, which was published on March 1, 1917, in the *Indiana (PA) Evening Gazette*.[36]

BEULAH AMIDON

> Beulah Amidon, Barnard girl has handed out the beauty whirls to all competing suffragettes in singles, doubles, and in sets, and being leader there has made her leader in the grand parade of college girls on Sunday next, when thousands of the not unsexed will march, regardless of the cold, to prove it is they want the vote and not alone to get man's goat, as anti-suffs have long averced in written speech and spoken word. Hail, Beulah, Belle of Beauty, hail! The cause you lead in cannot fail, and the compliment they give your beauty may be relative, what matters it when all must know that suffrage is no Beauty Show? What's beauty, anyhow? Skin deep and never warranted to keep! Is that to count among the gains requiring only nerve and brains? The melting eye, the luring lip, are they the signs of leadership? No, Beulah, no; and you may slam your beauty in the slats and ram your winsome

---

34 Ibid.
35 *Hymns and Their Authors* (London: Hodder and Stoughton, 1902).
36 *Indiana (PA) Evening Gazette*, March 1, 1917; See also W.J. Lampton obituary, *New York Times*, May 31, 1917.

ways into the mud if you can show true voting blood? That is the only stuff in sight to make the vote an equal right. And, Beulah, loveliest of the plain, Girl of the Suffrage West, your brain is what will set the franchise pace. Though beauty may be no disgrace, don't count on that a little, for no beauty ever won a war, and you, fair maid are out to fight for woman's constitutional right, which, tho the constitution fail to make it equal to the male, that instrument must undergo a female change to make it so. Ah, maiden fair, some day you'll stand secure inside the Beulahland, beneath the purple, gold, and white[37], and when you've found your heart's delight remember that the only rag of Freedom is our Starry Flag!!!

W.J. Lampton

And Beulah herself wrote a poem about standing in the picket line, which was published in the March 3, 1917, issue of *Suffragist Magazine* and reprinted in *The Story of the Woman's Party*.

THE PERPETUAL DELEGATION ON THE PICKET LINE

The avenue is misty gray,
And here beside the guarded gate
We hold our golden blowing flags
And wait.
The people pass in friendly wise;
They smile their greetings where we stand
And turn aside to recognize
The just demand.
Often the gates are swung aside:
The man whose power could free us now

---

[37] The colors of the Woman's Party. See Gillmore.

> Looks from his car to read our plea—
> And bow.
> Sometimes the little children laugh;
> The careless folk toss careless words,
> And scoff and turn away, and yet
> The people pass the whole long day
> Those golden flags against the gray
> And can't forget.
> Beulah Amidon.
> *The Suffragist,* March 3, 1917.

March 4, 1917, was a cold and rainy day. Nevertheless, between 500 and 1,000 women marched around outside the White House in support of women's suffrage. The March 5, 1917, *Washington Post* carried this headline:

RAIN SOAKED, 500 SUFFRAGISTS PARADE FOUR TIMES AROUND THE WHITE HOUSE AS 5,000 CHEER

> Wilsons in Carriage Ignore Dripping Ranks. Miss Amidon, "Prettiest" Picket Collapses. Unable to Present Letter and Resolution to the President – Jericho's Walls Fail to Fall.

The *Post* reported the following:

> Exhausted by the struggle with a heavy banner and two hours' exposure in the soaking rain, Miss Amidon collapsed shortly after returning to the headquarters at 21 Madison Place, and had to be removed to Emergency Hospital. Her condition was thought at first to be serious, but the hospital physicians later announced that she was resting comfortably, and pronounced her disposition as simply a case of shock.[38]

---

38 *Washington Post,* March 5, 1917.

Undaunted by the failure and presumably invigorated by the publicity brought to the picketing of President Wilson's inauguration, the National Woman's Party fought on. The headline in an article in the *Chillicothe (MO) Constitution* of March 31, 1917, read as follows:

WESTERN SUFFRAGISTS TO INVADE DIXIE ON BIG VOTE DRIVE

The newspaper reported that "six organizers have preceded the Invaders into the south. These include...Beulah Amidon of North Dakota..."[39]

Beginning in about April of 1917, the team was in North Carolina. From there, they went on to South Carolina and then to Alabama. And in May, they were in Vicksburg,[40] where Beulah would have met Paul Grady Ratliff and became engaged to be married.

With Grady having left for Canada, and then on to England and the war, Beulah was back in Washington. In an August 14, 1917, demonstration in Washington, a number of leading suffragists were arrested and sent to the infamous Occoquan Workhouse in Virginia. Demonstrations continued on August 15. The crowd turned rowdy, and the women were manhandled. Banners were torn out of women's hands. According to *The Story of the Woman's Party*, "Beulah Amidon of North Dakota was thrown down by a sailor, who stole her flag."[41]

---

39   *Chillicothe (MO) Constitution*, March 31, 1917.

40   Mary Walton, *A Woman's Crusade—Alice Paul and the Battle for the Ballot* (Palgrave Macmillan, 2010), 165–166. *A Woman's Crusade* makes numerous mentions of Beulah Amidon and her role in the movement.

41   Gillmore, 232.

Beulah Elizabeth Amidon 1916[42]

One must assume that Grady was in touch with Beulah by card or letter throughout his service in the RAF, including the seven months he was held in a prisoner of war camp in Austria. Though engaged, presumably they waited until Grady's release from prison camp and return to England before they set a date to be married. At some point after Grady's release, plans were soon made for the two to be wed in Beulah's hometown of Fargo, North Dakota, on February 27, 1919.

THE WEDDING IN FARGO

Grady arrived in Fargo on Monday, February 24, from his home in Drew, Mississippi. Soon after his arrival, he fell ill, and by Wednesday, the day before the wedding, he was diagnosed with influenza combined with pneumonia—possibly the strain of influenza that killed millions in the United States and abroad toward the end of World War I. In spite of his illness, rather than postpone the wedding, Beulah's family decided it should take place as scheduled, but without the hundreds of guests who had been

---

42 Harris and Ewing Photographers, 1916–1917, Records of The National Woman's Party, Manuscript Division, Library of Congress, Washington, DC. Photograph published in the *Suffragist*, 5, no. 70 (May 26, 1917): 4, and 6, no. 6 (Feb. 16, 1918): 11.

invited. Only family and a few intimate friends attended the wedding ceremony, which was said to have been held at Grady's bedside.

The headline of the article in the newspaper about the wedding read as follows:

Bridegroom's Illness Does Not Prevent Amidon-Ratliff Wedding[43]

The couple planned to settle in Drew, where two of Grady's brothers, John B. and Albert, lived. John B. gave the couple an automobile.[44] When told of the car gift many years later, John B.'s daughter Martha Ratliff Whetzel said that it was quite possible, since Grady was a special favorite of her father's. John B. named one of his sons after Grady—James Grady Ratliff, born in 1912.

Sometime after their marriage, Grady and Beulah were photographed together—both wearing Grady's RAF uniforms that he had brought home with him from the war. Perhaps it was Armistice Day (November 11) after their marriage, when war veterans were authorized and encouraged to wear their uniforms.[45]

---

43 *Fargo (ND) Forum*, February 27, 1919.
44 Information from Grady and Beulah's son Philip's widow, Patricia Everly Ratliff.
45 On a subsequent Armistice Day, Grady was also photographed in his uniform, holding his daughter Beulah.

Beulah and Grady in Grady's RAF uniforms

Although Grady is holding a cane in the photo, he is not known to have incurred any injuries in the war. After the war, Grady gave an identical cane to his brother John B., telling him that it was made from the propeller of his RAF airplane.[46]

Some months later, the 1920 census showed the couple living in Vicksburg. Beulah's occupation was "Writer of Books" and Grady's was "Cotton Buyer" for a cotton office.[47] Beulah was expecting their first child and went to Fargo to be with her parents sometime before her due date. Beulah Curtis Ratliff was born in Fargo on July 24, 1920. Grady, Beulah,

---

46 Told to the author by his Aunt Martha Whetzel, who showed him the cane given to her father.

47 1920 US Census, Ward 1, Vicksburg, Warren Co., Mississippi, ED 66, sheet 61B, National Archives Microfilm, T625, roll 897.

and their daughter returned to Vicksburg after the birth of their daughter,[48] but they would not remain in Mississippi much longer.

Cotton prices, which had begun to fall after WWI, plummeted so low that many farmers were wiped out, including Grady's older brother John B., who had held back his cotton from the market, anticipating a higher price. Presumably there was no longer a job for Grady as a cotton buyer in Vicksburg.

Of equal significance, however, could very well have been Beulah's reaction to life in Jim Crow-era[49] Mississippi. The January–June 1920 edition of the *Atlantic Monthly* published an article by Beulah entitled "'In the Delta' – The Story of a Man-hunt."[50] In the form of a letter to her father dated April 24, 1919, from Drew, Mississippi, Beulah described the shocking and casually cruel treatment of black people by some white residents in the Mississippi Delta, including beatings and killings. The account was so shocking that the editors of the *Atlantic Monthly* prefaced the letter by stating,

> [We print this genuine letter without alteration – The Editors]

According to her letter, when Beulah displayed shock at this inhuman treatment of their fellow human beings, she was told, "Don't be squeamish, Beulah. Remember, you've come to live in the delta."[51]

So, with their new baby, the couple decided to move to Los Angeles, where Beulah had earlier studied law and registered to vote. Initially, they

---

48 Family photo of daughter Beulah Curtis Ratliff, captioned as "age four months, Vicksburg."

49 "Jim Crow" laws were passed after the abolition of slavery with the sole objective of preventing black people from having equal rights.

50 Beulah Amidon Ratliff, "'In the Delta' – The Story of a Man-hunt," *The Atlantic Monthly*, January–June 1920. This article is courtesy of Beulah's granddaughter, Beulah Tacey Deyrup.

51 Ibid.

lived at 1056 W. Florence Avenue in Los Angeles.[52] At some point, Beulah's parents bought property in Inglewood, and by June of 1921, Grady, Beulah, and Beulah Curtis were living in a house on the same property as Beulah's parents, at 615 N. Prairie Avenue in Inglewood.[53]

Voter registration records show Beulah registered to vote in 1922 at the Prairie Avenue address. Though her occupation was listed as "housewife," she was already writing articles on social and education issues. Daughter Beulah Curtis was two years old.

The 1923 business section of the Los Angeles Directory lists Paul G. Ratliff as a cotton appraiser for Globe Cotton Oil Mills, with a residence in Inglewood.

On January 7, 1923, a son, Philip Grady Amidon Ratliff, was born. In the 1924 voter rolls, both Grady and Beulah are registered as living at the Prairie Avenue address. Beulah was listed as "housewife," while Grady was a "salesman."

A photo from this early period, taken about 1924, shows the happy family of four in a boat on a lake enjoying an outing.

---

52 Notation on a photo of Grady in his uniform, holding his daughter Beulah, on Armistice Day 1921, courtesy of Tacey Deyrup.

53 Notation on a photo of Beulah and daughter Beulah Curtis in June 1921; Patricia Everly Ratliff, widow of Grady and Beulah's son Philip Grady Amidon Ratliff, told the author that Philip took her to see the property on which he and his family lived when he was very young.

Beulah, Philip, Grady, Beulah Curtis

A later photo shows son Philip behind the wheel of the family's 1925 Franklin.[54] A similar automobile is on display at the Museum of American History, Smithsonian Institution, in Washington, DC.

Philip in the family's 1925 Franklin

Throughout the time that the family was in Los Angeles, Beulah continued her career as a writer, submitting articles and stories to a number

---

54 Perhaps this automobile replaced the one that Grady's brother John B. gave him in 1919.

of publications. In *St. Nicholas Magazine* of March 1921, she had a story published called "How the Money went to Bedford."[55] In the section "For the Children" of the *Woman's Home Companion* of February 1925, she was the author of a story entitled "The Wild Blue Jabby."[56] It is likely that she contributed many other articles to various publications.

The 1926 voter rolls do not show Beulah as registered to vote. Grady registered in 1926 but gave an address of 605 S. Harvard Boulevard in Los Angeles instead of the Prairie Avenue address in Inglewood, where the family had been living since 1921. Did the entire family move with Grady to Harvard Boulevard or could Grady have been separated from Beulah at this time? Could Grady's war experience have been so traumatic that it affected his marriage? It is impossible to determine the real story after more than eighty-five years.

Tragically, on October 31, 1926, Grady died of a self-inflicted gunshot wound. Although members of the Ratliff family were told that it was a hunting accident, some suspected suicide.

There was only one mention of his death in the newspapers. In the *Los Angeles Times* on November 1, 1926, under death notices, there was a terse statement of his death at age thirty-four with the name of the funeral home and, "Funeral Arrangements later."

No news report or follow-up death notice concerning funeral arrangements appeared in the newspapers. In 2009, requests for death records from both Los Angeles County and the State of California turned up neither a death certificate nor any other record of the death of a Paul Grady Ratliff. A call to the successor to the funeral home mentioned in Grady's newspaper death notice revealed that records for deaths/funerals in 1926 no longer existed.

All their lives, Grady's children were told their father died in a hunting accident. However, after Beulah's death in 1958, son Philip found documentation of Grady's suicide among his mother's effects.[57] Perhaps, with the influence of Beulah's father, Charles Fremont Amidon, a federal judge,

---

55 *St. Nicholas Magazine*, March 1921.
56 *Woman's Home Companion*, February 1925.
57 Conversation between Patricia Everly Ratliff and the author.

the family was able to keep the circumstances of Grady's death—even the announcement of his death—out of the newspapers and out of the public records. It is unlikely this mystery can ever be solved. Without question, whatever the cause and the circumstances, it was a family tragedy.

Beulah moved to New York with the children after Grady's death where she was an associate editor for *The Survey Graphic*, concentrating on labor and education issues.[58] She also edited a number of books and was instrumental in publishing the letters of her father to and from a variety of political figures of his day.[59] The 1930 census lists Beulah and her two children living at 85 Bedford Street in Manhattan.[60] Later, they also had a home in Westport, Connecticut.

Beulah and family 1935
Seated in front, Eleanor Amidon Clark; *from left,* Philip A.G. Ratliff, Beulah McHenry Amidon, Charles Fremont Amidon, Beulah Amidon Ratliff, Beulah Curtis Ratliff

---

58 *Survey Associate* Records, University of Minnesota Libraries, Amidon, Beulah 1925-1951, Box 51, Folder 346-350.

59 Beulah Amidon Ratliff, *Charles Fremont Amidon 1856-1937,* January 1, 1941. Out of print.

60 1930 US Census, Manhattan, New York, New York, ED 48, sheet 10A, National Archives Microfilm, T626, roll 1545.

The 1940 census found Beulah at the same address in New York City, with daughter Beulah, nineteen, and son Philip, seventeen. Mother Beulah was listed as an editor.[61]

Over the years Beulah maintained contact with the Ratliff family, sending children's books to great nephews and nieces at Christmas and birthdays.[62] According to Grady's niece, Martha Ratliff Whetzel, Beulah took her children to Mississippi from time to time to see their Ratliff relatives.

When Beulah's daughter, Beulah Curtis, got married in 1942, Beulah wrote an account of the wedding to Grady's brother John B. and his family. The letter began as follows:

85 Bedford Street
New York, NY
May 8, 1942

(Handwritten note) Please pass to the others.

Dear Miss Emma, John B., Paul, Barton and Mickey,[63] Anabel and Harry, Jimmy and Mary, Martha and Hilbert, and any others of the family who are interested:

I thought you all might like to know about Beulah's wedding so I am going to write one letter, and ask you to pass it around. I have neglected my work so much the last weeks, and there are so many things to do, at home and at the office just now, that I simply cannot write to each one, much as I should like to do so.

Of course, Beulah herself will want to write when she gets home. Many packages have come from our dear

---

61 1940 US Census, Manhattan, New York, New York, ED 31-51, sheet 65B, National Archives Microfilm, T627, roll 2626.

62 The author and his brother, Neil, were among the recipients of Beulah's gifts from the time when they were very young—about 1937—until the author was about twelve—in 1947.

63 The author's parents.

> Mississippi family—all but one of them after she left. But she will be back soon and then each one will hear from her. Meanwhile, you might like to have some of the details of the wedding, and those she never will find time to write, I'm sure. Also I am sure that she saw it all through a happy haze that she could not write about it as clearly as an onlooker could do…[64]

After describing how the newlyweds met and fell in love, and the details of the wedding itself, Beulah ends the letter as follows:

> We are all so sorry that none of Paul's[65] people could be here. I couldn't help hoping that someone might be able to—especially Bessie, who can get passes.[66] But I guess it was too sudden and too long a trip. We thought of you and wished that you could all be here, for to us it was a very important day.
>
> It seems very queer and lonesome here in the apartment. I can't seem to get around to making any plans. It seems foolish to go on here, just myself. But I can't seem to find the energy to do any real thinking on the subject. Maybe life itself will decide for me—it often does.
>
> Much love to you all,
>
> Beulah

Beulah's younger sister, Eleanor Amidon, married Sidney Clark, lived in Westport, Connecticut, and worked in New York City. The Clarks had no children. Judge and Mrs. Amidon had a home in Westport also—right

---

64 Letter from Beulah to Grady's family, May 8, 1942.
65 Paul Grady Ratliff.
66 Grady's sister Bessie's husband, Hall Causey, was a conductor for the railroad, so presumably they both could travel for free.

next door to Eleanor and Sidney Clark. Grady and Beulah's children, Beulah and Philip, would spend summers with their grandparents in Westport.

According to Dr. Kenneth Smemo, Professor Emeritus, Minnesota State University, when doing the research for his book about Beulah and Eleanor's father, Beulah's son, Philip, and his wife, Patricia, hosted a dinner for him at their home in Sherman, Connecticut, which Eleanor Amidon Clark also attended. He remembered the occasion fondly.[67]

Grady was the love of Beulah's life, and after his death, she remained a widow for the rest of her life, devoting herself to her children, grandchildren, and her work as a writer and editor. Beulah Elizabeth Amidon Ratliff passed away at the New York Infirmary in Manhattan on September 25, 1958, "after a long illness."[68] She was sixty-three years old. The headline of her obituary in the *New York Times* read as follows:

Beulah Amidon, Retired Editor Is Dead;
Labor, Education Expert For the Survey

---

67   Information from Professor Smemo by telephone, 2009.
68   *New York Times*, September 25, 1958.

THE CHILDREN OF
PAUL GRADY AND BEULAH AMIDON RATLIFF

Beulah Curtis Ratliff

Beulah Curtis Ratliff 1933

Beulah Curtis Ratliff was born in Fargo on July 24, 1920. She married Thorold Johnson Deyrup on May 3, 1942. Their son Curtis wrote of how his great-grandfather Jens Jensen Deyrup emigrated from Denmark and had his name changed by a US immigration official when he entered the country, and also how his mother and father came to meet:

> When my grandfather emigrated from Denmark to the U.S. around 1850, the immigration authorities admitted him under "Johnson" for reasons that have never been penetrated. The bureaucratic syllogism seems to have run: All

Scandinavians are Swedes and all Swedes are Johnsons, so this Scandinavian is Johnson. Eventually, Johnson's son Alvin Johnson, came to New York City, where he pursued an astonishing career. Starting as an impoverished Nebraska sodbuster, he gained a bachelor's degree from the University of Nebraska, advanced to Columbia University where he earned a Ph.D. in economics, and became a professor in the field and a journalist (he was a regular contributor to Herbert Croley's The New Republic). Later, he was a founding member of the New School for Social Research in New York City, with Thorstein Veblen, Charles Beard, and John Dewey, among others, and became its first President. As director of the New School, he created the University in Exile, which rescued many European scholars persecuted by the Nazis. Among the distinguished of the rescued scholars were the philosophers Hans Jonas and Hannah Arendt.

He had seven children, all originally born as Johnsons and all later had their names changed to "Deyrup," and thus the family patronymic was restored. One of his sons was Thorold Johnson Deyrup. As politically progressive intellectuals, Alvin Johnson and my grandmother Beulah became friends, and through this means, Thorold and my mother Beulah Curtis Ratliff were introduced.[69]

Beulah Curtis Ratliff and Thorold Johnson Deyrup had four children: Curtis Alden Deyrup, born 1943, John Thorold Deyrup, born 1945, Mark Amidon Deyrup, born 1947, and Beulah Tacey Deyrup, born 1951. John died of bone cancer on January 11, 1964, at age nineteen.

---

69   Letter from Curtis A. Deyrup to the author, November 18, 2011.

Thorold, Curtis, Beulah Curtis, John Deyrup 1945

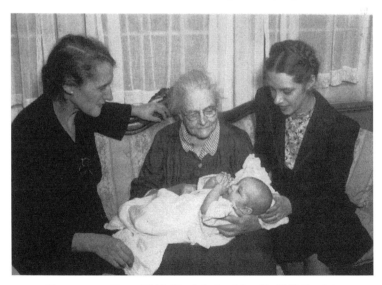

Four generations 1945: Beulah Amidon Ratliff, Beulah McHenry Amidon, John Deyrup, Beulah Curtis Deyrup

Christmas card photo at Grace Church, New York City 1954
From left, Curtis, Mark, Tacey, John

Curtis and his wife, Marta, have two children: Ivana and John. Mark and his wife, Nancy, have three children: Ingrith Elizabeth, Lief, and Steve. Tacey has never married.

Thorold died on March 25, 1984, and Beulah Curtis passed away on December 6, 1993, in Highlands County, Florida. Beulah and Thorold's ashes, along with those of their son John, were interred on the family property in Vermont.

Philip Grady Amidon Ratliff

Philip Grady Amidon Ratliff was born on January 7, 1923, in Los Angeles, California.

Philip Grady Amidon Ratliff

Lieutenant Philip Grady Amidon Ratliff 1944

US Army Lieutenant Philip Grady Amidon Ratliff married Patricia Browne Everly on November 27, 1944, in New York City, New York.

Patricia Brown Everly and Philip Grady Amidon Ratliff

Philip and Patricia had three daughters: Holly Everly Ratliff, Alison Amidon Ratliff, and Carol (Carey) Richardson Ratliff.

From left, Alison, Holly, Carey, Philip, Patricia

From left, Philip (with dog Sita), Carey, Alison, Holly (with cat Puri), Patricia (with dog Happy)

Philip held various offices in General Motors, both in New York City and abroad, which included tours with GM in both France and India. When Philip worked in New York, they lived in Sherman, Connecticut.

While Philip was working in GM's New York office, General Motors decided to move the office to the Midwest. All employees fifty-five years or older were offered early retirement. Philip happily accepted the offer, as did several others. Philip and Patricia kept their house in Sherman and later bought a winter home in Deland, Florida, subsequently moving to Naples, Florida.

Philip was keen on canoeing, and even got Patricia into it. They belonged to the Florida Paddling Club and paddled on all the rivers in Florida, branching out to the ones in Massachusetts and Connecticut.

They belonged to the Sailing Club in Deland and later to the one in Naples.[70]

None of the three daughters had children. Holly and Carey have passed away. Philip passed away suddenly of an aortic aneurysm in Naples, Florida, on March 6, 1992. His ashes were buried under the orange tree at the family home in Naples.

---

70   Letter from Patricia Everly Ratliff to the author, September 10, 2011.

10

BESSIE GRACE RATLIFF

Nokesville, Virginia - 1984

At age ninety-two, Bessie was encountering increasing problems living alone in her home in New Smyrna Beach, Florida. She found it difficult even to move around the house, much less go shopping for groceries or get herself to the doctor. Her niece Martha had offered to have Bessie come to Virginia and live with her so Martha could care for her. Bessie reluctantly agreed. Martha went down to Florida in order to help her close up the house, and then the two of them flew to Virginia. As the last remaining child of W.P. and Cornelia, Bessie had had a long life and had shared in her family's triumphs and tragedies. Martha went upstairs to check on her, where she lay in bed, no longer able to get up and move around. Martha asked Bessie if she would like a TV put in her bedroom. Bessie responded, "No, I don't need a TV. I have my memories."

THE LIFE OF BESSIE GRACE RATLIFF

Bessie Grace was born February 26, 1892, in Kosciusko, the youngest of the six daughters. At the age of eight, she was counted in the 1900 census with the family on the farm near Zilpha.[1] She was also with the family during their move first to Winona, where she would finish high school, and then on to the farm in western Illinois. The 1910 census confirms she was in Munson, Illinois, with her older sister Florence and younger brother Tom.[2]

Bessie Grace Ratliff

It is not likely that Bessie made the move with the family to Hope, Arkansas, in late 1910 or 1911 since no mention is made of her in letters to her brother Tom at the time. When she left Illinois, she must have gone

---

1   1900 US Census, Zilpha, Attala Co., Mississippi, ED 7, sheet 6B, National Archives Microfilm, T623, roll 800.
2   1910 US Census, Munson, Henry County, Illinois, ED 114, sheet 7A, National Archives Microfilm, T624, roll 291.

to college, though the name of the college and its location are not known. The 1940 census indicates that she had three years of college.[3]

Bessie married Kirby Hall Causey on January 20, 1915, back in Winona. At that time, her father was living in Arkansas and her mother in Texas. Perhaps Bessie married in Winona because of the presence of high school and family friends there. No other family members were known to be living in Winona in 1915.

Kirby Hall Causey, called "Hall" in the Ratliff family, was born October 3, 1889, in Seville, Florida. He was the youngest of the nine children of Leighton Erastus Causey and Frances Sophile Osteen. Leighton moved to Florida from Georgia just about the time of the Civil War, enlisting in Company F, Florida Ninth Infantry Regiment (CSA), on March 24, 1863.[4] He was a farmer.

According to the 1920 census, Bessie and Hall were living on Palmetto Street in New Smyrna Beach, Florida, near where Hall was raised.[5] Hall was a conductor for the railroad. A number of their neighbors also worked for the railroad in one capacity or another.

---

3   1940 US Census, New Smyrna Beach, Volusia Co., Florida, ED 62-42, sheet 9B, National Archives Microfilm, T627, roll 621.

4   American Civil War Soldiers, Historical Data Systems of Kingston, MA, comp. [database on-line]. Provo, UT, USA: Ancestry.com Operations Inc, 1999.

5   1920 US Census, New Smyrna, Volusia Co., Florida, ED 195, sheet 13A, National Archives Microfilm, T625, roll 230.

Bessie and Hall in New Smyrna Beach, Florida

On February 17, 1922, after seven years of marriage, Bessie gave birth to a son, Kirby Hall "Todd" Causey Jr. Tragically, Todd died of an illness January 15, 1926, in Daytona Beach, Florida, just before his fourth birthday.[6] Bessie and Hall would have no other children.

---

6   Florida Deaths 1877–1939.

Kirby Hall "Todd" Causey Jr. at age 2

The 1930 census records the couple at the same Palmetto Street address in New Smyrna Beach, Florida. Hall continued to work as a conductor on the railroad, and Bessie remained at home.[7]

In 1940, Bessie and Hall were still in the same house at 910 Palmetto Street in New Smyrna Beach, with Hall working as a conductor on the steam railroad. No employment was shown for Bessie.[8] The 1945 Florida census showed Hall continuing to work as a railroad conductor and Bessie working as a clerk.[9] Bessie worked for many years at City Hall in New Smyrna Beach, Florida.

---

7   1930 US Census, New Smyrna, Volusia Co., Florida, ED 38, sheet 8B, National Archives Microfilm, T626, roll 334.
8   1940 US Census, New Smyrna Beach, Volusia Co., Florida, ED 62-42, sheet 9B, National Archives Microfilm, T627, roll 621.
9   Eleventh census of the state of Florida, 1945; (Microfilm series S 1371, 43 reels); Record Group 001021; State Library and Archives of Florida, Tallahassee, Florida.

Kirby Hall Causey passed away on December 7, 1958, in St. Johns County, Florida. He was sixty-nine years old.

After Hall's death, Bessie continued to live at their house on Palmetto Street in New Smyrna Beach. Of all W.P. and Cornelia's eleven children, she took the most active role in preserving the Ratliff family history, keeping records on the birth and marriage of various family members. When her niece Bessie Ratliff Herrin (brother Tom's daughter) began to do research on the family, she turned to Aunt Bessie for assistance. Aunt Bessie responded with much information and photos that would have otherwise been unrecoverable. In an undated letter to her cousin Judith Ratliff Evans, granddaughter of Aunt Bessie's older brother Zack, Bessie Herrin wrote the following:

> Aunt Bessie gave me her college ring when I was 16. She and daddy were very close when they were children. I have the two doll quilts that Aunt Anna made her and daddy when they were 4 and 6 years old. When daddy died, she sent me all the pictures she had of my father. She said after she was gone, no one would be left to care about these but myself. I really do thank her for these. I have never seen her but once but I have always felt close to her. My father loved her very much.[10]

Bessie maintained a correspondence with her niece and namesake Bessie for some years. Bessie was particularly close to her siblings Tom and Sudie and maintained regular contact with them. In 1965, in a Christmas card to Tom, Bessie wrote the following:

> Dear Tom,
> So wish I could see you. Such a few of us left since losing Sudie. I miss her so. She was very dear to me. Love, your sister, Bessie

---

10   Undated letter from Bessie Ratliff Herrin to her cousin Judith Ratliff Evans.

Bessie was close to her niece Martha Ratliff Whetzel, the youngest daughter of Bessie's oldest brother, John B. In 1984, when it became clear that Bessie, who by then was ninety-two years old, could no longer live by herself, Martha went to New Smyrna Beach, closed up Bessie's house, and brought Aunt Bessie up to her home in Nokesville, Virginia. Bessie was largely bedridden by then and stayed in a large upstairs bedroom at Martha's house.

When the author visited his Aunt Martha's house shortly after his Great Aunt Bessie arrived, Martha took him upstairs to see her. Bessie perhaps had not seen him since the 1939 Ratliff Family Reunion in Kosciusko when he was four years old. Martha introduced the author as "Barton's son" (J. Barton Ratliff Jr., oldest son of Bessie's brother John B.), to which Bessie replied, "Well, hello, John. Do I look ninety-five years old?" The author assured her she did not. Bessie then responded, with her wit still sharp, "Well, I'm not!" (At the time, she was only ninety-two!)[11]

Bessie passed away on October 15, 1988, at the age of ninety-six. She had outlived all of her ten siblings by a minimum of sixteen and a maximum of sixty-two years. She was buried next to her husband, Hall, in the Edgewater New Smyrna Cemetery, Volusia County, Florida.

---

11 Conversation between the author and his great aunt Bessie, 1984.

11

TOM WATSON RATLIFF

The afternoon of April 15, 1917
On board the *Cameronia*
in the Mediterranean Sea

Tom was aboard the troopship *Cameronia*—filled with 3,000 soldiers—on his way to his new assignment with the British army in Thessaloniki. The day was sunny and the ocean was calm. Suddenly the troops heard a loud explosion, and men were running everywhere! The crew hurriedly prepared and lowered the lifeboats. Tom was in the last lifeboat to be lowered from the ship. One side of the lifeboat was lowered faster than the other, throwing the boat into the propellers. Tom was the only one to jump clear. He was in the water for hours, but no one came…

THE LIFE OF TOM WATSON RATLIFF

Tom Watson was born July 29, 1894, in Kosciusko—just four months after his father's deadly encounter with Sam Jackson. Tom was in Zilpha with his family in 1900,[1] and after moving to Winona in Montgomery County around 1906, the family, with Tom, then headed for a farm in western Illinois.

Tom Watson Ratliff

The 1910 Henry County, Illinois, census confirms Tom and sisters Bessie and Florence were still at home with their parents.[2]

By 1911, W.P., Cornelia, Tom, and sisters Kate and Florence were on a farm near Hope, Arkansas. Sister Bessie probably was off at college. In an April 22, 1911, letter to Tom, brother Grady asks how the schools were

---

1   1900 US Census, Zilpha, Attala Co., Mississippi, ED 7, sheet 6B, National Archives Microfilm, T623, roll 800.
2   1910 US Census, Munson, Henry County, Illinois, ED 114, sheet 7A, National Archives Microfilm, T624, roll 291.

compared to those in Winona, Mississippi. Grady also confirmed that he had received a letter from Florence and wrote, "Guess you are riding around a little since you all have a horse and buggy."³

In late 1911 or early 1912, when Tom was only seventeen years old, he sailed for England on a freighter loaded with bananas. He signed on as a ship steward, and for about three years he sailed to many ports, including in Latin America. Tom told his daughter Tommie many years later that in July 1915, with England already embroiled in World War I, he and a friend were in London watching a parade. He was moved by some children in the parade who were carrying a banner that read "SAVE US! JOIN THE ARMY!"⁴

On July 27, 1915, with the United States two years away from entering the fight, Tom joined the British army. His enlistment apparently was not to be effective until October. After enlisting, Tom sailed back to the United States, presumably to spend time with his family before going off to war. In October, he traveled from Galveston—where his mother was likely staying with her daughter Belle's family—to New Orleans, where he boarded a freighter filled with horses and sailed back to England.⁵

Tom's army pay book reveals that he wrote a will dated December 20, 1915, naming his mother as beneficiary.⁶ His entry-level pay was one shilling a day. In a January 1916 postcard to his mother in Sealy, Texas, he wrote, "Dear Mother, have had a fine time here Xmas. London was alive New Year's night. Will be here about two weeks. Tom."

The time line of Tom's military service is difficult to follow. However, according to an article in the *Washington (AR) Telegraph*,⁷ he first saw service with the British infantry in the trenches of France. He later told his

---

3   Letter from brother Grady in Evanston, Illinois, to Tom in Hope, Arkansas, April 22, 1911. As noted earlier, the author is grateful to Tom's daughter Tommie Jane Ratliff Allen for copies of the letters her father received from his siblings and parents over many years.
4   Conversation with Tom's daughter Tommie Jane Ratliff Allen, August 21, 2011.
5   Undated summary of "The Life of Tom Watson Ratliff" by his daughter Bessie Ratliff Herrin.
6   Conversation with Tommie, August 21, 2011.
7   *Washington (AR) Telegraph* article about Tom's return from WWI, October or November of 1919.

daughter Bessie that he got tired of walking and signed up for the cavalry. He further shared that there were times when the men were so hungry they ate some of the horses.

Tom in the British army

Tom was later sent to Palestine with the Egyptian Expeditionary Force under Field Marshal Edmund Henry Hynman Allenby. They crossed the River Jordan many times. Tom sent his mother a postcard (date illegible) with a photo of the pyramids in Egypt.

TOM WATSON RATLIFF

Tom *(standing on right)* and his fellow soldiers

The British forces were within seventy miles of Jerusalem when Tom contracted malaria and was sent to a hospital in India. After recovery, he was put on border patrol in India for about eighteen months. While there he learned to drive and was assigned as an armored car driver. His armored car was built on a Rolls Royce chassis, had wheels not tracks, and held three men, including a driver and a gunner. As driver, Tom sat on a cushion on the floor, with the gunner standing in the turret above him.

Tom W. and his Rolls Royce armored car
An almost identical vehicle is in The Tank Museum
Bovington, Dorset, England.

Tom with service ribbons

Tom's 1917 pay book noted that his pay had increased from an initial one shilling a day to one shilling, eleven pence, four. In April 1917, after receiving a transfer to Thessaloniki, Tom boarded the troopship *Cameronia*, which had provided steamship service between Glasgow, Scotland, and New York before being requisitioned for wartime use.

The May 19, 1917, *New York Times* published the following statement from the British Admiralty: "The British transport *Cameronia*, with troops, was torpedoed by an enemy submarine in the Eastern Mediterranean on April 15. One hundred and forty men are missing and are presumed to have been drowned."[8]

The *Times* went on to report as follows:

> ...A large number of the casualties were due to the explosion of the torpedo, which struck where there happened to be many soldiers. There was some excitement and confusion at

---

8   *New York Times*, May 19, 1917.

the outset after the torpedo had struck, but discipline soon prevailed. The boats were launched but one of them was smashed, and many lives were lost.

The *Cameronia* was afloat for forty minutes after she was torpedoed, which enabled several destroyers to run alongside. Soldiers from the crippled ship jumped on these boats in disciplined succession. The destroyers ceased taking on men as soon as they had obtained their complement. Many men from the *Cameronia* who jumped into the water were picked up...[9]

Daughter Bessie's account describes Tom's personal plight:

There were three thousand soldiers aboard the Cameronia. He was in the last life boat to be lowered from the ship. One side was lowered faster than the other and threw the boat into the propellers. He was the only one to jump clear. He was in the water for many hours before he was picked up by the crew in one of the other life boats. By that time, he was so frightened that he did not realize what was going on. He fought his rescuers and they had to knock him out with an oar in order to pull him into the life boat. They were picked up seven or eight hours later by a [Allied forces] U-boat chaser and taken to India.[10]

Tom returned to India. The United States entered the war on April 6, 1917, just before the torpedo attack on Tom's ship. According to the Arkansas newspaper article, Tom wanted to enlist in the American forces

---

9   Ibid.
10 Bessie Ratliff Herrin summary of "The Life of Tom Watson Ratliff," undated.

after the US declaration of war, but there were no US forces in India for him to join at that time.[11]

Tom remained in India from early 1917 until at least September 29, 1918, as indicated by the date on a letter addressed to Tom in Bangalore, India, from his father, W.P., in Washington, Arkansas.[12] His father referenced a letter that Tom had previously written in which Tom reported on hunting pheasants in India.

Just after receiving his father's letter, Tom also received a letter from a young lady, Indy B. (Indiabelle) Rowe, a resident of Ozan, Arkansas, who would have been about twenty years old in 1918, according to the 1920 census.[13] Perhaps she and Tom were in school together or were neighbors. She mentioned that "your father was here last Thursday and told Dad that it had been some time since he had had a letter from you. That was before your letter came." She also wrote, "Yes, I will be glad to have a photo of you and also some views of India. I know the country is so different from this. I am sorry but I haven't a picture of me to send. If I can, I will send one later."[14]

By the time he had received a letter from his father dated May 25, 1919, Tom was in Tiflis, Russia (present-day Tbilisi, Georgia),[15] and the war had been over for many months. A letter received later the same week from his sister Sudie was also addressed to Tom in Tiflis.[16] The address read, "Pvt. T.W. Ratliff, Transport Co., 7th Gloucester Regiment, Salonique Forces, Tiflis, Russia." Both letters expressed the hope that Tom would receive his discharge soon and be on his way home.

Sometime in July or August 1919, Tom's commanding officer, Lieutenant Colonel James Edwards, completed Army Form Z.18

---

11   *Washington (AR) Telegraph* article about Tom's return from WWI, about October or November 1919.
12   W.P. Ratliff letter to his son Tom, September 29, 1918.
13   1920 US Census, Ozan, Hempstead Co., Arkansas, ED 103, sheet 14B, National Archives Microfilm, T625, roll 64.
14   Letter to Tom at "Company G, 7th Gloucester Regiment, Bird Barracks, Bangalore, India" from Indy B. Rowe, September 30, 1918.
15   Letter from W.P. Ratliff to his son Tom, May 25, 1919.
16   Letter from Sudie Ratliff Spain to her brother Tom, May 28, 1919.

(certificate of employment during the war) for Private Tom Watson Ratliff. He identified Tom's regiment as the 2nd Gloucester, 11th Battalion, "B" Company and Tom's regiment number as #203286. His period of regimental employment was from July 1918 to July 1919. His occupation before enlistment was "Ship's Steward." Under "Military Qualifications," Edwards wrote "1st class shot" and "1st class M.O."[17]

Under "Special Remarks" as to qualifications, work done, or skill acquired during service with "the colours," he indicated, "Service in the field: (France 1 ½ years; Mesopotamia 2 ½ years).

"Comments: This man has been employed in Transport as a (illegible) Driver and proved himself an excellent driver. He is hardworking and thorough (illegible)."[18]

Although the war ended in 1918, Tom did not receive his discharge from the British army until October 11, 1919. For his service, he received the British War Medal.[19]

On the date of his discharge, October 11, 1919, Tom sailed from Glasgow on the S.S. *Saturnia*, arriving in Quebec on October 20. He crossed the border from Quebec at St. Albans, Vermont.[20] Many of the travelers on board the ship were current or former members of the British army, with their passage paid by the British government.

The border crossing records listed Tom's nationality as "English." Daughter Tommie said this was because when Tom was in line to enlist in the British army in London, he was asked his place of birth. When Tom told them, "Kosciusko, Mississippi, USA," he was sent to the back of the line. When it came his turn again, he simply told them he was born in England, arbitrarily picking the name of a city.

---

17 Certificate of employment during the war, British army Form Z.18 (undated).
18 Ibid.
19 British War Office: Service Medal and Award Rolls Index, First World War, Medal Card of Ratliff, Tom W.
20 Border Crossings: From Canada to US – October 20, 1919, Manifests of Passengers Arriving at St. Albans, VT, District through Canadian Pacific and Atlantic Ports, 1895-1954; National Archives Microfilm Publication: M1464; Roll: 380, Record Group Title: Records of the Immigration and Naturalization Service; Record Group Number: 85.

Tom listed his last permanent US residence as Galveston, Texas, where his mother, Cornelia, had been living with his sister Belle and her family. The form also confirmed that Tom had left the United States in 1915, as reported in the Arkansas newspaper after his discharge. By this time, the O.W. Wilson family had moved on to Sealy, Texas.

Upon arrival in the United States, Tom first went to see his father in Washington, Arkansas. During his October or November, 1919 visit, he was interviewed by the local newspaper regarding his war experiences. The article reported as follows:

> …Mr. Ratliff knows how it feels to have a ship blown from under you at sea and he has been wounded twice, receiving only flesh wounds, however. Many hardships were endured by him while in the service, but he says that he does not regret having gotten into the scrap.[21]

After visiting his father, Tom traveled around to see the country, including visits to his mother and siblings. In a December 3, 1919, letter from San Antonio, Texas, to Tom in Fort Worth, his mother wrote that she was soon moving to Jacksonville, Texas, with Tom's brother Albert and that she looked forward to having Tom visit her there where they would have a house, which she seemed excited about.[22]

Tom's daughter Bessie's summary of her father's life after he returned from WWI continues with this account:

> At one point in his travels, he found himself in Corsicana, Texas. He got a job as a barber there. He also met his bride-to-be, Rissie Corean Page in Corsicana. Tom was at the Palace Theater one night and was seated behind her. When she left her seat for a few minutes, he moved nearby and sat on her coat, so she had to ask him to move. He followed

---

21 *Washington (AR) Telegraph*, presumably in October or November 1919.
22 Letter to Tom in Fort Worth from his mother in Sealy, Texas, December 3, 1919.

her home after the show to see where she lived. The next day when he went to work, he discovered that she worked next door to the barbershop at a bakery. They began dating. Rissie's father kidded Tom about his being always dressed up. Rissie's brothers were laborers but Tom wore white pants and shirt and a straw hat after work.[23]

Rissie Corean Page was born on October 14, 1904, in Glen Rose, Texas. Her parents, Dan and Dora Page, came from Oklahoma. Rissie had three brothers and two sisters. Rissie's nickname "Ollie" was bestowed on her by her husband, Tom. No one knows how he came up with this nickname, but everyone in Corsicana called her "Ollie."[24]

Tom and Ollie

---

23 Bessie Ratliff Herrin summary of "The Life of Tom Watson Ratliff," undated.
24 Conversation with Tom's daughter Tommie, August 21, 2011.

Tom and Ollie married on March 20, 1921. Soon after they married, Tom purchased his own barbershop, which eventually grew to be the biggest in Corsicana. Tom named the barbershop "IXL."

Tom *(standing, left)* and his barbershop

A daughter, Bessie Corean, was born on July 25, 1922. A second daughter, Margaret Grace, was born on December 25, 1924. A third daughter, Tommie Jane, born in 1928, was named after her father, since there did not seem to be a prospect for any sons.

TOM WATSON RATLIFF

Tom and Ollie's three daughters, plus two cousins
at the 1939 Ratliff Family Reunion
On left, Bessie Corean Ratliff; *second from right,* Margaret Grace Ratliff;
far right, Tommie Jane Ratliff; *second from left,* Cousin Cornelia Ratliff;
in front, Cousin Roxana Ratliff

During the oil boom in Corsicana, Tom and Ollie rented out one of their bedrooms in their home on W. Eleventh Avenue for two dollars a week to some of the oil field workers. There was no running water on their street, so everyone used water from a common well about a block down the alley from their house. When water was brought to Eleventh Avenue, the Ratliff house was one of the first to have indoor running water—although the pipe was located on their back porch. The neighbors came to marvel as the water ran from the pipe.

They also had one of the first radios in their community. With no speaker, it came with a single set of earphones, and family members took turns listening to the news and music. The family didn't own a car, but the streetcar was only a block away so Tom rode it back and forth to work. He also owned some fighting gamecocks and made extra money betting on his roosters.

Around 1930, they bought a larger four-room house about a block from their first house. Later, Tom wanted his family to live in a better part of town, so they sold the four-room house and moved into a rental house until they could find the right house to buy.

In the 1930s, jukeboxes came on the market. Tom bought one of the first in Corsicana. It contained only eight records. The machine was a moneymaker, so he began to buy more and place them in dance halls, drugstores, cafes, etc. Jukeboxes continued to improve, from holding eight records, to ten, and then to fifty. Tom saw that his competitors were paying the proprietor of each establishment one-third of the profits from each machine. Tom went to the shopkeepers and offered to increase their share of the profits to 50 percent if they would sign up with his company, resulting in an even greater increase in the volume of business.[25]

Daughter Tommie fondly remembers going with her father to service the machines and helping count the coins. Each proprietor was given a number of nickels with red spots painted on each side. The coins with red spots were for the proprietor to play songs for his own enjoyment at no cost. When Tom came to service the jukebox, first the coins with the red paint were set aside and returned to the proprietor. Then the remaining coins were divided between Tom and the proprietor fifty-fifty.

The jukeboxes were so profitable that Tom sold the barbershop and worked full time on the coin-operated machines. Along with jukeboxes, he also bought slot machines, pinball, cigarette, peanut, and other coin-operated machines. At each of their homes Tom built a large workshop for the storage and repair of the machines.

Tom bought a house on W. Collin Avenue, where they lived for about eight years. He later purchased a house on N. Highway 75, surrounded by about a hundred acres. The house was just outside the city limits, but it had all the conveniences of town. All the rooms in the house were large. There were two large modern bathrooms, one upstairs and one down. It had a four-car garage and a long paved drive as wide as four cars. Tom had his office built behind the garage and the stable behind that. He hired people to take care of all of it. Everything was kept clean and in perfect condition. He bought four miniature horses and put them in the pasture next to the house. It was a beautiful modern two-story house: hardwood floors, a spiral staircase, and Tommie's room had a balcony and a walk-in closet. He bought and sold

---

25   Conversation with Tom's daughter Tommie, August 21, 2011.

many farms. He kept his 110 acres on the other side of town for his cattle. He also invested in rental property and made other investments as well.

A "self-made man" who came from a farm family in Mississippi, Tom became a wealthy man and was very much respected in Corsicana.

Tom Watson Ratliff died on October 28, 1969, at the age of seventy-five and was buried in Oakwood Cemetery in Corsicana. Ollie died April 1, 1989, in Ennis, Texas, at age eighty-four and was buried beside Tom.

For years after Tom's death, people in town would speak to daughter Tommie and her sisters about the many unsung kindnesses Tom had shown to people in need. Some told of his bringing groceries to them when they were strapped financially.

Tom's daughters loved him very much, and his daughter Bessie spoke for all three of his daughters when she wrote the following tribute to their father:

> He made life fun for his children. They never felt the depression. He gave his time as well as money, when he had it, to his family. They always had a bike or a horse to ride. He told them stories about his life and he always made it sound great. When times were bad, he played games with them when he came home from work. When he was home, it was like a party all the time. He was never too tried to share their problems or the things that happened to them during the day. He taught them good manners, and to be kind to others.
>
> We miss him very much and thank God that we had such a wonderful father. He was fun to be with and wonderful to know. He taught us much and we will always remember him with love. Although he is gone, he left a part of himself with each of his children and he will always be a part of us, in our lives and in our hearts.[26]

---

26 Bessie Ratliff Herrin, summary of "The Life of Tom Watson Ratliff," undated.

THE CHILDREN OF TOM WATSON AND RISSIE COREAN PAGE RATLIFF

Bessie Corean Ratliff
Bessie Corean was born in Corsicana, Texas, July 25, 1922. She married Jack Meredith Grooms, born December 24, 1923. They had a son, Michael Watson Grooms, born on June 17, 1941, in Corsicana, Texas, and a daughter, Meredith Kay Grooms, born in 1943.

Bessie Corean Ratliff

Son Michael married Mickie L. [Grooms] December 16, 1958. They had a daughter named Dana. Michael and Mickie divorced February 28, 1969, and Michael passed away July 31, 2006.

Daughter Meredith married Tommy L. Twomey October 15, 1961. They had a daughter, Tammy, and a son, Tommy (called "Chip"). Meredith and Tommy divorced January 26, 1995, and Meredith married Harold W. Davidson July 19, 1997.

Bessie and Jack Grooms divorced, and Bessie married Howell Jessie Herrin on April 12, 1945. He was born October 1, 1919, in Corbet, Texas, and was called "Jessie." They had a daughter, Beverly Lynn Herrin, born in 1946, and a son, Tom Howell Herrin, born in 1953.

Daughter Beverly married Larry Lynn Back on June 1, 1968. They adopted a son, Gregory Lynn Back (called "Gregg"), born on March 6, 1970. They had two more sons: Brian David Back, born in 1971, and Michael Howell Back, born in 1975. They also adopted a daughter, Keri Ann, born in 1982. Michael Back is married to Dacia Gonzalez, and they have a daughter, Isabella Celio, born in 2009. Keri Back is married to Clayton E. Coker, and they have a daughter, Alyssa Corean, born in 2009.

Larry Lynn Back passed away on May 30, 2005. Son Gregg passed away on October 24, 2012.

Son Tom married Beverly K. Smith on February 14, 1975. They have six children:

Jeramy, married to Kathleen Wilks, with sons Jessie and Kole; Zachary, married to Laura Janice Harshaw with daughters Elena and Audrey and son Levi; Virginia, married to Dave Dowden Laird with daughters Adri and Emryn; Genevieve, married to Tory Cunningham; Ethan, unmarried; and Lexi, unmarried.

Bessie and Jessie also adopted two daughters: Stacy Ann Herrin, born in 1963, and Lisa Renee Herrin, born in 1964.

Daughter Stacy married William A. "Tony" Rogers on November 26, 1985. They had two daughters, Hannah and Andrea. Stacy and Tony divorced. Stacy married Danny E. Edwards on February 5, 1991. They had a son, Brett. Stacy and Danny divorced on July 2, 1996.

Daughter Lisa married Randall E. Richards on August 21, 1981. They had a daughter, Mandy. Lisa and Randy divorced. Lisa married Joe N. Hernandez on November 22, 2002. They are divorced. Lisa also has another daughter, Schylar Rae.

Bessie Ratliff Herrin ran Bessie's Beauty Shop in Corsicana for almost forty years. She spent years researching the Ratliff family tree and developed more information about the family than anyone had done before. She conducted her research wherever she could, but she also benefited from memories, letters, and family records from her Aunt Bessie Grace Ratliff Causey, who also sent her old photos to preserve for the family.

Bessie's husband Jessie passed away on June 24, 1996. Bessie passed away on October 15, 2004. They were buried in Oakwood Cemetery in Corsicana.

Margaret Grace Ratliff

Margaret Grace Ratliff was born on December 25, 1924, in Corsicana, Texas. She married Frank Daniel Allen. He was called "Dan." He was born August 25, 1918, in Malakoff, Texas. They had a son, Frank Alton, born on November 20, 1946, and a daughter, Susie Irene, born in 1954. Margaret and Dan had four grandsons, one granddaughter, and four great-grandchildren.

Son Frank Alton married Karen Elaine Bolton on January 13, 1967. They had two sons: Frank Alton Jr. and Daniel Atwood Allen. Frank and Karen divorced on May 8, 1979. Frank married Sandra [Allen] on October 12, 1979. Frank Alton Allen Sr. died on May 11, 2010, in Dallas, Texas.

Daughter Susie married Edward (Eddie) L. Barber. Susie and Eddie divorced. Susie married Cecil Glynn Gracy. They later divorced. Susie has three children: Keith, Chad, and Misty.

Margaret's husband Dan was the owner/operator of Allen's Wholesale Meats for thirty-eight years. He served in the US Army Air Corps in WWII. He passed away on September 11, 1999. Margaret passed away two months later, on November 26, 1999. They were both buried at Oakwood Cemetery in Corsicana.

Tommie Jane Ratliff

Tommie Jane Ratliff was born in 1928 in Corsicana, Texas. Recalling her father, she spoke of his generosity to his children with both his time and material things that made childhood fun for all of his daughters. Tommie recalls the horses he bought for his daughters, as well as the red truck that she drove everywhere. When people saw that red truck, they knew it was Tommie.

Tommie riding Silver,
one of the family's horses, 1941

The red truck

Tommie's high school graduation photo

Tommie married Alton Atwood Allen on October 28, 1945. Atwood was born January 7, 1920, in Malakoff, Texas. He was the son of B.F. and Grace Irene Allen and the younger brother of Frank Daniel Allen, who married Tommie's older sister, Margaret Grace Ratliff.

Tommie and Atwood shortly after their marriage

Tommie and Atwood had two children: Gary Atwood Allen and Barbara Jane Allen.

Tommie, Atwood, Barbara, Gary

Barbara married Peter Sexton, and they had two sons and one daughter: Freddie Atwood, Gary Patrick, and Elizabeth Michelle. Barbara is presently married to J.C. Johnson. Her son Freddie married Suzanna, and daughter Elizabeth married James Young. Elizabeth and James had two sons: Aiden Gary and Colton Jason.

Tommie's husband, Atwood, was a foreman for forty years at the Oil City Iron Works in Corsicana. After a long illness he passed away at home with his family at the age of ninety on February 11, 2010. His nephew Tom Herrin, son of Tommie's older sister Bessie Herrin, officiated at the funeral. Atwood was buried at Oakwood Cemetery in Corsicana.

PART FOUR

THE SIBLINGS OF WILLIAM PINKNEY AND CORNELIA MITCHELL RATLIFF

1

THE SIBLINGS OF WILLIAM PINKNEY RATLIFF

William Pinkney Ratliff was the second child and oldest son of the ten children of Zachariah Lfonzo and Sarah Lucretia Adams Ratliff. Below is information about each of his siblings.

Early Attala County settlers 1887
Zachariah Lfonzo and Lucretia Adams Ratliff and their ten children

Top row, left to right, John Whitfield Ratliff, Louisa Matilda (Duck) Ratliff Hines, Dr. Rufus Winans Ratliff, Susanna Tatum (Sudie) Ratliff Gunter, Julia Permelia Ratliff Thompson, George Elfonzo Ratliff; *middle row, left to right,* Mary Jane Ratliff Wasson, Zachariah Lfonzo Ratliff, Sarah Lucretia Adams Ratliff, William Pinkney Ratliff; *front,* Sarah Elizabeth (Bettie) Ratliff, Zach Edmond Ratliff

Mary Jane Ratliff

Mary Jane Ratliff was born on August 2, 1845, in Leake County, Mississippi. She married Reverend Newton Copeland Wasson (born January 14, 1839, in Georgia) on September 7, 1865, in Attala County. They had eleven children, nine of whom lived to adulthood. Three of their sons became ministers. Newton passed away on November 25, 1886. Mary Jane died on October 10, 1938. Both were buried in Shady Grove Methodist Church Cemetery in Attala County.

Their eleven children:

Sally Andromeda Wasson (Moore, Crossley)*: Born November 1, 1866; died July 4, 1957.

Mary Eddie Wasson (Mitchell): Born January 17, 1868; died January 23, 1963.

Zachariah Alexander Wasson: Born February 5, 1870; died February 19, 1946.

Infant Daughter: Born and died December 10, 1871.

John Newton Wasson: Born November 6, 1872; died August 24, 1903.

Julia Matilda Wasson: Born April 25, 1875; died February 22, 1965.

Eliza Estelle Wasson (Harris): Born July 31, 1877; died June 21, 1969.

William Wasson: Born August 11, 1879; died August 22, 1879.

Rev. Lovick Pinkney Wasson: Born August 29, 1880; died December 29, 1973.

Rev. David Ratliff Wasson: Born May 1, 1883; died June 14, 1947.

Rev. James Carlisle Wasson: Born March 31, 1886; died November 14, 1966.

* Married name(s) in parentheses.

William Pinkney Ratliff

Born February 9, 1847: died May 10, 1927. See Part One for detailed information about his life, marriage and children.

Julia Permelia Ratliff

Julia Permelia Ratliff was born on December 3, 1848, in Leake County, Mississippi. She married George W. Thompson (born March 27, 1837, in Georgia) in 1885 in Attala County. They had one child, Lucius R. Thompson, born on March 3, 1887. Sadly, he passed away in 1897 at the age of ten. George died on October 14, 1905. Julia passed away on June 3, 1924. Julia, George, and son Lucius were buried at Springdale Cemetery, Attala County.

George Elfonzo Ratliff

George Elfonzo Ratliff was born on June 29, 1850, in Attala County. He married Elizabeth Exdothula "Exie" Noah (born on May 19, 1859, in Kosciusko, Attala County) about 1878. George and Exie had seven children together. Exie passed away on May 15, 1895. She was buried in Marvin Chapel Cemetery in Kosciusko.

George married Bessie Beatrice Lord (born on September 29, 1876, in Attala County) in 1896. They had three children together. Bessie passed away on January 30, 1912. She was buried in the Kosciusko City Cemetery. George passed away in 1921. He was buried next to his first wife, Exie, in Marvin Chapel Cemetery.

The seven children of George Elfonzo and Exie Noah Ratliff:

Zachariah Noah Ratliff: Born May 23, 1879; died November 29, 1925.

George Ernest Ratliff: Born November 23, 1880; died June 18, 1930.

William Lagrone Ratliff: Born April 21, 1882; died March 4, 1939.

Julius Everett Ratliff: Born February 14, 1884, died January 16, 1939.

Ruby Anola Ratliff (Comfort): Born February 9, 1887; died February 4, 1951.

Susan (Sudie) Kathryn Ratliff (Parcells): Born August 12, 1889; died April 22, 1976.

Esther Rebecca Ratliff (Sexton): Born February 1892; died January 26, 1963.

The three children of George Elfonzo and Bessie Beatrice Lord:

Newton L. Ratliff: Born July 16, 1898; died December 29, 1963.

Clay Lee Ratliff: Born November 5, 1900; died September 23, 1965.

Floy Kathleen Ratliff (Rush): Born August 25, 1902; died September 23, 1964.

Louisa Matilda (Duck) Ratliff

Louisa Matilda (Duck) Ratliff was born in Leake County, Mississippi, on November 19, 1852. On December 25, 1872, she married James Nathanial Hines (born January 25, 1852, in Greene County, Georgia). The couple had seven children, all born in Attala County.

Sometime before 1900, the family moved to Temple, Texas. James died on November 8, 1938, in Temple. Louisa passed away on July 9, 1942. They were buried in Hillcrest Cemetery in Temple.

Their seven children:

Kenneth Whitfield Hines: Born March 9, 1874; died January 13, 1929.

Ida Pearl Hines (Harrell): Born September 15, 1875; died June 7, 1963.

Ernest Earle Hines (Anderson): Born February 17, 1877; died December 14, 1972.

Sudie Bell Hines: Born September 1881; died April 25, 1908.

Zachariah Russell Hines: Born May 30, 1884; died October 13, 1948.

James Nathanial Hines: Born May 7, 1886; died September 28, 1950.

Hugh Fulton Ratliff

Hugh Fulton Ratliff was born on December 22, 1854, in Attala County. He died at the age of four on March 9, 1859, and was buried in Liberty Chapel Cemetery in Attala County.

John Whitfield Ratliff

John Whitfield Ratliff was born on April 19, 1857, in Attala County. He married Laura Turner (born in Mississippi on February 14, 1860) in 1879 in Attala County. They had eight children.

John passed away on October 22, 1924. Laura passed away on February 13, 1929. Both were buried in Springdale Cemetery.

Their eight children:

Hattie Sue Ratliff: Born October 31, 1880; died December 3, 1912.

William Turner Ratliff: Born December 1, 1882; died January 19, 1955.

Mary Ella Ratliff (Oakes): Born February 24, 1885; died July 14, 1967.

John Arthur Ratliff: Born July 12, 1887; died July 20, 1967.

Charles Douglas Ratliff: Born January 11, 1889; died December 29, 1954.

Leslie Ratliff (Ewing): Born April 1, 1892; died September 3, 1975.

Bessie Ratliff (Abernethy): Born July 15, 1894; died September 19, 1969.

Sally Kate Ratliff (Jamison): Born November 1900; died July 15, 2000.

Zachariah Edmond Ratliff

Zachariah Edmond Ratliff was born on August 22, 1859, in Attala County. He married Zenobia Lily "Zena" Crosby (born on June 18, 1872, in Mississippi) on March 14, 1900. They had four daughters—three lived into their nineties and one of the three lived to be 101.

Edmond died on October 26, 1951. He was buried in Springdale Cemetery. Zenobia passed away on May 10, 1952, in Leon County, Florida. She was buried next to Edmond in Springdale Cemetery.

Their four daughters:

Edna Willena Ratliff: Born January 15, 1901; died September 10, 1995.

Aileen Ratliff (Lee): Born February 5, 1905; died March 11, 1981.

Mary Lou Ratliff (Sanderson): Born May 23, 1903; died December 17, 1993.

Ruby Ratliff (Gamblin): Born November 3, 1907; died June 26, 2009.

Susanna Tatum (Sudie) Ratliff

Susanna Tatum (Sudie) Ratliff was born on September 19, 1861, in Attala County. On December 11, 1884, Sudie married Alexander Gallasby Gunter (born in March of 1859 in Attala County). They had three children: James, born in 1886, Stacy, born in 1889, and George, born in 1894. There are no records for James, who seems to have died as a child.

Sudie died on September 19, 1896, at the age of thirty-five. She was buried in Springdale Cemetery. Sudie's older sister Julia Permelia Ratliff Thompson and her husband, George, took over the raising of Sudie's daughter Stacy. Son George initially lived with his grandparents Zachariah Lfonzo and Sara Lucretia Adams Ratliff but later joined his sister Stacy at his Aunt Julia's.

The widower Alexander Gallasby Gunter moved to Prairie, Arkansas, where he is believed to have passed away in 1900 at the age of forty-one. His date of death and place of burial are unknown.

Sudie and Alexander's three children:

James Gunter: Born 1886. No other information.

Stacy Gunter (Woods): Born August 16, 1889; died July 30, 1992.

George A. Gunter: Born March 3, 1894; died December 1978.

Dr. Rufus Winans Ratliff

Dr. Rufus Winans Ratliff was born in Attala County on December 1, 1863. In 1891, he married Ida Roberts (born in Mississippi in June 1870). They had one child, Rufus Winans Ratliff Jr., born on August 12, 1902, in Arkansas.

Ida Roberts Ratliff seems to have passed away in 1938, though no record can be found. In 1939, Rufus married Lovie C. Turner (born in Kentucky on September 13, 1892). Rufus died on June 23, 1942, in

Jonesboro, Arkansas. Lovie lived another thirty-two years and passed away on September 5, 1974, in Memphis, Tennessee. Both Rufus and Lovie were buried in City Cemetery, Jonesboro, Arkansas.

Rufus Jr. married Margaret Deering Dismukes Trull, born on July 27, 1889. Margaret passed away on May 11, 1980. Rufus Jr. passed away two months later on July 8, 1980, in Durham, North Carolina. They were both buried in St. Matthews Episcopal Church Cemetery in Hillsborough, North Carolina.

Sarah Elizabeth (Bettie) Ratliff

Sarah Elizabeth (Bettie) Ratliff, the youngest of Z.L. and Sarah Lucretia Adams Ratliff's eleven children, was born in Attala County on August 25, 1868. She was a respected and beloved public school teacher much of her adult life. She never married. As was the practice of the time, as an unmarried woman she lived with her parents until their death in 1905–1906. She then moved in with her sister Julia Permelia Ratliff Thompson and lived with her and her family until Julia's death in 1924.

Sometime before 1935, she bought a house on Fairgrounds Road in Kosciusko. In 1939, when she attended the reunion of the extended family of her oldest brother William Pinkney and his wife Cornelia on Bettie's nephew Zack Mitchell Ratliff's farm, she was one of only three children of Z.L. and Sarah who were still living. Bettie passed away twenty years later, on November 19, 1959, at the age of ninety-one. She was buried in Springdale Cemetery.

2

THE SIBLINGS OF CORNELIA MITCHELL

As mentioned earlier, Cornelia Mitchell was the youngest of the eight children of Albert Washington and Susan Cone Mitchell. Below is information about each of her siblings.

Whitman William Mitchell

Whitman William Mitchell was born in Georgia about 1833. He married Alice Jane Davis about 1859. They had a daughter, Eulah Davis Mitchell, born on July 19, 1860. Whitman joined the Confederate army at the outbreak of the Civil War. He was killed on December 31, 1862, at the Battle at Murfreesboro, Tennessee.[1]

His widow, Alice, married David Lewis Brown, a widower with two daughters. Whitman and Alice's daughter, Eulah, married William Smith Adams on December 16, 1885. Between 1887 and 1896, Eulah and William had five children, all born in Attala County.

David Lewis Brown passed away on August 6, 1903. Alice Davis Mitchell Brown died on December 8, 1907. Both were buried at Shady Grove Methodist Cemetery.

---

[1] Joe and Lavon Ashley, *The Civil War Record and Diary of Captain William V. Davis, 30th Mississippi Infantry, C.S.A - "Oh for Dixie"* (Colorado Springs: Standing Pine Press, 2001). Thanks to Joe and Lavon Ashley for permission to use this information from their book.

Daughter Eulah died on September 2, 1937. Her husband, William, died on December 8, 1953. Both were also buried at Shady Grove Methodist Cemetery.

George Fellows Mitchell

George Fellows Mitchell was born in Georgia in March of 1835. He married Nancy Merritt Davis (born in 1835 in Holmes County, Mississippi) in 1862. He served in the Confederate army during the Civil War.[2] George and Nancy had three children. George died on October 24, 1914. Nancy passed away in 1917. Both were buried at Shady Grove Methodist Cemetery.

Their three children:

James Walter Mitchell: Born September 16, 1866; died Nov. 28, 1943.

Mary Sue Mitchell (Adams): Born February 1872; died April 3, 1910.

John Frank Mitchell: Born September 30, 1873; died June 24, 1910.

Lucy Ann Mitchell

Lucy Ann Mitchell was born in Georgia on August 12, 1837. She married James Riley Duncan (born in Georgia on February 18, 1835) about 1856. They had four children.

James joined the Confederate army in the Civil War. He was captured by Union forces and died of illness in Rock Island County, Illinois, on February 12, 1864.[3] He was buried in the Rock Island Confederate Cemetery in Rock Island, Illinois.

Left a widow with four children, Lucy married Thomas Adam Gallaway in 1867 (born on June 12, 1834, in Warren County, Mississippi). Thomas also served in the Confederate army during the Civil War. Lucy and Thomas had four children. Thomas died on August 29, 1897. Lucy passed away on October 28, 1918. Both were buried at Shady Grove Methodist Cemetery.

---

2 Ibid.
3 Selected Records of the War Department Relating to Confederate Prisoners of War, 1861-1865, Roll: 598_10, National Archives Microfilm Series (M1303, M598, M2702, and M918).

The children of Lucy Mitchell and James Duncan:

Ida A. Duncan: Born January 7, 1858; died December 31, 1945.

Henrietta Duncan: Born January 26, 1860; died October 5, 1875.

Susan Louella Duncan (Pender): Born February 28, 1862; died July 12, 1959.

Albert Ross Duncan: Born November 15, 1863; died December 25, 1942.

The children of Lucy Mitchell and Thomas Gallaway:

Tallulah Walton Gallaway (Ricketts): Born January 25, 1868; died October 12, 1941.

Robert Lee Gallaway: Born June 4, 1869; died September 30, 1875.

Thomas George Gallaway: Born July 29, 1873; died August 15, 1909.

William Franklin Gallaway: Born October 12, 1876; died March 26, 1943.

John A. Mitchell

John A. Mitchell was born on June 14, 1840, in Georgia. He died in Attala County at the age of only nineteen on June 30, 1859. He was buried at Liberty Chapel Cemetery.

Albert Pierce Mitchell

Albert Pierce Mitchell was born in 1844 in Georgia. He was wounded in the Civil War, fighting for Confederate forces, and was later a prisoner of war.[4] He married Frances Hines (born on December 28, 1841, in Greene County, Georgia) sometime after the Civil War ended. They had one child, Leona Mitchell, born on May 1, 1868, in Kosciusko. Albert seems to have passed away a few years later. The date and place of his death and burial have not been found.

His widow Frances Hines Mitchell married Frank M. Harper (born on February 4, 1836, in Mississippi) on August 6, 1874. Harper served with the Confederate forces during the Civil War. Based on the 1880 census,

---

4   Ashley.

Harper was probably a widower, with a daughter named M.E. Harper, born in 1866. Frances and Frank had two daughters together.

Frances Hines Mitchell Harper passed away on July 6, 1902. Husband Frank died on August 20, 1924. Both Frances and Frank were buried in the Kosciusko City Cemetery. Albert Pierce Mitchell and Frances Hines's daughter Leona Mitchell married William Ransom Wilson on December 16, 1885. They had eight children. Leona died on March 31, 1930.

Benjamin Franklin Mitchell

Benjamin Franklin Mitchell was born in 1846 in Georgia. He joined the Confederate forces and was killed in the Atlanta, Georgia, area in August 1864 at the age of eighteen.[5] His burial site is unknown.

Charles Robert Mitchell

Charles Robert Mitchell was born in 1848 in Georgia. He married Permelie Ann Elizabeth Britt (born in Mississippi on March 4, 1851) about 1872. They had four children. Charles is said to have been killed in 1895 while hunting bear in Sunflower County, Mississippi. His burial place is unknown. Permelie passed away on November 5, 1911, and was buried in the New Hope Church Cemetery in Gravel Hill, Carroll County, Mississippi. Her son Archie Clay Mitchell was buried in the same cemetery, so it is likely that she had moved to Carroll County to be near her son and his family.

The children of Charles Mitchell and Permelie Ann Elizabeth Britt:

Malcolm Mitchell: Born about 1873; died (unknown).

Eula Kate Mitchell (Bush): Born August 11, 1875; died October 25, 1929.

Archie Clay Mitchell: Born July 23, 1877; died December 22, 1948.

John H. Mitchell: Born December 19, 1879; died June 4, 1969.

Cornelia Mitchell

Born October 11, 1851: died June 18, 1942. See Part Two for detailed information about her life, marriage and children.

---

5   Ibid.

EPILOGUE

Although the last surviving child of William Pinkney and Cornelia Mitchell Ratliff died in 1988, the story goes on. Seven of their eleven children have living descendants who are at this very moment living the future history of the *William Pinkney Ratliff Family Saga*. In addition, there are hundreds of descendants of the siblings of W.P and Cornelia.

It is hoped that this book will help each one of those descendants and the descendants' descendants know the lives and legacies of their Ratliff and Mitchell ancestors.

APPENDICES

APPENDIX ONE

WILLIAM PINKNEY RATLIFF, WRITING IN THE *ALLIANCE VINDICATOR* JULY 14, 1891

"RATLIFF'S ATTEMPT TO REPLY TO THE NINE QUESTIONS"

In replying to Bro. J.H. Wallace, who signed his name "An Alliance Man," I wish to say to Bro. Wallace, you need not try to hide behind a fictitious name, for if you are after information along that line I will cheerfully give it to you, so I take up your questions as they are expounded.

1st. No, I bought my bagging in July before the bagging fight began, and my neighbors instructed me to buy for them, which I did and wrapped their cotton at cost which I have done for years, and at less than they could buy themselves. Charged my father and brothers just the same I did the poorest colored man in the country.

2nd. It would be presumption in me to say I was a true Alliance man. I will let my Alliance answer that. However I would say, they have elected me three times President of Springdale Alliance, and I have always had an official position in the Alliance. That speaks louder for me than any words of self praise I could offer.

And as to the desertion of my calling, you are reckoning without your host. I preached to an appreciative audience last Sunday and expect to fill an appointment at Forest on next Sunday; and as for the slum and mud in politics you are right. I let my political bucket down too deep when I went after some of these candidates. I brought up mud slime, vipers, and hideous reptiles, and creeping things of the earth; in fact Brother Wallace, our political wells need cleaning out. They will create contagious diseases and cause an epidemic among the candidates before the end of the next month. Then Brother Wallace, they don't like for these old pits to be uncovered, people smell the stench and hunt it up and remove (them). Then those preachers have read so much in the Bible about crime, they are watching everything they see or hear. You know Judas sold his master for thirty pieces of silver; and Uriah had a good wife and David wanted her, and he had Uriah killed so he might get his wife. Then Delilah made as though she loved Samson, and she married him and nursed him to sleep in her arms, and the Philistines put his eyes out, then she was happy. Bro. Wallace, don't you let the Philistines dandle you on their knees--the first thing you know they will have their fingers in your eyes. Don't you know Christ said "Woe unto ye Scribes (editors), Pharisees, hypocrites! Woe unto ye lawyers for ye bind heavy burdens and grievous to be born upon men's shoulders and will not touch them with one of your fingers."

3rd. and 4th. I am a Jeffersonian Democrat. I believe in a government of the people, by the people and for the people. [some lines illegible]... was for their interest, I would do it and let the responsibility rest where I belonged. To do otherwise would be saying the people are fools; they don't know what they want. I believe Representatives ought to be servants of the people and not their masters. I have confidence in the honesty of the people. If they had the money they would pay every cent they owe, hence I never press a man for what he owes me, and I can prove that by you Bro. Wallace, for when I sold you that lumber to build your room, although it has been six or seven years ago, I have never dunned you for it. You know you offered to pay for it in corn once, but I told you that you needed the corn and I would not take it. I know if you ever get able to pay it you will do it. If you and I could get a fair price for what we make we would have been

APPENDIX ONE

out of debt long ago. And as to voting against our Democratic nominees, I would tell you that the charge you heard was some of their campaign lies; if it is was not for my modesty, you know when a preacher gets into politics he must not tell the truth on people all the time, the truth hurts – they can't stand the truth. Who was it that said it was the hit dog that hollers?

5th. I would not do either for it's all sold and gone to pay credit and then I didn't have enough to pay my debts. We did not save out any spinning cotton. They found that out though, and so when it went to the warehouse they picked out enough to last several years for table use, and they were very kind, they did not charge us anything for picking it out, and they just took the cotton and knocked it off of the bale. Did you ever see a woman fix up her children to go visiting? You know it would not do to send that cotton over to Europe until they took off its dirty clothes and dried it.

6th. We never have any trouble along that line. Frequently it don't take 80 per cent to pay their debts, but if we can't get some relief somewhere and get a better price than they pay, (then even) 100 per cent won't pay the bills.

7th. No. He has been a true friend to the farmer. But he has made a mistake, and no doubt his prayer is—if I can get forgiveness for this, I'll never do so again. He tackled a bigger thing than he bargained for. He needs help to turn it loose. Then we think it is undemocratic to disregard the wishes of his constituents. He ought to have treated us respectfully; and when our leaders went to Washington to discuss our bill instead of giving them thirty minutes to discuss the sub-treasury bill[1] and then telling them to retire, they should have had one whole day if necessary.

8th. I did my duty precisely as the law directed. The Legislature of 1876 said the salary of the Assessor was too low; but they wanted to pare expenses, so instead of increasing his salary, they passed a law for the people to meet the Assessor and give in their taxes, and provided for the Assessor to go and see those that did not come and said the Assessor should charge up seventy five cents extra on the books, and the Sheriff should collect and pay the Assessor the same. In 1878, the Legislature repealed the law and

---

1 The bill to establish federal warehouses for cotton farmers.

increased the Assessor's salary, and said, you go to the people's houses and assess them.

9th. I will just refer you to the men who work my land. They are honorable gentlemen, and will tell you the truth. Bro. Fosse tackled one of them the other day, just ask him how it is he can answer better than I can. They are Ratliff men, dyed in the wool—all wool and a yard wide.

Now Bro. Wallace, I would give you a "skull cracker" if I thought you concocted those questions, but I am certain you did not; it don't sound like you. Now you look out, you are too clever a fellow to be made a tool of. If these editors want to slander anybody let them come out over their own signature. They are doing their best to down our noble order; they claim they are in favor of equal justice to all. But that is not true. Now I will tell you a secret if you will promise not to tell it. Did you know they charged all the sub-treasury candidates for their announcement in their papers, and published the Hon. D. T. Guyton's free of charge? Now it wouldn't do for this to get out for they would say we were slandering them; and if they admitted it was true and said there was nothing wrong in that they would want us to prove it. Now Bro. Wallace, I won't let my bucket any deeper in the political well just now. I want this to soak in. Did anybody ever hear of a preacher in politics? Gentlemen, let me know when you run dry.

Respectively,
W.P. Ratliff
July 14th, 1891[2]

---

2   Typed from a copy of the original by Ed Ratliff.

APPENDIX TWO

WILLIAM PINKNEY RATLIFF, WRITING IN THE *ALLIANCE VINDICATOR* SOMETIME AFTER JULY 14, 1891

"RATLIFF PUT ON ANOTHER BLISTER"

The Star put me upon the witness stand, and puts me on oath, to answer some questions this week, but refuses me space in its columns unless it is in the way of retraction or it suits them after they read it, so I write this especially for the Vindicator.

They say I transcended the bounds of propriety and truth last week, in my articles. As to propriety, perhaps it was not proper to tell an editor of his shortcomings, for Mr. Haden said lying was a prerogative... [illegible]...And if he is correct in that, it might be well to allow them unlimited latitude along other lines as well. Now as to transcending the bounds of truth, we will give the facts to the public and let the people say who told the truth. I wrote the answer to Mr. Wallace on the 10th, and dated it accordingly. It was set up in the Vindicator office and a proof carried to the Star office. The editor read it, and showed me the ledger, where Guyton was charged with the announcement. So when I answered Guyton's piece three days later, I stated in plain English, this question: Why did you tell your announcement did not cost you anything? For I see the Star has you charged with the announcement and the Messenger expects you to pay him; thus throwing the responsibility on Mr. Guyton. And all this in the same issue of the Star. Then they say, they came to me and gave me an opportunity to withdraw the charge before it went into print. But I say, there never was a word uttered about such withdrawal between us, and no one knows it better than the editors of that paper. Of course they were not under oath. Then another strange thing is why they changed the date to my article. My article to Wallace was set up in the VINDICATOR office and a proof furnished them, and my answer to Guyton was set up in the Star office and furnished to the VINDICATOR. THE VINDICATOR has it correct, why not the Star? I called on them, and they could not explain.

Then you say my charge about your trying to (put) down the Alliance, is false. Here we differ again: perhaps we had better go to the record and see who is telling the truth. If you were not making a fight with the Alliance, what does this editorial in the Star, on the…[illegible]…(?)

"A strong effort will be made by the Alliance in this State to elect a sub-treasury Legislature. If they are victorious, consistency and justice seem to point out that Barksdale and Burkins should be their candidates for U.S… [illegible].

In view of such a situation it behooves all straight-out Democrats who are honestly opposed to the sub-treasury measure to come out and fight for their convictions. Let the issue be strictly drawn and squarely fought and the opposers of the scheme will win."

May the 29th, the Star says: "Why does the Alliance propose to displace a true and tried servant of the people who is a practical farmer and whose interests are identical with the people; especially why does the Alliance propose to displace him by putting in his place one who is not a practical farmer? – and yet the Farmers Alliance proposes to put out a farmer for the purpose of reviling the farmers."

Now I would like you would be either a bird or a beast. Quit blowing hot and cold out of the same mouth. You said on the 24th of April, "Let the issue be strictly drawn and squarely fought." You have made the issue and have been fighting it out on the line marked cut above. Yet you say you are dependent on the men who compose the Alliance for support; and they are the bone and sinew of the land. Well, if that is your dependence, perhaps you had better be making friends of the mammon of unrighteousness, then when you fail they may receive you into their habitations.

Then again, you say as to the boycotting proposition and the exposing of my record, you let the matter drop. Is this one of your prerogatives or do you mean to let the matter…[illegible]…your columns over the signature of [illegible] Allianceman?" The very identical charges you threatened are in the questions. Now if you don't mind [illegible] bottom will be out of the Chancery Clerk's office, and you will drop down into the cellar among the rubbish; take care young man.

What about that prayer? Do you think if the Lord was going to deliver you from charity he could bring into requisition all his omnipotence and cause the sun to stand still while [illegible] unwrought a wonderful miracle in the land? Or do you suppose He would say, "Oh well that's a small job. I'll just [illegible] that over to you, boys; answer your own prayer, you won't have to go [illegible]." It's all right for Mr. Wallace to delve into my private affairs; but if I bring him upon the stand to answer his own questions, I am very uncharitable. It makes a great deal of difference as to whose ox is getting gored…You were very charitable in giving me space in your columns. You invited discussion and published charges against and said your columns are open to Ratliff for [illegible].

The Doctors are not agreed on this case. You say I realized the weakness of my cause and that public sentiment was against me, and I wanted to shift the battlefield. Others say we are in favor of the sub-treasury scheme because it is popular and we want to get into office; who is right?

You say in conclusion, that it is difficult to see that I am a Democrat. Now there is one thing you boys will learn later on; and that is, your being unable to see a thing, don't change the facts. The fellow who did not believe the world was round was honest in it, but [illegible]. He said if it turned over every twenty four, that rock would fall off that stump. But she continued to revolve on her axis. So you see we may be ignorant about a thing and it don't change the facts. If what I knew and what I don't know was put in a book it would be a whopper.

Now boys, if you were farmers, I would just take you across my knees and I would spank you—well, I'd fairly blister you. That could be done on a farmer, but these people who are fighting the sub-treasury—well they sit down so much they are tough, right? Spanking would just make them mad; as I will just pat you on the head and dandle you on my knee, and say: now boys look around on the world and take in the situation. It may be that all the charity and all the brains and all the patriotism are not found in the towns. It may be fun for you to ridicule the old farmers and call them "red necks" and "Hillbillies" but sir, like Belshazzar of old, when he was reveling with his lords, the hand-writing was being traced on the wall: "Thou art weighed in the balance and found wanting."[1]

Respectively,
W.P. Ratliff

---

1   Book of Daniel, Old Testament.

APPENDIX THREE

AN EDITORIAL IN SUPPORT OF WILLIAM PINKNEY RATLIFF AND THE SUB-TREASURY PLAN

PROBABLY W.P. RATLIFF IN THE *ALLIANCE VINDICATOR*, SOMETIME AFTER JULY 14, 1891

"WHO COMMENCED IT?"

We are very sorry to see the excitement that now seems imminent before the termination of the present political campaign now going on in this county.

For some weeks past a hot correspondence has been carried on, through the columns of the town papers, between Hon. D.T. Guyton and W.P. Ratliff. Mr. Guyton opposing the Sub-treasury and Mr. Ratliff favoring. Mr. Guyton in his first article, said that he could not see how any Christian could indorse the Sub-treasury, a slur as it seemed at Mr. Ratliff. In our mind it seems very fair and just that Mr. Ratliff should answer this charge, for his honest convictions led him to believe this scheme to be a just and honorable measure; and hence of course he would be expected to defend his honest convictions. But it seems that Mr. Ratliff defended this unjust and uncalled for attack upon the Christian people who favored the Sub-treasury so well that Mr. Guyton must hunt up someone to help keep back the foe; and in the next issue, his reinforcement came out in full force, with some very hard questions over the signature of "Alliance Man." Mr. Ratliff again came to the front and answered every question exactly as propounded to him. His answers were perfectly satisfactory to all unprejudiced minds of the best thinking people of the country; but alas! This was not enough. He must be attacked editorially as having "transcended the bounds of propriety and truth" and that he had "insulted others and disgraced himself."

Now we call upon the good intelligent thinking people of Attala county to pass judgment as to whether or not Mr. Ratliff has ever insulted any one? He is well known throughout the country; his honesty is unquestioned, and his character irreproachable. Christian, have you ever suspected this man to be a traitor and insulter of others, as he is accused? Farmers of Attala, have you ever found in this man, your valiant leader, anything that is mean, low down, unjust and disgraceful? We hear the voice of many, coming up from the four corners of the county, crying NO! NO! a thousand times no.

He is also accused of being an "Artful Dodger." Yes, he is such an artful dodger of those who would seek unjustly to down him that his political enemies have resorted to slander in its worst stage, in the grasping and gaping hope that they might vindicate themselves.

Resolved by Salem Alliance

Resolved by Salem Alliance No. 9: That we condemn the Kosciusko Messenger for its unjust criticism and utterances against the Alliance, as unwarranted; and we think it comes with poor grace from a man that is supported largely by our membership, we therefore discontinue the Messenger and earnestly request the co-operation of every Sub-Alliance in the county.

J.M. Sandridge, Pres.

W.B. Lee, Secty.

Resolved, that we endorse and approve the Sub Treasury bill now pending before the Congress of the United States of America, believing as we do that by this measure or its equivalent we can be freed from the shackles of the moneyed shylocks and plutocrats who are striving to impoverish and degrade the farmers of our county.

Resolved second, that this Alliance condemn the course pursued by Bro. Guyton as unpatriotic, as he has the reputation of being the leader of the Alliance in the county; we ask the aid of all true Alliancemen in the county to help us stamp it as a falsehood.

J.M. Sandridge, Pres

W.B. Lee, Secty

The above resolutions were passed by Salem Alliance, and were sent to us with a special request to be published.

LOOK OUT

Never, in the history of politics, have there been more spurious counterfeit party platform planks than will now appear in the old party platforms. Each old party platform will contain planks that will be nicely engraved and stereotyped in imitation of certain planks in the People's party platform. Already the Ohio Republican platform has one in it, nicely engraved, "opposition to trusts and combines." So you see each old party will attempt to fill the country with a circulating medium of counterfeit platform planks, hoping that by doing so they can get a new grip on the people, and thereby check the mighty hosts of people that are moving into Washington. Friends of reform, be on the lookout for the aforesaid counterfeit planks. They will be like all the other counterfeits – no good. Accept no party plank for your vote that is not engrafted in the people's party platform, approved, signed and countersigned by the People's national political party of the United States. –

Kansas Agitator.

APPENDIX FOUR

EDITORIAL IN THE *MERIDIAN MISSISSIPPI NEWS* ADVOCATING A POLICY OF REFUSAL TO PUBLISH INFLAMMATORY ATTACKS

REPRINT IN THE *MEMPHIS APPEAL-AVALANCHE* (SOMETIME AFTER MARCH 3, 1894)

"EDITORIAL RESPONSIBLITY"

The Meridian, Miss. News says:

The terrible tragedy at Kosciusko Saturday last was the direct result of a pernicious custom that has prevailed all too long, especially in the South, of making newspapers the vehicle of offensive personalities. It is the fruit of publishing cards reflecting upon the character and reputation of citizens, and whatever may have been the nature of the quarrel between Ratcliff *(sic)* and Jackson, it is safe to say that had it been kept out of the newspapers, two men now dead would today be living and a third strong and well, instead of lingering between life and death from a bullet wound. Had the parties to this quarrel met each other on the streets and exchanged the same epithets and offensive language as was printed, a fight, in all probability, would have ensued, but the chances are that neither would have been armed and the difficulty would have been settled without bloodshed. A few blows on either side would have vindicated the honor and courage of each and the interposition of friends would have done the rest. But the moment that a man prints an insulting card he puts his gun in his pocket and goes hunting for trouble. It is tantamount to a public challenge to his enemy and a warning to him to prepare for a fight, and it is superfluous to say that this challenge in Mississippi is nearly always accepted. Nor is the party who signs such a card alone responsible. The newspaper that prints it is *particeps criminis* in any serious consequences that may ensue, and cannot escape its share of moral accountability. But for its cooperation, the deed could not be done, and everybody knows that the lie given in print is different from that delivered individually, inasmuch as it is almost impossible to make retraction or apology except through the same medium of insult, and this few men will consent to do. *The News* long ago adopted a rule to refuse publication, under any and all circumstances, to this class of cards. We have repeatedly said that nothing should appear in these columns that might induce a personal difficulty between citizens and the awful tragedy at Kosciusko only affords another confirmation of the wisdom of this policy.

APPENDIX FOUR

We reprint this article, which is exactly in line with the Appeal-Avalanche's comment of last Monday, because we would assist in its circulation. The editor of the *News* has an accurate idea of editorial responsibility. No editor has the right to allow any man or any set of men to denounce any other man or any set of men in the columns of his paper, signature or no signature. In behalf of all self-respecting journalists, the Appeal-Avalanche thanks the News for its article.

APPENDIX FIVE

DUELING NEWSPAPER ARTICLES BETWEEN W.P. RATLIFF AND SAM JACKSON

LATE FEBRUARY 1894

W.P. RATLIFF IN THE *ALLIANCE VINDICATOR*, RESPONDING TO SAM JACKSON'S STATEMENT IN THE *KOSCIUSKO STAR* CALLING RATLIFF A LIAR

A STATEMENT - Mr. S.A. Jackson says we misrepresented him when we said he voted for Col. Nugent in the caucus. If it is any gratification to Mr. Jackson we will say he voted for Col. Nugent in the joint convention. He may have voted for him in the caucus; nobody knows for that was by secret ballot. What we said about the incident was in a spirit of levity, but Mr. Jackson seems to make something else out of it.

We will now give him the opportunity by emphasizing that he has the distinction of being the only Democrat who voted for a Populist for United States Senator. We reiterate every statement in our last week's article save that it all happened in the joint convention instead of the caucus, which fact only places him in a more ridiculous attitude. If there is any consolation in this correction to Mr. Jackson, he is welcome to it, but lest he should think it is subject to comment we will now call the previous question on the whole concern.

(Signed)   W.P. RATLIFF[1]

---

1   *Alliance Vindicator*, late February 1894.

APPENDIX FIVE

SAM JACKSON'S PAID RESPONSE IN THE *KOSCIUSKO STAR* TO RATLIFF'S STATEMENT ABOVE

When Andrew Jackson was president he appointed in this state one John Smith as Indian agent. John Smith was detected in some crookedness by the lamented Greenwood Leflore,[2] who preferred charges before the administration without avail. The chief, not satisfied, went on to Washington and confronted the president, when this colloquy ensued:

> 'I, Andrew Jackson, president of the United States, know Mr. Smith to be an honest man.'

The chief drew himself up to his full height and with his keen-searching black eyes steadily fixed on the old hero, said:

> 'I, Greenwood Leflore, chief of the Choctaw Nation, know Mr. Smith to be a damned rascal.'

It is unnecessary to say that the previous was lost and Mr. Smith was removed.

In citing the above history I will add an amendment to be future history in Attala County, to wit:

> 'I, W.P. Ratliff, Populite representative from Attala County in the Mississippi legislature, emphasize that S.A. Jackson, Democratic representative from Attala County in the Mississippi legislature, voted for a Populite for the United States senate.'

> 'I, S. A. Jackson, Democratic representative of Attala County in the Mississippi legislature, emphasize that W.P. Ratliff,

---

[2] Principal chief of the Choctaw Nation.

Populite representative from Attala County, is an infernal damned liar.'

As to the previous question on this amendment, Ratliff can make any move he desires.

(Signed) S.A. Jackson[3]

---

[3] *Kosciusko Star*, late February 1894.

APPENDIX SIX

LETTER OF RESPONSE TO W.P. RATLIFF FROM COL. WILLIAM LEWIS NUGENT

FEBRUARY 26, 1894[1]

Jackson, Miss., Feb. 26, 1894
Hon. W.P. Ratliff, Kosciusko, Miss.:

Dear Sir:—I am in receipt, on my return from the seacoast, of your letter of the 24th, and have carefully read it. As understood by me, the vote of Mr. Jackson was wholly accidental and complimentary, and was given to further the resolution of the caucus, not to elect anyone in the joint session of the Legislature. In consequence I regret it should be made the basis of the article in your paper and thus give rise to a controversy so unpleasant between you and him. I am not a politician and have no aspiration for public office. I view economic questions from a comparatively

---

1   Reprinted in the *Kosciusko Star*, probably late February or early March 1894.

NON-PARTISAN STANDPOINT

but in doing thus I have never swerved in my allegiance to the Democratic party, nor have I ever voted any other ticket, State or national.

I am, as the phrase goes, a "Cleveland Democrat, [words missing]" to the free and unlimited coinage of silver with unlimited legal tender capacity. That being the shibboleth of the People's party or the Populites, the gulf between me and that party is impassable. I am a bimetalist, but until the question is settled by a monetary congress, would only agree to the free coinage of silver dollars on the condition that they should be limited as a legal tender to a single debt of $100 or under. In my humble judgment any economic or practical reforms in the doctrines or policy of the Democratic party ought to be worked out in party lines, and this has always been my course in the private ranks.

I have never sulked because I could not control. The *Clarion* letter, to which you kindly refer, according to my recollection, was a discussion or criticism of the Stanford loan scheme as to its constitutionality and expediency. In that letter I pointed out objections that could be obviated, and it is but just to say that those judgments could be relieved, personally and within my the lines of my party, I would favor the measure. It is true that I am in sympathy with the farmers of the country, who constitute its bone and sinew, but it is not true that I endorse my brother's views[2]. Indeed, I regretted to see him leave the party when his influence was so great as to justify the conclusion that he might have modified its points on economic questions.

---

2 Thomas Lewis Nugent, who was the Populist Party candidate for governor of Texas in 1892.

APPENDIX SIX

I must express my regrets again that any misunderstanding between you and Mr. Jackson touching the trivial circumstances of the vote cast by him for me in the late joint session of the Legislature.

Yours truly,

W.L. Nugent

APPENDIX SEVEN

THE ANCESTORS OF WILLIAM PINKNEY RATLIFF

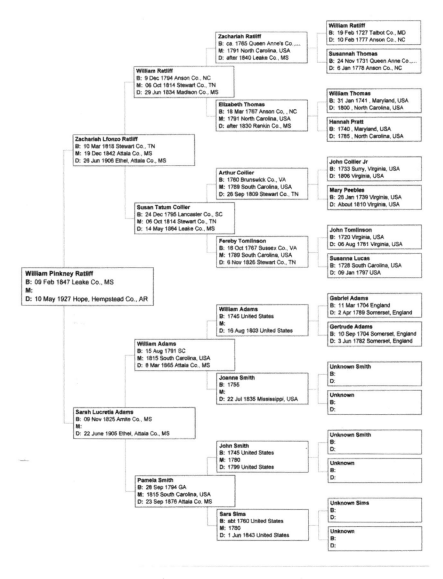

(continued on next page)

THE WILLIAM PINKNEY RATLIFF FAMILY SAGA 1847-1988

THE ANCESTORS OF
WILLIAM PINKNEY RATLIFF
(CONTINUING WITH WILLIAM RATLIFF'S
WIFE SUSANNAH THOMAS)

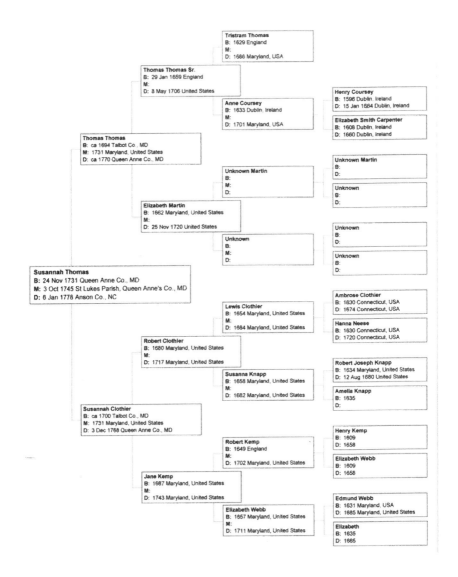

APPENDIX EIGHT

THE ANCESTORS OF CORNELIA MITCHELL

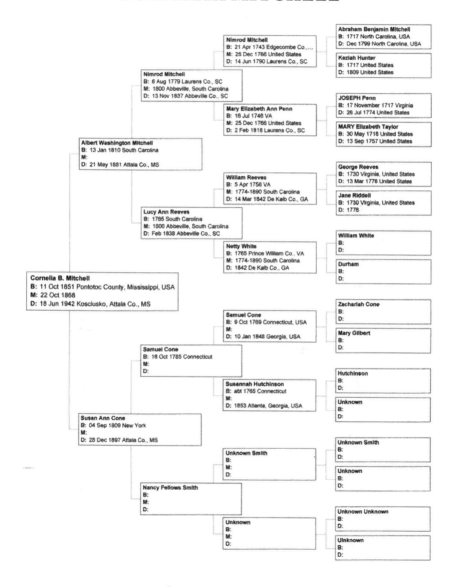

(continued on next page)

THE WILLIAM PINKNEY RATLIFF FAMILY SAGA 1847-1988

THE ANCESTORS OF CORNELIA MITCHELL (CONTINUING WITH ABRAHAM BENJAMIN MITCHELL)

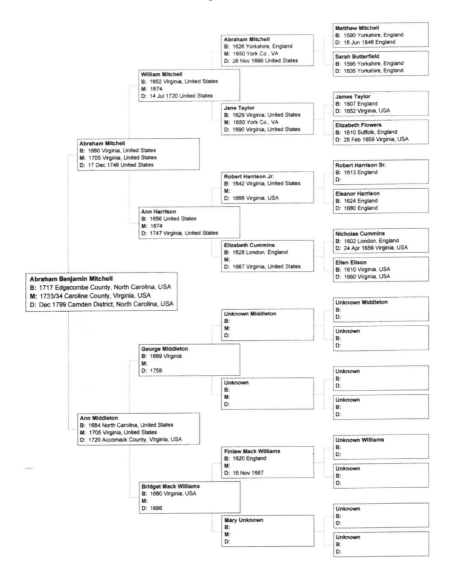

BIBLIOGRAPHY

PUBLISHED SOURCES

Ashley, Joe and Lavon. *The Civil War Record and Diary of Captain William V. Davis, 30th Mississippi Infantry, C.S.A - "Oh for Dixie."* Colorado Springs: Standing Pine Press, 2001.

Biographical and Historical Memoirs of Mississippi. Chicago: The Goodspeed Publishing Company, 1891.

Brien, Barbara Gail Russell and Bill Gary Russell. *The Russell and May Family History.* Greenville, Mississippi: BGR Brien, 1997. Out of print.

Carson, Betty J. Ratliff and Howard S. Hazlewood. *The William Ratcliff/ Ratliff Family of Maryland and Anson County, North Carolina.* Sun Valley, Arizona, 1989.

Cresswell, Stephen. *Multi-Party Politics in Mississippi 1877-1902.* Oxford, Mississippi: University Press of Mississippi, 1995.

Gillmore, Inez Haynes. *The Story of the Woman's Party.* New York: Harcourt, Brace, and Company, 1921.

Hemphill, Marie M. *Fevers, Floods, and Faith – A History of Sunflower County: 1844-1976*. Indianola, Mississippi, 1980.

Hymns and Their Authors. London: Hodder and Stoughton, 1902.

Kosciusko-Attala Historical Society, *Kosciusko-Attala History.* Walsworth Publishing Company, 1976.

"Meet a Pro." *Bankers Life and Casualty Company internal newsletter.* Portland, Oregon: Bankers Life and Casualty, 1984-1985.

Moss, Bobby G. *Roster of South Carolina Patriots in the American Revolution.* Baltimore, Maryland: Genealogical Publishing Company, 1983.

Ratliff, Beulah Amidon. *Charles Fremont Amidon 1856-1937.* January 1, 1941. Out of print.

Smemo, Kenneth. *Against the Tide: The Life and Times of Federal Judge Charles F. Amidon, North Dakota Progressive.* Garland Publishing, Inc., 1986. Out of print.

Walton, Mary. *A Woman's Crusade - Alice Paul and the Battle for the Ballot.* Palgrave Macmillan, 2010.

UNPUBLISHED SOURCES

Trippett, Bernard L. *The Jackson-Ratliff Duel: A Memoir of Family History* (unpublished manuscript, 1991).

OFFICIAL RECORDS

American Civil War Soldiers, Historical Data Systems of Kingston, MA, comp. [database on-line]. Provo, UT, USA: Ancestry.com Operations Inc, 1999.

BIBLIOGRAPHY

British War Office: Service Medal and Award Rolls Index.

California Death Index 1940-1997.

Census of the State of Florida, 1945; (Microfilm series S 1371, 43 reels); Record Group 001021; State Library and Archives of Florida, Tallahassee, Florida.

Certificate of Employment during the War – British Army Form Z.18. for Ratliff, Tom W.

Confederate Prisoners of War, 1861-1865, Roll: 598_10, National Archives Microfilm Series (M1303, M598, M2702, and M918).

CSA Muster Roll.

First World War, Medal Card of Ratliff, Tom W.

Florida Deaths 1877-1939.

Illinois Deaths and Stillbirths Index 1916-1947.

National Archives and Records Administration: Border Crossings from Canada to US, 1895-1956.

Records of The National Woman's Party, Manuscript Division, Library of Congress, Washington, DC.

Selected Records of the War Department Relating to Confederate Prisoners of War, 1861-1865, Roll: 598_10, National Archives Microfilm Series (M1303, M598, M2702, and M918).

Texas Death Index 1903-2000.

Texas State Library and Archives Commission.

The National Archives (UK), Air Ministry: Department of the Master-General of Personnel: Officers' Service Records.

US Census, National Archives Microfilm.

US Dept. of Veterans Affairs BIRLS Death File, 1850-2010.

US World War II Army Enlistment Records, 1938-1946.

Victoria (Texas) District Court Criminal Docket.

Washington State Marriage Records.

WWI Draft Registrations.

NEWSPAPERS

Atlanta Constitution.

Biloxi (MS) Herald.

Bismarck (ND) Daily Tribune.

Chicago Daily Blade.

Chillicothe (MO) Constitution.

Connellsville (PA) Daily Courier.

Eau Claire (WI) Leader.

Fargo (ND) Forum and Daily Republican.

BIBLIOGRAPHY

Hammond (LA) Daily Star.

Helena (MT) Independent.

Honolulu (HI) Advertiser.

Indiana (PA) Evening Gazette.

Jackson (MS) Clarion-Ledger.

Kosciusko (MS) Alliance Vindicator.

Kosciusko (MS) Star.

Kosciusko (MS) Star-Herald.

Kosciusko (MS) Star-Ledger.

Los Angeles Times.

Marshall (TX) News-Messenger.

Miami Herald.

New Orleans Times-Democrat.

New York Times.

Phoenix Arizona Republic.

Ponchatoula (LA) Enterprise.

San Antonio (TX) Express-News.

Tyler (TX) Morning Telegraph.

Victoria (TX) Daily Advocate.

Washington Post.

Washington (AR) Telegraph.

MAGAZINES

Atlantic Monthly, January to June 1920.

Family Business Magazine, June 2006.

Houston Artletter, February 15, 1996.

Inc. Magazine, 2002.

St. Nicholas Magazine, March 1921.

The Suffragist from the Congressional Union for Woman's Suffrage (later National Woman's Party) in Washington, DC, 1913-1920.

The Survey Graphic from Survey Associates of East Stroudsburg, Pennsylvania.

Woman's Home Companion, February 1925.

CITY DIRECTORIES

1930 Arizona Directory of Phoenix and Surrounding Towns.

1947 City Directory, Phoenix, Arizona, and Vicinity.

ABOUT THE AUTHOR

JOHN BARTON RATLIFF III earned his BS in Japanese from Georgetown University, followed by graduate studies in linguistics under a Defense Department fellowship. After a distinguished twenty-three-year career with the US Department of State as an expert in foreign-language training for US government personnel, he founded his own highly successful language services company and directed it for sixteen years, retiring in 2001.

This is his first book. He and his wife, Diane, live in Northern Virginia, near their four sons, their wives, and eight grandchildren.

Visit *www.ratliffsaga.com*.

INDEX OF NAMES

Abernathy, Anna S., 214
Abernathy, Baird, 214
Abernathy, Brownie, 214
Abernathy, Frances B. (Mrs. Zack Mitchell Ratliff), 66, 69, 75, 213-220, 230, 233
Abernathy, Joseph Luther, 214
Abernathy, Laura (Lolly) (Mrs. Robert A. Landry), 213-14, 216, 220-21, 228
Abernathy, Mercer, 214
Abernathy, Robert, 214
Abernathy, Sophia Georgia (Georgie) Carruth. *See* Carruth, Sophia Georgia
Adams, Sarah Lucretia (Mrs. Zachariah Lfonzo Ratliff), 7, 86, 187, 353-4, 360, 393
Adams, William, 7
Adams, William Smith, 361
Alexander, Rev. J.H., 28
Allen, Alton Atwood, 349-50

Allen, Barbara Jane (Mrs. J.C. Johnson), 350
Allen, Daniel Atwood, 347
Allen, Earnest, 23, 34
Allen, Frank Alton, 347
Allen, Frank Alton Jr., 347
Allen, Frank Daniel, 347, 349
Allen, Gary Atwood, 350
Allen, Susie Irene (Mrs. Eddie L. Barber; Mrs. Cecil Gray), 347
Allenby, Field Marshal Edmund Henry Hynman, 332
Allgood, W. L., 34
Amidon, Beulah Elizabeth (Mrs. Paul Grady Ratliff), ix, 282-3, 286-8, 291-315
Amidon, Beulah Richardson McHenry. *See* McHenry, Beulah Richardson
Amidon, Eleanor F. (Ms. Sidney Clark), 292, 309, 311-12

Amidon, Judge Charles Fremont, 286-7, 291-2, 308-9, 398
Arrington, Frank, 19, 34
Ashley, Joe and Lavon, 60, 361-4, 397

Back, Brian David, 345
Back, Gregory Lynn, 345
Back, Isabella Celio, 345
Back, Keri Ann (Mrs. Clayton E. Coker), 345
Back, Larry Lynn, 345
Back, Michael Howell, 345
Barber, Chad, 347
Barber, Eddie L., 347
Barber, Keith, 347
Barber, Misty, 347
Barr, Lester Ethel, 14
Bechtold, Marvin, 108
Bell, George W. and Joanna, 47
Bengel, Elaine (Mrs. Albert Wade "Bevo" Ratliff), 197-200
Blackstock, L. S., 34
Boissevain, Inez Milholland. *See* Milholland, Inez
Bolton, Karen Elaine, 347
Bopp, Kate. *See* Ratliff, Katherine Elaine
Bopp, Robert "Bob" Henry, 75, 242-4
Brien, Barbara Gail Russell, 25, 397
Britt, Permelie Ann Elizabeth (Mrs. Charles Robert Mitchell), 364
Brooks, Alicia, 176
Brooks, Peggy Elizabeth. *See* Green, Peggy Elizabeth

Brooks, Stephen, 176
Brooks, Stephen Jr., 176
Brown, Connie "Cissy" Elaine Hazelwood. *See* Hazelwood, Connie "Cissy" Elaine
Brown, David Lewis, 361
Brown, Rev. Olympia, 297
Bruce, C.M., 34
Bullock, Delilah Quin (Mrs. Joseph T. Bullock), 265
Bullock, George, 35
Bullock, Joseph T., 265
Bullock, Ruth (Mrs. Albert Wade Ratliff), 75, 143, 265-70
Butler, Marianna Dine Rathke, 271
Butler, Marianna Elizabeth, 271

Carruth, Sophia Georgia (Mrs. Joseph Luther Abernathy), 213-14, 228
Carson, Betty J. *See* Ratliff, Betty J.
Casey, H.P., 23-4, 34
Causey, Bessie. *See* Ratliff, Bessie Grace
Causey, K.H. *See* Causey, Kirby Hall
Causey, Kirby Hall, 75, 311, 323-7
Causey, Kirby Hall Jr. "Todd", 324-5
Causey, Leighton Erastus, 323
Causey, Mrs. K.H. *See* Ratliff, Bessie Grace
Clark, Bessie, 49
Clark, Eleanor Amidon. *See* Amidon, Eleanor F.
Clark, J. C., 19, 34

INDEX OF NAMES

Clark, Sidney, 311-12
Clawson, Leah Britton (Mrs. Barton Wade Ratliff), 259, 262, 273-5
Clower, Lillie P. (Mrs. Samuel Anderson Jackson), 14
Clower, Susan (Mrs. Samuel Anderson Jackson), 14
Coker, Alyssa Corean, 345
Coker, Clayton E., 345
Cole, Alison Jane (Mrs. Joshua Murray Thompson), 200
Cole, Runie Bevly (Mrs. Mitchell Carruth Ratliff), 228-9
Cole, Trenton Cecil, 228
Cole, Trenton Cecil Jr., xii, 228-9
Cole, Trenton Cecil III, 229
Cone, Susan Anne (Mrs. Albert Washington Mitchell), 60, 361
Cooke, Pamela Joyce Hazelwood. *See* Hazelwood, Pamela Joyce
Cooper, W.M., 35
Cosgrove, Lydia, 160
Cottrell, Dick, 35
Cresswell, Stephen, 6, 397
Crosby, Zenobia Lily "Zena" (Mrs. Zachariah Edmond Ratliff), 358
Cunningham, Tory, 345
Curry, G.W., 35
Curry, Will, 35

Dailey, Zack, 34
Davenport, Bill, 231
Davidson, Harold W., 345

Davis, Alice Jane (Mrs. Whitman William Mitchell; Mrs. David Lewis Brown), 361
Davis, Nancy Merritt (Mrs. George Fellows Mitchell), 362
Deal, Sandra (Mrs. Joseph Pinckney Ratliff Jr.), 227
Deyrup, Beulah Tacey, xii, 305-6, 314, 316
Deyrup, Curtis Alden, xi, 286-7, 313-16
Deyrup, Ingrith Elizabeth, 316
Deyrup, Ivana, 316
Deyrup, Jens Jensen, 313
Deyrup, John, 316
Deyrup, John Thorold, 314
Deyrup, Lief, 316
Deyrup, Mark Amidon, 314, 316
Deyrup, Marta (Mrs. Curtis Alden Deyrup), 316
Deyrup, Nancy, 316
Deyrup, Thorold Johnson, 313-16
Dodd, Ephraim, 34
Dodd, S.L., 4
Donoho, Anna Ratliff. *See* Ratliff, Sarah Anna Lee
Donoho, Mary Lee (Mrs. Arthur Lee Hazlewood), 48, 75, 77, 87-9, 92-5, 97-9, 101-3, 108, 116
Donoho, Robert E. Lee, 63, 85-92, 96
Donoho, Sarah Elizabeth (Mrs. Marvin Bechtold; Mrs. William Henry Kimberlin Jr.), xi, 56, 86-9, 91-2, 94, 108-16

Donoho, W. B., 87
Dorrill, W. N., 34
Downs, Callie Crawford, 185
Downs, Jimmy, 185
Downs, Susan Harrison (Mrs. Wilks Wood), 185
Duncan, Albert Ross, 363
Duncan, Henrietta, 363
Duncan, Ida A., 363
Duncan, James Riley, 362-3
Duncan, Susan Louella (Mrs. Susan Louella Duncan Pender), 363
Durfy, Elizabeth (Mrs. Frederick Zollicoffer), 14

Eakin, Martha (Mrs. W.B. Donoho), 87
Edwards, Brett, 345
Edwards, Danny E., 345
Edwards, Lt. Col. James, 336-7
Eller, Michael John, 276
Emerson, J. A., 34
Evans, Charlotte (Mrs. Tom Jerome Ratliff), 276
Evans, Judith Camille Ratliff. *See* Ratliff, Judith Camille
Everly, Patricia Browne (Mrs. Philip Grady Amidon Ratliff), ix, 282-3, 288-90, 303, 306, 308, 318-20

Fowler, T.J., 10
Furr, J. J., 34

Gage, Betty (Mrs. Barton Wade Ratliff), 272-3

Gallaway, Robert Lee, 363
Gallaway, Tallulah Walton (Mrs. Tallulah Walton Gallaway Ricketts), 363
Gallaway, Thomas Adam, 362-3
Gallaway, Thomas George, 363
Gallaway, William Franklin, 363
George, Rev. J. B., 34
Gillmore, Inez Haynes, 293, 297-9, 301, 397
Glazier, L., 34
Gonzales, Enrique, 211-12
Gonzalez, Dacia (Mrs. Michael Howell Back), 345
Gracy, Cecil Glynn, 347
Gray, Mary Garrott (Mrs. James Grady Ratliff), 183-5
Green, Brandon, 177
Green, Candice, 177
Green, Cody, 177
Green, David Barton, 176
Green, Debbie Ree. *See* Shifflett, Debbie Ree
Green, Frances Roxana Ratliff. *See* Ratliff, Frances Roxana
Green, Heather, 176
Green, Herbert Lee, 177
Green, Jessica, 176
Green, Lloyd Alan, 177
Green, Lloyd Wright, 176-8
Green, Maye Lynne (Mrs. Ronald "Ronnie" Whitfield), 176
Green, Peggy Elizabeth (Mrs. Steven Brooks), 176

INDEX OF NAMES

Green, Samantha, 176
Green, Travis, 176
Green, Wanda. *See* Stanley, Wanda
Green, William "Billy", 176
Green, William Brooks "Buddy", 176
Grooms, Dana, 344
Grooms, Jack Meredith, 344-5
Grooms, Meredith Kay (Mrs. Tommy L. Twomey; Mrs. Harold W. Davidson), 344
Grooms, Michael Watson, 344
Grooms, Mickie L. (Mrs. Michael Watson Grooms), 344
Gunter, Alexander Gallasby, 359
Gunter, Bob, 23, 34
Gunter, George A., 359
Gunter, James, 359
Gunter, Stacey, 359
Gustafson, Adolph, 47

Hacksworth, W. R., 91
Harper, Frank M., 363-4
Harper, M.E., 364
Harshaw, Laura Janice (Mrs. Zachary Herrin), 345
Hartman, Alan, x, 120, 125-6, 128-33
Hartman, Bill, 126, 128, 130, 132
Hartman, Miriam (Mrs. Robert William Hartman), 129-31
Hartman, Robert William, 129-32
Harvey, Emma Wilson, 119
Havens, Allen Lee, Jr., 185
Havens, Anna Patrick, 185
Havens, Elizabeth Gray, 185
Havens, William Allen, 185
Hawks, Dawn Trese (Mrs. Jerome Clay Ratliff), 276
Hawthorne, Candy (Mrs. Brent Edward Ratliff), 167
Hazelwood, Arthur Robert, 75, 78, 92-5, 98-105
Hazelwood, Connie "Cissy" Elaine (Mrs. Connie Elaine Brown), x, 86, 89, 91-4, 97-100, 102, 104-5
Hazelwood, Joe Walter, 104
Hazelwood, Kathryn Anne (Mrs. Kathryn Hazelwood Roy), x, 104
Hazelwood, Kenneth Clyde, 104
Hazelwood, Martin Keith, 104
Hazelwood, Mary Elizabeth, 104
Hazelwood, Pamela Joyce (Mrs. Pamela Joyce Hazelwood Cooke), x, 104
Hazelwood, Robert Charles, x, 104
Hazlewood, Arthur Lee, 75, 77, 85, 89-94, 97-103
Hazlewood, Darrell Austin, 106
Hazlewood, Edward Lee, x, 75, 78, 86, 91-5, 97-103, 106-7
Hazlewood, Fred, 97
Hazlewood, Howard S., viii, 7, 397
Hazlewood, Joseph, 97-8
Hazlewood, Lee and Jodie, 97-8
Hazlewood, Mary Lee Donoho. *See* Donoho, Mary Lee

Hazlewood, Maude, 97
Hazlewood, Walter, 97
Hemphill, Marie M., 142, 398
Herrin, Audrey, 345
Herrin, Bessie Corean. See Ratliff, Bessie Corean
Herrin, Beverly Lynn (Mrs. Larry Lynn Back), 345
Herrin, Elena, 345
Herrin, Ethan, 345
Herrin, Genevieve (Mrs. Tory Cunningham), 345
Herrin, Howell Jessie, 345-6
Herrin, Jeramy, 345
Herrin, Jessie, 345
Herrin, Kole, 345
Herrin, Levi, 345
Herrin, Lexi, 345
Herrin, Lisa Renee (Mrs. Randall E. Richards; Mrs. Joe N. Hernandez), 345
Herrin, Schylar Rae, 345
Herrin, Stacy Ann (Mrs. William A. Rogers; Mrs. Danny E. Edwards), 345
Herrin, Tom Howell, 345
Herrin, Virginia (Mrs. Dave Dowden Laird), 345
Herrin, Zachary, 345
Hill, District Attorney W.S., 29, 40
Hillebrandt, Oskar Barton, 173
Hillebrandt, Vera Vanessa, 173
Hines, Ernest Earle (Mrs. Ernest Earle Hines Anderson), 357

Hines, Frances (Mrs. Albert Pierce Mitchell; Mrs. Frank M. Harper), 363-4
Hines, Ida Pearl (Mrs. Ida Pearl Hines Harrell), 357
Hines, James Nathanial, 357
Hines, Kenneth Whitfield, 357
Hines, Louisa Matilda "Duck" Ratliff. See Ratliff, Louisa Matilda "Duck"
Hines, Sudie Bell, 357
Hines, Zachariah Russell, 357
Hitt, Tina (Mrs. Herbert Lee Green), 177
Hoffman, L.W., 34
Hoffman, Mary Eva (Mrs. William Rodgers Ratliff), 146, 189-91
Hollien, Maxine (Mrs. Peter Frederick Naylor), 243, 248-253
Hughes, J.M., 23, 35
Hughes, John, 35
Hull, M.M., 23, 35
Hull, Will, 34
Hurt, Garrett, 185
Hutchinsons, Dave and Eldry, 249

Imai, Yoshiko (Mrs. John Barton Ratliff IV), 166-7

Jackson, Claude, 44
Jackson, Doty, 44
Jackson, Eva Lillian (Mrs. Lester Ethel Barr), 14

INDEX OF NAMES

Jackson, Frederick Zollicoffer, 14
Jackson, John Anderson, 13
Jackson, John Felix, 14
Jackson, Lavinia Ethel (Mrs. Dalton McBee), 14
Jackson, Lillie Clower. *See* Clower, Lillie
Jackson, Martin, 212
Jackson, Sam. *See* Jackson, Samuel Anderson
Jackson, Samuel Anderson, vii, xiii, 5-6, 9-10, 13-15, 17-44, 62
Jamison, Sally Kate Ratliff. *See* Ratliff, Sally Kate
Jamison, Will, 21, 34
Jenkins, Alice, 137-8
Jenkins, Ben J., 136, 138
Jenkins, Danah, 137-8
Jenkins, Eliza Light, 137
Jenkins, Elois L., 136, 138
Jenkins, Emma Roxana (Mrs. John Barton Ratliff), xii, 63, 75, 137-48, 162-3, 175, 177, 189, 195, 267, 310
Jenkins, Fannie, 137-8
Jenkins-Hartman, Patricia (Mrs. Alan Hartman), x, 120, 125-6, 128-32
Jenkins, Hattie, 138
Jenkins, James L., 137-8
Jenkins, Netta, 138
Jenkins, Thomas ("Uncle T"), 137-8
Jenkins, Wessie, 138

Jennings, Jenny (Mrs. Jack Ratliff Thomas), 182
Johnson, Alvin, 314
Johnson, Beverly Grace (Mrs. Harry Milton Thomas Jr.), 181-2
Johnson, Emily (Mrs. Harry Milton Thomas III), 182
Johnson, F. P., 21
Johnson, J.C., 350
Jones, T.V., 34

Kimberlin, James, 112
Kimberlin, Mary "Lena", 111
Kimberlin, Sarah Elizabeth Donoho. *See* Donoho, Sarah Elizabeth
Kimberlin, Tom, 112
Kimberlin, William Henry Jr., xi, 86, 108-16, 207
Kimberlin, William Henry Sr., 109
Kimberlin, Wilma (Mrs. John McNeil Sr.), 109, 111
Kuykendall, C. G., 34

Laird, Adri, 345
Laird, Dave Dowden, 345
Laird, Emryn, 345
Lampton, W.J., 298-9
Landry, Laura "Lolly" Abernathy. *See* Abernathy, Laura "Lolly"
Landry, Robert A., 221
Lansdale, Isaac, 35
Leflore, Greenwood, 387
Listner, Charles, 22, 34

Lord, Bessie Beatrice (Mrs. George Elfonzo Ratliff), 356-7
Love, Deputy Sheriff Newt, 22, 24, 26
Love, Sheriff David F., 22, 24, 26, 34-5
Love, Tracy Diane (Mrs. Christopher Barton Ratliff), 235

MacCallum, May, viii
Marcum, Gary Lavell, 235
Marcum, Gary Lavell Jr., 235
Marcum, Jason Donavan, 235
Marcum, Kary Denise, 235
Marcum, Martin Lee, 235
Marcum, Michelle Lynn, 235
McBee, Dalton, 14
McCool, J. F., 34
McDade, Deborah (Mrs. Andrew Michael Ratliff), 166-7
McDaniel, Bobby Horace, 106
McDaniel, Darrell Austin. *See* Hazlewood, Darrell Austin
McHenry, Beulah Richardson (Mrs. Charles Fremont Amidon), 291-2, 309, 315
McMillan, George, 34
McNeil, Barbara Ann (Mrs. Barbara Ann McNeil Mingee), xi, 56, 86, 90-1, 98, 111-16, 207
McNeil, Henry, 112
McNeil, John Jr., 112
McNeil, John Sr., 111
McNeil, Wilma Kimberlin. *See* Kimberlin, Wilma
Meek, R.B., 35

Milholland, Inez (Mrs. Inez Milholland Boissevain), 296-7
Miller, Nathan, 267
Mingee, Barbara Ann. *See* McNeil, Barbara Ann
Mingee, Susan, xi, 56, 86, 90-1, 98, 111, 113-14, 207
Mitchell, Abraham, 60
Mitchell, Albert Pierce, 60, 363-4
Mitchell, Albert Washington, 60, 361
Mitchell, Archie Clay, 364
Mitchell, Benjamin Franklin, 60, 364
Mitchell, Bill, 18
Mitchell, Charles Robert, 364
Mitchell, Cornelia,
   The Early Life of Cornelia Mitchell, 59-63
   Moving On, 65-7
   Back Home in Kosciusko, 69-79
   The Siblings of Cornelia Mitchell, 361-4, 3, 8-9, 45-50, 55, 83, 94-5, 118, 122, 136, 143, 154-5, 167, 175, 192, 201, 206, 210, 217, 228, 237, 256, 262-3, 265-6, 321, 326, 330-1, 338, 364-5, 395-6
Mitchell, Eula Kate (Mrs. Eula Kate Mitchell Bush), 364
Mitchell, Eulah Davis (Mrs. William Smith Adams), 361-2
Mitchell, George Fellows, 60, 362
Mitchell, James Walter, 362
Mitchell, John A., 363
Mitchell, John Frank, 362

INDEX OF NAMES

Mitchell, John H., 364
Mitchell, Leona (Mrs. William Ransom Wilson), 363-4
Mitchell, Lucy Ann (Mrs. James Riley Duncan; Mrs. Thomas Allen Gallaway), 362-3
Mitchell, Malcolm, 364
Mitchell, Mary Sue (Mrs. Mary Sue Mitchell Adams), 362
Mitchell, Nimrod, 60
Mitchell, Whitman William, 60, 361
Mixon, Elsie Vera (Mrs. John Barton Ratliff Jr.), 75, 77, 79, 151-61
Mixon, James Sidney, 157
Mixon, Neil Holton, 153
Moffat, Mary Diane (Mrs. John Barton Ratliff III), v, x, xii, 162-8, 171, 403
Montgomery, Callie. *See* Thompson, Callie
Moss, Bobby G., 60, 398
Mullen, David, 185

Naylor, Bradford Joseph, 251, 254
Naylor, Frances Christine, 241
Naylor, Kate Ratliff. *See* Ratliff, Katherine Elaine
Naylor, Kathryn Ann, xi, 241, 244, 251, 253-4
Naylor, Maxine Hollien. *See* Hollien, Maxine
Naylor, Michael Robert, 241, 246, 251, 253
Naylor, Peter Francis, 241-2

Naylor, Peter Frederick, 241-53
Naylor, Peter Frederick Jr., 70, 245, 251
Naylor, Ruth (Mrs. Peter Frederick Naylor), 245
Noah, Elizabeth Exdothula "Exie" (Mrs. George Elfonzo Ratliff), 356

Oakes, Charles "Charlie" Franklin, 23-4
Oakes, Ellen, x, 23, 31, 120
Osteen, Frances Sophile (Mrs. Leighton Erastus Causey), 323
Owens, Frances, 182
Owens, Sam, 182

Page, Dan and Dora, 339
Page, Rissie Corean (Mrs. Tom Watson Ratliff), 75, 338-44
Pender, Susan Louella Duncan. *See* Duncan, Susan Louella
Peterson, Laura (Mrs. Timothy Moffat Ratliff), 167
Pettit, Ellen Oakes. *See* Oakes, Ellen
Potter, Doreen Faye (Mrs. Edward Lee Hazlewood), 106
Prenevost, Kathryn Ann "Kathy". *See* Naylor, Kathryn Ann

Quick, George, 88
Quick, John, 88

Randazzo, Alexandra Leah, 275
Randazzo, Gregory John, 275

Randazzo, Isabelle Angela, 275
Randazzo, Jack Gregory, 275
Ratcliff, Clarence Earl, ix
Ratcliff, Polly Ann. *See* Ratliff, Pollyanna
Rathke, Chaco Devlin Butler, 271
Rathke, Cornelia Ratliff. *See* Ratliff, Cornelia Ruth
Rathke, Dale Lawrence, 270-1
Rathke, Edmann Jacob, 270-1
Rathke, Stephen Wade, 270-1
Ratliff, Aileen (Mrs. Aileen Ratliff Lee), 358
Ratliff, Albert Wade, ix, 45-6, 48, 62, 66-7, 69, 75-8, 122, 143, 148, 206, 215, 259, 261-70, 303, 338
Ratliff, Albert Wade "Bevo", xii, 75, 77, 143-4, 197-200
Ratliff, Alison (daughter of Barton Wade Ratliff), 273, 275
Ratliff, Alison Amidon, x, 278, 318-20
Ratliff, Anna Belle (Anabel), xii, 75, 77, 140-1, 147, 179-81
Ratliff, Andrew Michael, xii, 163-8
Ratliff, Barton Bullock, 273-5
Ratliff, Barton Wade, ix, 19, 34, 75, 77, 143, 148-9, 156, 259, 262, 266-9, 271-5
Ratliff, Bennett Justin, 167
Ratliff, Bessie Corean (Mrs. Jack Meredith Grooms; Mrs. Howell Jessie Herrin), ix-x, 75, 77, 123, 326, 331-2, 335, 338-41, 343-6, 350
Ratliff, Bessie (Mrs. Bessie Ratliff Abernethy), 358
Ratliff, Bessie Grace (Mrs. Kirby Hall Causey), 45-7, 62, 65, 75-6, 113, 190, 202, 207, 226-7, 244, 256, 259-60, 264-5, 282, 311, 321-7, 330, 346
Ratliff, Betty J. (Mrs. Betty Ratliff Carson), viii, 7, 397
Ratliff, Beulah Amidon. *See* Amidon, Beulah Elizabeth
Ratliff, Beulah Curtis (Mrs. Thorold Johnson Deyrup), xi, xii, 286, 304-16
Ratliff, Brent Edward, 163-8
Ratliff, Brian, 273-4
Ratliff, Brooks Allan, 199-200
Ratliff, Carla, 273-4
Ratliff, Carol (Carey) Richardson, 318-19
Ratliff, Charles, viii-ix
Ratliff, Charles Douglas, 358
Ratliff, Charles Peterson, 167
Ratliff, Christopher Barton, 235
Ratliff, Clarence Harold, 140-1
Ratliff, Clay Lee, 357
Ratliff, Cornelia Ruth (Mrs. Edmann Jacob Rathke), 75, 77, 148-9, 266-8, 270-1, 341
Ratliff, Daniel David Mead, 235-6
Ratliff, Dawn Alane, 276
Ratliff, Ed, vii-viii
Ratliff, Edna Willena, 358

INDEX OF NAMES

Ratliff, Elaine Bengel (Mrs. Albert Wade "Bevo" Ratliff), 197-200
Ratliff, Elise Marie, 200
Ratliff, Emily Catherine, 167
Ratliff, Emily Eugene (Mrs. Lee Havens), 184
Ratliff, Emma Roxana Jenkins. See Jenkins, Emma Roxana
Ratliff, Eric McDade, 167
Ratliff, Esther Rebecca (Mrs. Esther Rebecca Ratliff Sexton) 357
Ratliff, Florence Cornelia (Mrs. David Franklin Romine) 4, 34, 45-8, 62, 65-6, 75-6, 117, 122-5, 127-8, 140, 255-60, 262, 265, 322, 330-1
Ratliff, Floy Kathleen (Mrs. Floy Kathleen Ratliff Rush), 357
Ratliff, Frances Abernathy. See Abernathy, Frances B.
Ratliff, Frances Roxana (Mrs. Lloyd Wright Green), xii, 75, 78, 146, 175-8, 341
Ratliff, George Elfonzo, 354, 356-7
Ratliff, George Ernest, 356
Ratliff, Hailey Marjorie, 167
Ratliff, Hattie Maye Sanders. See Sanders, Hattie Maye
Ratliff, Hattie Sue, 358
Ratliff, Hillary Diane (Mrs. Jeffrey Thelin), 167
Ratliff, Holly Everly, 318-20
Ratliff, Hugh Fulton, 357

Ratliff, Jack William, 199-200
Ratliff, James Grady, xii, 75, 77, 140, 183-5, 303
Ratliff, James Grady Jr., xii, 184-6
Ratliff, Jerome Clay, 276
Ratliff, John (son of Barton Wade Ratliff), 273-4
Ratliff, John Arthur, 358
Ratliff, John Barton (son of W.P. Ratliff), ix, xii, 8, 45-6, 49, 61-3, 66, 69-70, 75-8, 118, 135-48, 155, 161-3, 175, 177, 190, 193-4, 215, 253, 257, 265-7, 278, 285-7, 304-5, 310, 327
Ratliff, John Barton Ratliff Jr. (grandson of W.P. Ratliff), vii, 63, 75, 77, 79, 140-1, 147-61, 163
Ratliff, John Barton III (great grandson of W.P. Ratliff), 8, 75, 78, 153-6, 158-67, 171, 403
Ratliff, John Barton IV (great great grandson of W.P. Ratliff), 163-8
Ratliff, John Gray, 184-6
Ratliff, John Whitfield, 23, 120, 354, 358
Ratliff, Joseph Pinckney, xiii, 214, 220-7
Ratliff, Joseph Pinckney III, 227
Ratliff, Joseph Pinckney Jr., 223, 227
Ratliff, Judith Camille (Mrs. Judith Camille Evans), xi, 211-14, 217, 220-1, 223-7, 229-30, 326

Ratliff, Julia Permelia (Mrs. George W. Thompson), 354, 356, 359-60
Ratliff, Julius Everett, 356
Ratliff, Kate. *See* Ratliff, Katherine Elaine,
Ratliff, Katherine Elaine, xi, 4, 45-6, 61, 70, 75-6, 210, 239-45, 253, 330
Ratliff, Lee, 273-4
Ratliff, Leslie (Mrs. Leslie Ratliff Ewing), 358
Ratliff, Lisa Vann (Mrs. Jimmy Downs), 185
Ratliff, Lori Lynn (Mrs. Michael John Eller), 276
Ratliff, Louisa Matilda "Duck" (Mrs. James Nathanial Hines), 28, 354, 357
Ratliff, Margaret Grace (Mrs. Frank Daniel Allen), 75, 77, 340-3, 347, 349
Ratliff, Margaret Wade (Mrs. Gregory John Randazzo), 273-5
Ratliff, Marion, viii
Ratliff, Maris Jewel, 167
Ratliff, Martha Cornelia (Mrs. Hilbert Wilkinson; Mrs. Harry Allen Whetzel), ix, xii, 60, 69, 75, 77, 137, 139, 141-7, 150-1, 162, 179, 192-6, 250, 253, 257, 266-7, 303-4, 310, 321, 327
Ratliff, Mary Belle (Mrs. Overton Welch Wilson), x, 45-6, 61, 63, 65-6, 76, 117-28, 132-3, 139-40, 256-9, 263, 265, 331, 338
Ratliff, Mary Ella (Mrs. Charles Franklin Oakes), 24, 358
Ratliff, Mary Eva Hoffman. *See* Hoffman, Mary Eva
Ratliff, Mary Jane (Mrs. Newton Copeland Wasson), 136, 354-5
Ratliff, Mary Lou (Mrs. Mary Lou Ratliff Sanderson), 358
Ratliff, Mava, xii, 162, 189-91
Ratliff, Melissa Frances (Mrs. Gary Lavell Marcum), 235-7
Ratliff, Miki Jo, 227
Ratliff, Mildred, 49-50
Ratliff, Mitchell Carruth, xii, 65, 214, 228-9
Ratliff, Mrs. J.B. *See* Jenkins, Emma Roxana
Ratliff, Mrs. Zack Mitchell. *See* Abernathy, Frances B.
Ratliff, Nancy (Mrs. James Grady Ratliff Jr.), 185
Ratliff, Neil Mixon, 153-9, 169-71
Ratliff, Newton L., 357
Ratliff, Pamala Roxana (Mrs. Pat Tvrdik), 185
Ratliff, Patricia Browne Everly. *See* Everly, Patricia Browne
Ratliff, Paul Adams, vii, 141, 161, 187-8
Ratliff, Paul Grady, ix-xii, 45-7, 62, 65, 76, 187, 202, 241, 256, 277-90, 301-13, 330-1

INDEX OF NAMES

Ratliff, Philip Grady Amidon, ix-x, 282, 303, 306-10, 312, 317-20
Ratliff, Pinkney Brooks, vii, xii, 23, 49, 75, 77, 140-1, 145-7, 161, 175-8, 187, 197
Ratliff, Pollyanna, 49-50
Ratliff, Rebecca Ann (Mrs. Allan P. Johnson IV), 235
Ratliff, Rissie Corean. *See* Page, Rissie Corean
Ratliff, Robert Edmond, xi, 66-7, 70, 75, 77-8, 144, 204-5, 210-11, 214, 216-20, 225, 229, 231-7
Ratliff, Ruby (Mrs. Ruby Ratliff Gamblin), 358
Ratliff, Ruby Anola (Mrs. Ruby Anola Ratliff Comfort), 356
Ratliff, Rufus Winans, 354, 359
Ratliff, Rufus Winans Jr., 359-400
Ratliff, Ruth Bullock. *See* Bullock, Ruth
Ratliff, Sally Kate (Mrs. Sally Kate Ratliff Jamison), 358
Ratliff, Sallye (Mrs. William (Billy) Hubert Ratliff, 185
Ratliff, Sarah Elizabeth (Aunt Bettie), 71, 75, 108, 354, 360
Ratliff, Sarah Anna Lee (Mrs. Robert E. Lee Donoho), x-xi, 45-6, 48, 55-6, 61-3, 75-8, 85-99, 102-3, 108-9, 112, 118, 140, 206, 240, 243, 326
Ratliff, Sean Dee, 227
Ratliff, Sidney Joy. 157-9, 171-4
Ratliff, Sudie (Mrs. Ernest Claude Spain), 45-6, 54-5, 61, 66,69, 75-6, 95, 118, 122, 143, 201-7, 265, 326, 336
Ratliff, Susan (Sudie) Kathryn (Mrs. Susan Kathryn Ratliff Parcells), 356
Ratliff, Susan Elaine (Mrs. W. Murray Thompson Jr.), 199-200
Ratliff, Susanna Tatum (Sudie) (Mrs. Alexander Gallasby Gunter), 354, 359
Ratliff, Timothy Moffat, 163-8
Ratliff, Tom Jerome, 75, 77-8, 266-8, 276
Ratliff, Tom Watson, ix-x, 46-55, 62, 65-6, 75-7, 95, 122, 125, 205, 215, 240-1, 256, 263-5, 278-81, 322, 326, 329-44, 348, 399
Ratliff, Tommie Jane (Mrs. Alton Atwood Allen), ix, 47, 66, 75, 77, 125, 278, 331, 337, 339-43, 348-50
Ratliff, Vera Mixon. *See* Mixon, Elsie Vera
Ratliff, W.P. *See* Ratliff, William Pinkney
Ratliff, Wade Allan, 200
Ratliff, Wesley Garrett, 235
Ratliff, William "Billie" Rodgers, xii, 144-7, 162, 189-91, 194
Ratliff, William (1727-1777), 7
Ratliff, William Franklin, 8
Ratliff, William Hubert, 184-6

Ratliff, William Lagrone, 356
Ratliff, William Patrick, 167
Ratliff, William Pinkney, vii, xii
   A Tribute, 3-4
   March 3, 1894, 5-6
   Who was William Pinkney Ratliff?, 7-12
   Who was Samuel Anderson Jackson?, 13-15
   Showdown at the Courthouse, 17-28
   On Trial for Murder, 29-42
   Life as a Farmer, 43-56
   The Siblings of William Pinkney Ratliff, 353-60
   Appendices, 369-94, 61-3, 65, 69, 71, 76-9, 86, 120, 124, 136, 167, 210, 216-17, 220, 256, 262, 281, 287, 321, 326, 330, 336, 338
Ratliff, William Turner, 358
Ratliff, Z.M. *See* Ratliff, Zack Mitchell
Ratliff, Zachariah Edmond, 55, 233, 354, 358
Ratliff, Zachariah Lfonzo, 7, 353-4, 359, 393
Ratliff, Zachariah Noah, 356
Ratliff, Zack Abernathy, 49, 67, 75, 77-8, 216-18, 230-2
Ratliff, Zack Mitchell, xi, 44-7, 49, 61, 65-7, 69-71, 75-8, 94, 204, 209-20, 360
Ray, W.L., 34

Redding, J. H., 34
Richards, Mandy, 345
Richards, Randall E., 345
Richards, Shirley (Mrs. Paul Adams Ratliff), 188
Riley, Julia (Mrs. John Felix Jackson), 14
Riley, W.T., 34
Roberts, Ida (Mrs. Rufus Winans Ratliff), 359
Robinson, Asa, 35
Roby, Dr. J. R., 19, 24, 34
Rogers, Andrea, 345
Rogers, Hannah, 345
Rogers, William A. "Tony", 345
Romine, David Franklin, 255, 258-60
Romine, Florence Ratliff. *See* Ratliff, Florence
Romine, J. Helen (Mrs. David Franklin Romine), 258, 260
Rowe, Indy B. (Indiabelle), 336
Rowell, C.F., 35
Russell, Allen, 25
Russell, Bill Gary, 25, 397
Russell, Sam, 24-6, 33
Russell, Seborn, 25
Ryan, Sam, 229

Sanders, Edgar, 34
Sanders, Hattie Maye (Mrs. Pinkney Brooks Ratliff), 75, 175-6
Sanders, W.J., 34
Sanders, Will, 24-5, 34
Sexton, Elizabeth Michelle, 350

INDEX OF NAMES

Sexton, Freddie Atwood, 350
Sexton, Gary Patrick, 350
Sexton, Peter, 350
Sexton, Suzanna (Mrs. Freddie Atwood Sexton), 350
Shaw, Mary Katherine (Mrs. Arthur Robert Hazelwood), 104
Shelley, Rosalind Smith, 136
Shifflett, Debbie Ree (Mrs. David Barton Green), 176
Sisson, Prof., 44
Sklar, Pincus, 266
Sloss, Sarah "Sally" (Mrs. William "Billie" Eugene Wasson), x, 18, 22, 28, 136
Smemo, Kenneth, 291-2, 312, 398
Smith, Beverly K. (Mrs. Tom Howell Herrin), x, 345
Smith, Charlotte, 200
Smith, Jazmine, 235
Smith, Keith, 200
Smith, Victoria, 235
Smythe, Dr. F.D., 35
Spain, Claude, 4, 55, 69, 75, 203-7
Spain, David, 203
Spain, Ernest Claude. *See* Claude Spain
Spain, Major Johnson, 203
Spain, Mrs. Claude. *See* Ratliff, Sudie
Spain, Mrs. K.H. *See* Ratliff, Sudie
Spain, Sudie. *See* Ratliff, Sudie
Stacy, L. D., 156
Stanley, Wanda (Mrs. William Brooks Green), 176

Stingley, Ed, 34
Stingley, Will, 34
Sullivant, J.H., 35

Taylor, Jane (Mrs. Abraham Mitchell), 60
Terry, Maj. L. S., 10
Thelin, Hillary Diane Ratliff. *See* Ratliff, Hillary Diane
Thelin, Jeffrey, 167
Thomas, Christopher William, 182
Thomas, Harry Milton Jr., 181-2
Thomas, Harry Milton III, 182
Thomas, Harry Milton Sr., 179-81
Thomas, Jack Ratliff, 181-3
Thomas, Kally, 182
Thomas, Molly, 182
Thomas, Rachel (Mrs. Sam Owens), 182
Thomas, Susannah (Mrs. William Ratliff), 7, 393-4
Thomas, Tristram, 8, 394
Thompson, Callie, 49-50
Thompson, George W., 356
Thompson, Joshua Murray, 200
Thompson, Lucius R., 356
Thompson, Mildred. *See* Ratliff, Mildred
Thompson, N.O., 34
Thompson, Pollyanna. *See* Ratliff, Pollyanna
Thompson, Rebecca Susan (Mrs. Keith Lee Smith), 200
Thompson, Violet May, 200

Thompson, Vivian. *See* Ratliff, Vivian
Thompson, W. Murray Jr., 199-200
Tollefson, Belle (Mrs. Joseph Hazlewood), 97-8
Trcka, Larry, xi, 227
Trippett, Bernard L., 9, 11, 13-15, 28, 398
Trull, Margaret Deering Dismukes (Mrs. Rufus Winans Ratliff, Jr.), 360
Turner, Laura (Mrs. John Whitfield Ratliff), 358
Turner, Lovie C. (Mrs. Rufus Winans Ratliff, Sr.), 359
Tvrdik, Patrick Thomas, 185
Twomey, Tammy, 244
Twomey, Tommy "Chip", 244
Twomey, Tommy L., 244

Wallace, Deputy Sheriff, 19
Wallace, V.H., 34
Walton, Mary, 301, 398
Ward, W.A., 35
Wasson, Eliza Estelle (Mrs. Eliza Estelle Wasson Harris), 355
Wasson, John Newton, 355
Wasson, Julia Matilda, 355
Wasson, Mary Eddie (Mrs. Mary Eddie Wasson Mitchell), 136, 355
Wasson, Mary Jane Ratliff. *See* Ratliff, Mary Jane
Wasson, Newton Copeland, 355
Wasson, Rev. David Ratliff, 355
Wasson, Rev. James Carlisle, 355
Wasson, Rev. Lovick Pinkney, 355
Wasson, Sally Andromeda (Mrs. Andrew Alonzo Moore; Mrs. William Anderson Crossley), 355
Wasson, Sally. *See* Sloss, Sarah "Sally"
Wasson, William (Billie) Eugene, 28, 136
Wasson, William (son of Mary Jane Ratliff and Newton Copeland Wasson), 355
Wasson, Zachariah Alexander "Zack", 355
Weakley, Dianna Dawn (Mrs. Lloyd Alan Green), 177
Whetzel, Christopher, 196
Whetzel, Harry Allen, 194-5
Whetzel, Harry Allen Jr., 194, 196
Whetzel, Martha Ratliff. *See* Ratliff, Martha
Whetzel, Matthew, 196
Whetzel, Sheila (Mrs. Harry Allen Whetzel Jr.), 195
Whidden, Joyce Ann (Mrs. Robert Edmond Ratliff), 235-7
White, J. W. D., 34
Whitehead, W. C., 34
Whitfield, Maye Lynne. *See* Green, Maye Lynne
Whitfield, Ronald "Ronnie", 176
Whitworth, Brandon Lee, 235

INDEX OF NAMES

Whitworth, Bridget Kelly, 235
Wilkinson, Hilbert, 144, 193-4, 310
Wilkinson, Marlyn Frances, ix, xii, 139, 144-6, 162, 193-6
Wilkinson, Martha Ratliff. *See* Ratliff, Martha
Wilks, Kathleen (Mrs. Jeramy Herrin), 345
Williams, Sam, 35
Williams, Sen. John Sharpe, 11, 287
Wilson, Belle. *See* Ratliff, Mary Belle
Wilson, Frank H., 119
Wilson, Jefferson Clay, 121, 124, 128, 133
Wilson, Jessie T. (Mrs. O.W. Wilson Jr.), 124, 127
Wilson, Mrs. O.W. *See* Ratliff, Mary Belle
Wilson, Overton Welch "O.W.", 63, 65-6, 117-25, 139, 256-8, 338
Wilson, Overton Welch Jr., 117, 119-25, 127-8
Wilson, Sudie (Mrs. Robert William Hartman), x, 117, 120-6, 128-33
Wilson, Tom, 119
Wilson, William Ransom, 364
Wollesen, Virginia Mae (Mrs. Joseph Pinckney Ratliff), 223-7
Wood, Wilks, 185

Yandell, W. M., Sr., 34
Young, Aiden Gary, 350
Young, Colton Jason, 350
Young, Elizabeth Michelle Sexton. *See* Sexton, Elizabeth Michelle
Young, James, 350

Zollicoffer, Gen. Felix Kirk, 13
Zollicoffer, Susan Anna (Mrs. John Anderson Jackson), 14

Made in the USA
Middletown, DE
18 November 2014